Cosmo Innes

Lectures on Scotch Legal Antiquities

Cosmo Innes

Lectures on Scotch Legal Antiquities

ISBN/EAN: 9783337397296

Printed in Europe, USA, Canada, Australia, Japan

Cover: Foto ©Thomas Meinert / pixelio.de

More available books at **www.hansebooks.com**

LECTURES

ON

SCOTCH LEGAL ANTIQUITIES

INTRODUCTORY.
CHARTERS.
PARLIAMENT.
THE OLD CHURCH.

OLD FORMS OF LAW.
RURAL OCCUPATION.
STUDENTS' GUIDE BOOKS.
APPENDIX.

BY

COSMO INNES

EDINBURGH:
EDMONSTON AND DOUGLAS.
1872.

TO THE RIGHT HONOURABLE JOHN INGLIS,

LORD JUSTICE-GENERAL OF SCOTLAND.

My Dear Lord Justice-General,

    Allow me to dedicate to you this little book, which owes its existence very much to your Lordship's precept and example.

    I have the honour to be,

        Your most obedient Servant,

            C. INNES.

INVERLEITH,
    Oct. 14, 1872.

CONTENTS.

I.—INTRODUCTORY.

Lectures delivered first in the Advocates' Library—next before the Juridical Society—Scotch Legal Antiquaries—Sir Thomas Craig—Sir John Skene—Sir George Mackenzie—Dirleton and Stewart—Sir Thomas Hope—Stair — Erskine — Sir James Dalrymple — Lord Hailes—Lord Kames—Alexander Wight—Thomas Thomson—Joseph Robertson—George Chalmers—John Riddell—Learned Writers to the Signet—David Erskine—John Russell—William Tytler—Charles Gordon—Isaac Grant—Samuel Mitchelson—James Anderson—George Home—Walter Ross — John Davidson — Archibald Swinton — David Wemys — Colin Mackenzie — Sir James Gibson-Craig—Styles of Dallas of St. Martin—Styles selected by the Juridical Society—Disadvantages under which our early Antiquaries laboured—Outline of the subjects of the Course—Bolingbroke on the importance of historical study for lawyers, ... 1

II.—CHARTERS.

Styles and terms of ancient Charters—Charters commence with David I.—Title of the King—Mode of Address—Scotch Charters founded on Saxon models—Early Charters undated—how the period of an undated Charter may be ascertained—sometimes by an incident in contemporary history—sometimes by the name of granter, grantee, witness—Chronology of the Charters of David II.—Charters to Monasteries very elaborate—Charters to Laymen short—Bruce's Charters—the clauses of a Charter analysed—Style and Title of the Granter—Persons addressed—*Dreng*—"Goodmen"—Motives inductive of ancient Grants—to Laymen—to Churchmen—Subjects granted—The *quæquidem* clause—The Tenure, *modus tenendi*—Grant of Regality—Grant of Earldom—Grant *in liberam forestam*—Mode of constituting the right of Forest—Apparent extent of the right—Right of Pannage—Grant *in liberam warennam*—Nature and extent of this right—Grant *in liberam baroniam*—What it conveyed :—Territorial rights—Parts and Pertinents : Woods and plains—Meadows and pastures—Roads and Paths—Moors and marshes—*in aquis et stagnis*—Fish-stanks or ponds—Vineyards—Parks—Brushwood or jungle—Petaries and turbaries—Coal pits, quarries, stone and lime—Pigeons and dovecots—Wrak, waith and wair—Huntings, hawkings and fishings—Mills, multure dues, sucken—Smithy—brew-house—saltworks—Rights seignorial: tenants, tenandries—Homage, ward, relief—Bondsmen, neyf or serf—Marchetæ mulierum—Heriot—Rights of Jurisdiction : sac and soc—Thol and them—Infangthief and outfangthief—Pit and gallows—Courts, issues of Courts, pleas—Bludwite—The Four Points of the Crown—Ordeal : *examen aquæ, ferri calidi et duelli*—Reddendo or faciendo—Different kinds of services—Tenure by serjeantry—Money rent seldom stipulated—Origin of the word "sterling"—Blench duties—Valuations of blench terms—Authentication of ancient Charters: seldom subscribed by the granter—completed by fixing his seal—Crown writs, how sealed—Affixing of Great Seal implied the presence of the King—The Signature—Charter of Terregles—Sorryn—Fachalos (? Frithalos)—The state of society revealed by the Charter—Sale of an Earldom—

CONTENTS. ix

PAGE

Grant of Chiefship—Officers mentioned in Charters — Steward — Constable — Marischal — Justiciar — Chancellor—Chamberlain—Treasurer — Comptroller —Lord Privy Seal—Lord President of the Council—Secretary—Lord Clerk Register—King's Advocate—Justice-Clerk—Master of Household—Doorward or Usher — Almoner — Maor, Maormor — Toschach — Thane—List of thanedoms—Bailie—Crowner—Constable—Investitures—Spurious Charters, . . 29

III.—PARLIAMENT.

Ancient divisions of the Kingdom—Uncertain tenure by the Kings, of Cumbria, Galloway, Caithness, Moray —Malcolm Canmore—Early differences between the Constitutions of England and Scotland—Royal Progresses—Influence of Queen Margaret upon Scotch Customs: Southern Immigration—The Officers of State during the reign of Canmore—Celtic Institutions —Earliest Court in Scotland—The Kings of Scotland not absolute—Origines Parliamentariæ: Alexander I.—Malcolm IV.—William the Lion—Alexander II.—John Balliol—William Wallace—Robert Bruce—Parliament complete—Similar Constitutions abroad—Parliament in the reign of David II. and Robert II.—Succession to the Crown—Robert III.—Records of Parliament in Scots—Taxing the test of supreme power of Parliament: taxation under Malcolm IV.—under William the Lion—State and Constitution of ancient Scotch Burghs—The Court of the Four Burghs the beginning of the Third Estate—Burghs in Parliament—Constitutional Government: Constitution of the Cambuskenneth Parliament—Name of "Parliament"—Commencement of the regular Records of Parliament—Powers of Parliament delegated, especially in judicial matters—Parliament held at Perth A.D. 1369—Lords of the Articles — Court of Session — Parliament of James I.—

Speaker of Parliament—Attempts at representation—Parliament of James II.—Act in favour of the "Pure pepil that labouris the grunde"—Early Sederunt of Parliament—Parliament of James III.—Power of Parliament intrusted to a Committee—Parliament of James IV.—Act for the benefit of Burghs—Act for compulsory Education—Act appointing Sang-schools in Burghs—Act establishing and endowing Parish Schools—Parliament in the reign of James V.—Representation of the lesser Barons—Parliament in the reign of Queen Mary and James VI.—Power of Parliament in the reign of Charles I.—The Commonwealth—Scotland represented in the British Parliament—Grouping of Shires—Grouping of Burghs—The Clergy as one of the Estates of Parliament—Act in regard to the Representation of Burghs—Forms of Parliament: Sitting of Parliament—Riding of Parliament—No debates in Parliament—How measures were carried through Parliament—Life Peerages—Defects in the political Constitution: Officers of State Members of Parliament *ex officiis*—The Committee of the Articles—Their Election—Usurpation of the power of Parliament—Revocation of Grants—Annexation—Heritable jurisdictions—The Act abolishing them—Excommunication by the Church—Liberty more protected in England than in Scotland—Law of treason—Styles of Parliamentary writs—Payment to Members of Parliament—Language of the Scotch Acts—Notice of some unjust Laws: Commonty—Sea shores—Clan-holding—Trout-fishing—Rights of road and way—Wise legislators in Parliament—Dying out of slavery first in Scotland, ... 92

IV.—THE OLD CHURCH.

Secular and regular clergy distinguished—Regulars: Monks (Cluniacs—Cistercians—Valliscaulium)—Culdees—Canons Regulars of St. Augustine—Priory of St.

Andrews—the Abbey of Scone—Benedictines of the unreformed rule of St. Bernard—Abbey of Dunfermline—Disputes about coal-levels between Dunfermline and Newbattle—Benedictines of Tiron—Abbey of Kelso—Cell of Lesmahago—Great Charter of Kelso—Abbey of Arbroath—Brecbennach—Cluniac Benedictines—Abbey of Paisley—Chartulary of Paisley—Pedigree of the Royal Stewarts—Abbey of Melrose—Royal Charters preserved by this house—Deathbed letter of Robert Bruce—Newbattle Abbey—Cistercians—Knights Templars—Knights of St. John of Jerusalem—Heads of Monasteries sat in Parliament—Officers of the Monastery—Abbot—Prior—Sub-Prior—Cellarer—Porter—Friars—Dominicans (Friars Preachers)—Franciscans (Friars Minors)—Carmelites—Nunneries—Augustinian Nuns of Sciennes—Nuns of St. Clare—Hospitals—Their intention—Seculars—Government and discipline of the Church—Notice of *Statuta Ecclesiæ Scoticanæ*—Bishoprics in Scotland—Archbishopric of St. Andrews—Suffragans of St. Andrews: Dunkeld, Aberdeen, Moray, Brechin, Dunblane or Stratherne, Ross, Caithness, Orkney Islands—Archbishopric of Glasgow—Archdeaconry of Glasgow proper: Deaneries of Rutherglen, Lennox, Lanark, Kyle and Cuninghame, Carrick—Archdeaconry of Teviotdale: Deaneries of Teviotdale, Peebles, Nithsdale, Anandale—Suffragans of Glasgow: Galloway, Argyle: (Deaneries of Cantyre, Glassary, Lorne, Morven), the Isles—How bishops appointed—The Pope's usurpation of patronage of Bishoprics—Constitution of the Chapter of Cathedrals—Dignified Canons: Dean—Archdeacon—Official—Precentor or Cantor—Song-schools—Chancellor—Treasurer—Numerous inferior dignitaries—Rural dean—Prebendaries—Distinction between *vicarii stallarii* and *vicarii parochiales*—Property of the Church—Mensal churches—Common churches—Parson or Rector—Appropriation—Impropriation—Great and small Tithes—Other sources of church revenue—Temporality—Spirituality

—Church rentals—Chartularies—Bagimond's Roll—
Valuation of benefices—Registers of Bishoprics—
Printed Chartularies of Monasteries—Monastic Registers still in MS.—Lost registers—Chartulary—Distinction between rectorial and vicarial Tithes—
Valuation of Vicarages—Valuation of Tithes—Settlement of Tithes—Church Foundations—Collegiate
Churches—Soltra—Trinity College, Edinburgh—Kirk
of Field—Restalrig—Corstorphine—Crichton—Dalkeith—Roslin—Commendator—Mitred Abbot—
Curate—Titular—Grant of *ecclesia*—Can and conveth
—Pleas at Dull—Dedications of churches, . . . 161

V.—OLD FORMS OF LAW.

Institutions common to the whole Anglo-Saxon peoples
omitted—Compurgation—*Judicium Dei*: Ordeal of
hot iron, of water, wager of battle—Church and
Crown procedure—Jury trial originated in Church
courts—Juries in use in England and Scotland
about the same time—Jury trial in its infancy—
Brieves from the Ayr MS. and Bute MS.—Case of
Monachkeneran—Lay process—The King at first
judging in person—Royal Brieves addressed to the
sheriffs—Inquests upon the Brieves—Early Juries—
Appeals—*Auditores causarum et querelarum*—*Acta
dominorum concilii domini regis*—Court of Session—
Early subjects of controversy—Notice of Brieves for
compelling payment of debts—Implement of contracts
—Brieves of mortancestry, of novel diseisin, of recognition, of perambulation, of partition, of ward—
Brief *de nativis et fugitivis*—Brief of emancipation—
Brief to compel payment of church rents—Brief against
excommunicates and apostates—Brief limiting the
jurisdiction of the Church—Brief prohibiting process
in Consistorial Court concerning a lay tenement—
Brieves concerning Seisin, Terce, Dowry, Tutory—
Brief to compel friends to support a pauper—Brief to

distinguish between aforethocht felony and *chaude melee*—Brief of right—Brief *in re mercatoria*—Brief ordering inquiry as to the disease of sheep—Brief for putting down cruives—Civil and Church Courts—Jurisdiction of the civil magistrate maintained by the Scotch Kings—The Consistorial Court—Its extensive jurisdiction—Henryson's Fable, ... 209

VI.—RURAL OCCUPATION.

Early information chiefly from religious houses—Rental of Monastery of Kelso, A.D. 1290—Teviotdale husbandry—Measures of Land: Oxgate—Husbandland—Ploughgate—Crops cultivated—Vehicles used—Roads and bridges—Flocks and herds—Wool, the great produce—The Grange or homestead—Inhabitants of the Grange: Native, Neyf or villein—Cottar—Husbandman—Services performed and rent paid—Description of horse-load—Exemption of women from field labour—*Stuht* equivalent to *steel-bow*—Kindly tenants of the Abbey—Church vassals, their condition and privileges—Mills and brewhouses—their rents—Lands granted for support of bridges—Public burdens—Military service from a ploughgate in 1327—Early contract of lease, A.D. 1312—Its language—Conditions of the lease—Rental of the Bishopric of Aberdeen, A.D. 1511—Services and rents—Rent of a ploughgate in the parish of Clatt—Parish of Fetternear—Conditions of Subletting—Rent of a croft—Rent of a mill—Forest of Glenrinnes reserved "to my lord" the Bishop—Good neighbourhood—Improvements by tenants—Runrig—Rent of the foggage of the forest of Birss—Rent in kind for the farm of Dulsak—Rental of the barony of Forbes 1532—Measures of land—Good neighbourhood—Office of "birleymen"—Rent of a ploughgate—Customs—Number of tenants on a ploughgate—Disappearance of the *nativi*—Rental of the Gordon estates, A.D. 1600—Holdings in joint occupancy—Maill or silver-maill—Ferme—Customs —Mart—Reek-hen—Ells of cloth—Specimens of rentals—West Highland tenants—Rent of a ploughgate in a Highland parish (Kingussie)—Rent of a ploughgate in a Lowland parish (Bellie)—Teinds—Fishings—Cattle and sheep—Leases—Sub-tenancy—Report on the Perth forfeited estates, 1762—Classes of Sub-tenants: Bowman—Steel-bowman—Pendicler —Cottar—Crofter—Dry-house-cottar—Rental of Struan, 1755—Items of rent—Souming—Rouming—Excessive population in the Highlands—Old Extent —Money measures established by this valuation—Money extent of a ploughgate—Where money measures of land most used—Davach of land: a division chiefly found in the North-Eastern Shires—*Terra ecclesiastica*—Etymology of Davach—Its extent—The "Aucht-and-forty Dauch of Huntly"—Earliest marks of national taxation—Ploughgate, oxgate, marks of taxation?—Money measures of land (poundland, markland, shillingland, pennyland, farthingland) more likely—Money measures found on the West—The valuation, whether for tax or rent on the West Coast and Isles, in money—The oldest Island rental preserved—Valuations in merks or multiples of merks—The rental of the Bishopric of the Isles—Rentals of Orkney and Shetland—No measure of land, agricultural or pastoral, there—Orcadian customs—Attempt to balance agricultural against money divisions—One oxgate = 13 acres—4 oxgates = one pound of Old Extent—40 shilling land of Old Extent = one ploughgate—1 merkland = $34\frac{2}{3}$ acres, 241

VII.—BOOKS.

Plea for the Study of Records—Guide books for the study: Diplomata et Numismata Scociæ—Kemble's collection of Anglo-Saxon Charters—Thorpe's collection of the Ancient Laws of England—L'Art de vérifier les Dates—Nicolas's Chronology of History—Chalmers's Caledonia—Origines Parochiales—Scotland in the Middle Ages—E. W. Robertson's Scotland under her Early Kings—Hailes's Annals—Thomas Innes's Critical Essay—Keith's Catalogue of Scottish Bishops — Crawford's Lives of the Great Officers of State—Chronicles of Melrose and Holyrood—Fordun's Scotichronicon—Barbour's Chronicle—Wyntoun's Chronicle—Chronicle of Lanercost—Reeves's Adomnan's Life of St. Columba—His History of the Culdees—The Registers of Bishoprics and Monasteries—Joseph Robertson's Antiquities of the Shires of Aberdeen and Banff—His Inventories of Queen Mary's Jewels—His Statutes and Councils of the Scotch Church—Henry Laing's Scottish Seals—Mr. David Laing on the Reformed Church and the old Scots poets—Du Cange's Dictionary of Mediæval Latin—Acts of the Parliaments of Scotland—General Index to the Acts of Parliament of Scotland—Barrington's Observations on the Statutes—Blount's Ancient Tenures and Jocular Customs of Manors—Oughton upon Consistorial Form of Process—White Kennet's Law of Parishes — The Works of Madox, Spelman, etc.—Stubbs's Documents of English Constitutional History—English and Scotch Record Publications, . . 286

APPENDIX.

Henryson's Fable, illustrating the Forms of the old Consistorial Court, ... 299

INDEX, ... 303

LECTURES

ON

LEGAL ANTIQUITIES.

LECTURE I.

INTRODUCTORY.

These Lectures have been twice read, with some variations. On the first occasion my audience consisted chiefly of a few gentlemen of my own profession, who gathered in our Library before the meeting of the Court in the cold and dark mornings of winter 1868-9, to hear what I could tell them of the antiquities of our law. Two years later, the Juridical Society did me the honour to ask me to repeat the course, and were so obliging as to change their evening hour and accustomed place of meeting, for mid-day in the Advocates' Library, to suit my convenience.

Before reading the Lectures at all, I thought fit to circulate a programme or table of contents, which attracted some attention and criticism. More than one of the heads of the profession took up my project favourably, and suggested subjects deserving of elucidation, which I had omitted. It is to one of these, whose least suggestion commands our respect, that I owe perhaps my most important chapter, that on the Parliamentary Constitution of Scotland. I hope my readers may think I have been well advised. Rude and unsuccessful as our early efforts at Parliamentary government were, there are things in the legislation of Scotland of which a Scotchman may well be proud, and even precedents which a learned Englishman may find useful for solving some of the acknowledged difficulties in the working of the great machine—institutions which even the British Parliament might borrow with advantage.

We have not had many legal antiquaries in Scotland; and if you criticise them, you will find that as you go farther back the writers are the more ignorant of the precedents and practice of early times in their own country. I should perhaps except Sir Thomas Craig, whose admirable book, the 'Jus Feodale,' must always be spoken of with respect. But Craig wrote less as a Scotch lawyer, than as a learned student of the civil and canon and feudal law. He quotes cases that happened in his own day and a little before, in Scotland, but he had no care to distinguish the history of our law from that of any other feudal nation; and whenever he makes a general assertion, I think you will find that he draws it from the Roman law or the book 'De Feudis'—which, united, were in fact the common law—the law of civilized Europe in his time.

Quite in an opposite direction was the failing of Sir John Skene, who, being employed to collect the old laws of Scotland, set his wits to *make* a respectable code of Scotch law, taking the materials wherever he could find them in lawyers' books, whether they were Scotch or English. Skene says very much of his labour in collecting and digesting his code, but it never occurred to him that the old laws of a country hitherto unpublished are to be found, or at least can best be tested and proved, in the written transactions of the people. I have tracked him and his manner of working, and I have not observed that he ever quotes an old charter, a brieve, or a step of old court procedure. He was satisfied with transferring to his work whole pages of the rambling note-books of nameless lawyers, and to attribute them to the legislation of fabulous kings from Malcolm Mackenneth downwards, while he put on his margins references to English books, wishing his reader to believe that these were borrowed from ours.

I have never found much satisfaction in consulting Sir George Mackenzie's 'Observations on the Statutes.' That accomplished scholar to whom we owe, I suppose, the first foundation of our noble library, directed his studies for the most part to more congenial pursuits. Neither his studies nor the bent of his mind were very historical, and not at all constitutional. His 'Observations on the Statutes,' published in the worst time of our history (1686), are unfortunately suited to that bad time.

Books like Dirleton and Stewart (Dirleton's 'Doubts and Questions in Law,' and Stewart's 'Answers') are rather ingenious elucidations of the subtleties of the law than works of legal and historical antiquities. Dirleton, speaking of Sir Thomas Hope, calls him *juris nostri peritissimus*, but qualifies his praise by telling us that he was generally thought of extreme and captious subtlety (*nimiae et captiosae subtilitatis*); but it was the age of such subtlety, and the ingenious writer is himself open to the same blame. You will find some curious speculation in these books with regard to Crown lawyers stretching the royal prerogative—doubly interesting when you reflect that the Lord Advocate of Charles the Second, writing just before the Revolution, is explained and criticised by the Lord Advocate of William and Mary.[1] Stewart reproaches Dirleton for taking his notion of *prerogative* from the Roman law.

[1] Voce *Prerogative*.

"As to questions," he says, "of state and government, the Civil Law is of no use with us." But neither of these ingenious writers thought of solving any doubt or problem by seeking back to the origins and history of law in our country. Observe, that during the time we have yet looked to, there were none of the facilities for study which the modern lawyer possesses. There were no printed Collections of Decisions, no institutional writer had yet ventured to speak of the law of Scotland as a peculiar system, well defined by long series of precedents, and worthy to be called the common law of our country. Thin MS. volumes of 'Practicks,' collected by old lawyers, still passed from hand to hand, and were copied by young students and clerks with more or less accuracy. These were quoted and received as authorities; and indeed it is matter of admiration how lawyers have in all times admitted any precedents and authorities, as if to save them from the dreaded discussion of principles.

At length arose Stair, of whom we Scotsmen speak with some of the superstitious respect which the English show for Littleton and his great Commentator, and, I think, with better reason. But the object of Lord Stair was very different from that of Sir Edward Coke, who was a thorough lawyer, and, be it said—*pace tanti viri*—nothing more. Before coming to the bar Dalrymple had *regented* for ten years at Glasgow, and was deeply imbued with the philosophy and divinity of the schools, as well as with all the learning of the Civil and Canon law. So armed and accomplished, and with the practical experience of a well employed Scotch lawyer, he employed his leisure— his forced leisure—in building up a great fabric of national jurisprudence. His vigorous and well-trained intellect was directed to the philosophy of his youth, to the Divine law and the law of Nature, as the foundations of his system, and he wished to prove that the decisions of the Scotch Courts were not inconsistent with these. But a very slight attention to his great work will show that he had not bestowed much thought upon the historical foundations—the origin and progress of our peculiar law.[1] There were, in truth, no materials for such a study in Scotland. If we set aside the books of Skene as we do the fables of Hector Boece, I say there were no materials in Stair's time for a busy lawyer to work out the foundations of legal history. I need not say that there was as yet no taste or call for such studies.

Unfortunately the taste for historical antiquities had not yet arisen when our *second* great institutionalist produced his well-known work. Erskine

---

[1] 'Stair's Institutes,' ed. Brodie; Brieve, p. 608.

found the law of Scotland much elaborated since the days of Stair, and settled by printed decisions. These he quotes, and supports his positions with citations from Craig's 'Jus Feodale,' Balfour's 'Practicks,' Bankton's 'Institutes,' Kames's works and Mackenzie's. He had the good fortune and the good sense to use 'Blackstone,' and he made full use of the civil law and civilians, including Grotius. But I suspect he was ignorant of our Scotch history; and for our peculiar and national law he is content to take it as given by Skene, and admits all Skene's materials as of excellent use towards understanding the history and gradual progress of our law. I do not find that Erskine himself anywhere seeks back to the antique original of any branch of Scotch law; and now that we have so much printed of old styles and forms and examples of early litigation, Erskine's few contributions to legal antiquities seem to us very trifling.

Two Baronets, lawyers, of the great legal name of Dalrymple, have done much to remove the reproach of want of reasonable research concerning the *origines* and history of Scotch law. You will excuse me for placing them together, although they lived, the one at the beginning, the other at the end of last century. In two things only do they agree. They were both zealous Presbyterians, and both founded their historical statements upon proofs from ancient writs, though I doubt if either of them could actually read an old charter with ease.[1] Sir James Dalrymple collected copies of charters which he considered useful for proving that Presbytery was the most ancient form of Christianity; and he threw them into his book in such wild confusion that it is impossible to follow his purpose except from the headings of his chapters. His book was published just before the Union (1705). He calls it 'Collections concerning the Scottish History preceding 1153, wherein the Sovereignty of the Crown and Independence of the Church are cleared—with an account of *the Antiquity and Purity of the Scottish British Church, and the Noveltie of Popery in this Kingdom.*'

His namesake and kinsman, Sir David Dalrymple, better known as Lord Hailes, was in some respects the very ideal of a historical inquirer. His mind was fair and dispassionate, and he reasoned with excellent logic. You will seldom find a mistake in fact or a conclusion not warranted by the premisses in Lord Hailes's 'Annals.' He had some defects, too, and the greatest of them is an unnecessary and repulsive dryness of narrative. You know Dr. Johnson, though

[1] Mr. Thomas Thomson always doubted Hailes's ability to read charter-hand.

loving nothing Scotch, admired the accuracy of our Scotch annalist. What he did was of inestimable value. But surely it was not necessary that an author using the same title which Tacitus gave to his greatest historical work, should make his 'Annals' little better than a chronicle of kings and queens and battles, and births and deaths—a sort of almanac of history.

The second fault which I—a humble follower at such a distance—venture to charge against Lord Hailes, is his slighting of the great subject of Church antiquities—as important a chapter of national history as any; and I think Lord Hailes would have confessed so much. But the materials were not in his hands. You observe that he wrote chiefly from English chroniclers, and with them, of course, the Church of Scotland is little more than a name, whilst the real materials for Church history were still to be gathered from neglected MSS., Chartularies, fragments of Church Books, cases in Church Courts, which had never come in Lord Hailes's way. I am aware that he gives such scraps of Scotch Church history as he found in Fordun, and that he even bestows a dissertation upon the Canons of the Church of Scotland, one copy of which—a very imperfect copy, a mere fragment indeed—he found in the Chartulary of Aberdeen. But these are only proofs how little the Presbyterian lawyer had thought it worth his while to investigate the history of a superstitious Church. I am unwilling by even these small deductions to appear to lessen the fame of him who was really the first to investigate accurately, and state honestly, the early history of our country.

We moderns are hardly enough aware how much the Scotch lawyer is indebted to Henry Home, Lord Kames. His versatile and truly philosophical mind neglected nothing. He enriched the law of Scotland by his collection of remarkable decisions, by his abridgment of the Statutes, and by a large body of ingenious speculations and criticisms upon law and legal decisions. I think you will find his opinions sagacious, and for the most part sound. They would have had more weight with the profession if written in more technical language, and if he had thought it worth his while to hide the marks of his early philosophical studies. A Scotch lawyer is roused to a little jealousy, if not to laughter, when he reads in a treatise on the law of Prescription, that the writer found it "indispensable to examine what the law of Nature, or in other words, common law, dictated on that subject;" or when he begins a commentary on an Act of Parliament concerning procuratories of resignation and precepts of sasine, with words like the following:—
" Man, a voluntary agent, governs himself and his

concerns by his own will, and, in order to fulfil it, he exerts external acts," etc.[1]

This most ingenious, most suggestive of our legal writers, perceived all the importance of *our* studies, and in one or two instances he actually dug out an old record and used it. In his inquiries he had the invaluable assistance of John Davidson, Writer to the Signet, or, as he chose to write himself, Clerk to the Signet, a lawyer following in the footsteps and imitating even the uninviting manner of Lord Hailes. But neither he nor any man *then* had access to the whole stores of our records, which were indeed unknown to their keepers.

If we did not know his unhappy end, we should call Alexander Wight, the author of the 'Law of Elections' and 'History of Parliament,' the most sensible, dispassionate, and clear-headed of historical lawyers. He had great difficulties to contend with in writing too early for correct versions of our Acts of Parliament; and the curious charters appended to his volume lose much of their value by the extreme inaccuracy of the only readings which he could procure.

I now come to the best and greatest of our historical lawyers, Thomas Thomson. With great sense and sagacity, with ample preliminary study,

[1] 'Elucidations,' Articles 33, 39.

and very uncommon legal learning, Thomson might have risen to the head of his profession in any of its more trodden paths, but some circumstances of the day—a considerable Record movement spreading from England to us, and, more than any circumstances, "the strong propensity of nature,"— urged him to the study of legal and historical antiquities. Some of his pleadings while still at the bar are very masterly. I need not remind you of that one which carried the Court in the great Craigengillan marriage case, nor of the dissertation in the case of Cranston *v.* Gibson (1818), which most of us have on our shelves, titled 'Old Extent,' and the study of which Lord Glenlee said was like reading a lost decade of Livy. In that pleading, regarding a vote in this county, Mr. Thomson laid before the Court the most learned and accurate history of Scotch taxation that has ever been written. No wonder that it cost much time and much reproof for delay. The fines for the delay of that paper— *amendes* they called them then—amounted to £20. The materials for the paper were to a large extent unprinted. Mr. Thomson will be remembered always by the Scotch lawyer for having rescued our Records from impending decay and ruin, and for having given, in almost a complete series, the body of the legislation of Scotland, as well as shown the way, in the beginnings of works like the great collection of the Chamberlain Rolls, one volume of the 'Registrum Magni Sigilli,' and a digested edition of the first century of Scotch Retours. These are noble works, of importance to all the professions of the law, and still serve as examples—such examples as men are slow to follow—of how a system of national Records can be turned to great popular use.

Mr. Thomson, who was educated for the Church —the Presbyterian Church of Scotland—like his master Hailes had somewhat neglected the study of middle-age Church history; and you will find the same neglect running through the works of all our modern historians, from Pinkerton and Tytler down to our friend Mr. Burton, who eschews superstition of all kinds.

We had lately to regret the premature loss of a Record scholar and historical inquirer of quite a different stamp. Mr. Joseph Robertson was as scrupulous about his facts as Lord Hailes, as careful and correct in reading and editing as Mr. Thomson. He had, however, with the most catholic love of antiquities, a strong feeling of the importance of the ecclesiastical element in Scotch history, and his book 'Concilia et Statuta Scotiae' has gone far to supply the short-comings of Hailes and Thomson in Church history, while his 'Inventories of Queen Mary' have improved a dry list of the Queen's jewels and clothes into a very picturesque and, I think, a very true view of the life of the unhappy Queen.

Hitherto, and with only the last remarkable exception, the writers of our legal history, of *applied* history, as we may call it—history applied to the investigations of law—have been all Advocates —a profession which has won and kept the foremost place in the literature as well as in the law of this country. It is an unenvied pre-eminence: for who does not know the long and laborious education required before the student can enter the profession of an advocate? who but must see the strain of the intellect, not to mention the natural gifts, required to take any prominent position at the bar? But the sister profession of Scotch Conveyancers has also had men of historical research, who have adorned the drier work of their peculiar study with some of the legal learning which suits it so well. From the time of Dallas of St. Martin's there has been a succession of learned conveyancers, who have, indeed, been generally content to feel the position their learning had given them among lawyers, without giving the world the benefit of their studies.

John Clerk, in his pleading in the great "Old Extent" case, mentions Mr. D. Erskine, Mr. John Russell, Mr. William Tytler, Mr. Charles Gordon, Mr. Isaac Grant, and Mr. Samuel Mitchelson, as the most eminent conveyancers of their time—that is, of Lord Eldin's own; and upon some doubt being thrown on his statement, the great lawyer's junior (afterwards Lord Murray) returns to these names. Can there be, he says, any higher authorities in the profession than Mr. D. Erskine and Mr. John Russell, senior?[1]

[1] The first in the above list, Mr. David Erskine, has left the highest reputation as a feudalist and conveyancer of any man of his time. He was son of John Erskine of Carnock, the author of the 'Institutes,' and I believe he edited that book after his father's death. His mother was Miss Stirling of Keir, the second wife of the author of the 'Institutes;' of his former marriage with Miss Melville was born Dr. John Erskine, so well remembered as minister of the Greyfriars.

Mr. David Erskine was the head of that house well known for two generations afterwards under the name of Dundas and Wilson, Clerks to the Signet. It is pleasant to trace the transmission of personal qualities and professional eminence in the same house.

John Russell, senior, was the author of two works—'Forms of the Court of Session and Teinds,' 1768, and the 'Theory of Conveyancing,' 1788.

I wish to add the names of a few other Writers to the Signet who have left a memory honoured in the profession. James Anderson, Writer to the Signet, whose literary and patriotic works injured, I fear, his professional business, was the author of several books, occasioned by the proposed Union of the kingdoms, and asserting the ancient independence of Scotland. He was the compiler of the 'Diplomata et Numismata Scotiae,' a noble collection of Charters and Coins, to which Thomas Ruddiman contributed the Latin introduction.

George Home of Wedderburn and Paxton was learned, especially in commercial law. He managed the affairs of the Douglas, Heron and Co. Bank, after its bankruptcy—the most noted bankruptcy, I suppose, in Scotland previous to the failure of the Western Bank. There is a tradition that it was the general wish of his profession that Mr. Home should be raised to the Bench. I think Sir Walter Scott succeeded him as Clerk of Session. He

Almost all these learned conveyancers have avoided publishing the results of their studies, content to let their names be handed down in the tradition of their profession.

To this over-modest silence, however, there have been some exceptions, and prominent among these was Mr. Walter Ross, the author of Lectures on Conveyancing, and especially of a preliminary or specimen Lecture on the narrow subject—though on principles of humanity a very important one—of "Removing of Tenants," which he treated with such learning and research as give importance to any subject.

George Chalmers, the author of 'Caledonia,' the enemy of Pinkerton, the champion of the Celts, has contributed some papers to the 'Mirror.'

John Davidson was W.S. and Crown Agent. Hume in his Lectures used to mention his Treatise on the Roman Law, discussing whether it should be quoted as *our* law. I know him better for what I believe is the first correction of the fable of the 'Regiam Majestatem,' where he tells us, what is now well known, that the "Regiam Majestatem is a book copied from Glanvill." Davidson was succeeded in his business and the office of Crown Agent by Hugh Warrender.

Archibald Swinton was an able conveyancer. He managed the great estates of the York Building Co.,—that is, in fact, all the Forfeited Estates.

David Wemyss has left the tradition of a learned and eminent conveyancer.

Colin Mackenzie was considered a learned conveyancer, but withdrew from business when he became Clerk of Session.

Sir James Gibson-Craig, though so eminent and influential in the profession, was, I think, better known for his management and organization of business than for any deep study of technical conveyancing.

done more than any one man for the topography and family history of Scotland. He laboured under the disadvantage of defective scholarship, of which he was quite unconscious; and he is not more strong in Gaelic and British, I believe, than in Latin. In charter study, where everything depends on accuracy of text, he worked with faulty copies, but yet, if he had bestowed the time he wasted on Lollius Urbicus and the Roman period of our history on the parts of modern Scotland which he left untouched, he might, with his astonishing perseverance, have completed what seems an undertaking too great for one life.

Among Scotch legal antiquaries I must not omit the name of John Riddell, who spent a long

---

I have thought that it might be interesting to preserve the names of some of those eminent men, who founded houses of law business, where the traditions of their conveyancing must have continued to guide their successors in business. It is very long since the *Styles* of Dallas of St. Martin's could have formed the rule of practice amongst us. After his and Spottiswood's subsequent book became antiquated, the necessary forms and styles of writs were no doubt preserved and handed down in the chambers of such men as I have enumerated, until Russell's books supplied the more modern conveyancing required by the last two generations. The happy idea of making a selection of styles from actual instances of writs used in all the great conveyancing houses is due to the Juridical Society; and although some of the earlier forms inserted in that work show strange symptoms of insufficient care, the work, as it now stands, meets, I believe, with general approbation. It seems to me that the style of the present day would bear a vigorous pruning.

life in searching and noting the contents of charter-chests. I once heard him say—"I assure you that to spend one's time in seeking for a name or date in a bit of crabbed old writing does not improve the reasoning powers." And perhaps it is not in reasoning that Mr. Riddell excels; his style too is hardly English; but his two volumes contain a vast mass of new facts on Peerage and Consistorial Law; and his collected MSS., which our Library owes to the generosity of Lord Lindsay, will be found, no doubt, a treasure to the pedigree-hunter, especially if he loves a little old scandal to season the dish.

Using the sources which these men have opened to us, using other materials which the taste created by them has brought before the world, taking my examples and illustrations often from MSS., often from printed books of that kind of rarity which the book-fancier holds to be "as good as MS.," I undertake to lay before you, and to strip of their mysterious obscurity, in the first place, some of those early charters, the first writing of our forefathers, records of their first transactions, documents which show how they held their property, how they settled with or fought with their neighbours, what jurisdiction they exercised over their vassals, and all *that* in a language which, though Latin, is only Saxon Latinized. You will find in those charters the best explanation of modern conveyancing. We shall get beyond the difficulties which impede the reader of 'Waverley' when the Baron of Bradwardine pours out his charter-learning, how the lands of "Bradwardine and Tully-Veolan had been erected into a free barony by a charter from David the First, cum liberali potestate habendi curias et justicias, cum fossa et furca (*lie* pit and gallows) et saka et soka, et thol et them, et infangthef et outfangthef, sive hand-habend sive bak-barand." "The peculiar meaning of all these cabalistical words few or none could explain," says Scott, who had some of the learning of the writer's chamber as well as of the bar. I modestly propose to undertake the task.

In connexion with these old charters I once thought of saying something of the manner of giving possession—taking heritable state and seisin—whether *per fustem et baculum*, by staff and baton, or in the homely form which Bailie Macwheeble would have recognised—*per terrae et lapidis traditionem*—by giving of earth and stone. In short, I had planned a little discussion on the curious, now forgotten, learning of symbols—the symbolism of feudal investiture. I wished to tell you how King Alexander the Fierce—elder brother of the good King David—invested the Cathedral of Saint Andrews in the *cursus apri*,—the "bares rayke" Wynton calls it—who tells us how at Saint Andrews, the King offered it on the high altar in symbol, and how he gave investiture by such symbols of investiture:

> " Hys cumly sted of Araby,
> Sadelyd and brydelyd costlykly,
> Wyth hys armwrys off Turky,
> That pryncys than oysid generaly,
> And chesyd mast for thare delyte,
> Wyth scheld and spere off sylver qwhyt,
> Wyth mony a precyows fayre Jowele."

Or I might tell you a yet older story, which I have always thought to be the very first instance of symbolical seisin:—Saint Columba wished to take heritable state and seisin of his little island of Hy, and resolved it would be best done by the interment there of one of his followers; but the question was who should die and be buried for this end. Then Oran arose quickly, and thus spoke:—" If you accept me, I am ready for that." " Oh, Oran," said Columkille, " you shall receive the reward of this." Oran then died, and was buried, and Columba founded the church of Hy close to the grave of Oran. Some of you may know that even yet the cemetery of Iona is known by the name of " Relig-Oran." But I fear your patience would fail, as well as my time, if we were to trace our poor seisins back so far.

Then you will pass with me into the august presence of an ancient and defunct Parliament. I will try to show you how an unbroken line of Celtic monarchs framed the constitution of their kingdom on Saxon models. You will see the Three Estates intermingled, taking their places round the throne, in no less hopeful form than the Parliament of England, before it resolved in its wisdom to divide into two Houses. When bad days had come, and the spirit of Scotland had taken another direction than the constitutional, you will still see convulsive struggles after freedom and good government, and will observe how some men at least in that anomalous assemblage were wise and good enough to pass the earliest laws that we read of in favour of the poor people that labour the ground—in favour of education of all classes—first the Barons' sons, and, later, the class that required an endowment of parish schools, which endowment was not withheld by poor Scotland.

I cannot show you a form of process so ancient as that of the County Courts of England, where, they tell us, in the days of Alfred, the Earl and the Bishop sat side by side, administering justice and directing proceedings, by which suitors obtained the judgment of their peers; but we can get back to that time when civil justice in its infancy was already vigorous enough to support the rights of the Church, and could yet peremptorily limit the jurisdiction of Churchmen seeking to meddle in civil matters. For this purpose I shall report for your special use one entire process, keenly contested on the banks of the Clyde in the year of grace 1233. I will lay before you, too, I may say for the first time, some of those Brieves, which, in this country as well as in England, are the oldest remaining traces of civil process, though with us the change of form, the abandonment of the ancient trial by jury in civil cases, have thrown these writs out of the notice of lawyers.

I will detain you but a short time upon the ramifications of the King's Council, our first Supreme Civil Court of common origin, if not originally identical, with the High Court of Parliament. And then come the committees of Parliament, upon whom the rustic Barons gladly devolved their judicial powers, and you will see how for some generations the Lords of the Council and the Parliamentary Committee, known as the Lords Auditors of Complaints and Causes, carried on a concurrent and undistinguishable jurisdiction, until the power and jurisdiction of both were merged in one by the Act which created the Court of Session, and furnished the subject of our fine window up-stairs.

All law students must feel the difficulties which men of our National Church have to encounter in dealing with old Church law and practice, having to speak of the functions, offices, persons of an ecclesiastical system *quorum ipsa nomina perdidi-*

mus—whose very names we have forgotten. You will forgive me if, in my endeavours to supply the defect in our books—to join on the old system of Church and Churchman to the modern more simple order of things, and especially to make the legal phraseology intelligible which had to deal with the benefices and properties, the title-deeds, as I may say, of a great hierarchy now defunct,—you will forgive me if, with these objects, I seem to run very elementary.

To some of you much that I shall say upon this subject will be the repetition of a well-known lesson; but those who know it best will agree with me that it is very useful, and that it is not all to be found in any of our text-books.

The endeavour to restore to the Reformed Church some adequate living for its clergy, and also to provide from the plunder of the old Church in lay hands some help to the slender resources of the Crown, gave rise to the remarkable undertaking of Charles the First to induce, or almost compel, the great holders of the spirituality of the ancient Church to place at his royal disposal, on equitable terms, the whole tithes of Scotland. It was to carry out that great undertaking that the successive Commissions were issued for surrender, valuation, allocation of teinds. I need not tell you that questions relating to teinds are now the great questions of the antiquarian lawyer in Scotland. The learning of the bar is no longer exercised in setting up a 40 shilling land of old extent or a £400 Scots of valued rent; even the antiquity of entails has no longer to be studied—no man values a county franchise now—the fetters of a strict entail are of little value since the Rutherfurd Act—but in teinds there still lurks that mysterious and alluring obscurity that furnishes the best field-days at our bar, and requires the deepest investigation thoroughly to master. I hope the last Lecture to which I have alluded—I mean the history and nomenclature of the old Church—will be found useful here, and that the knowledge of the old possessors, their tenures and varying interests, will help us to comprehend the footing upon which the settlement was intended to be carried through by Charles and his successive Parliaments.

To myself personally the most interesting subject which I have to bring under your notice is the state of our rural population. I think a notice of the tenures, service, rents, measures of land—the whole system of agricultural life—may be rendered very useful to lawyers on very many occasions of practice. But I shall not hold myself precluded from speaking of the state of the people, their social condition, even the signs of their intelligence; I shall not avoid such matter merely because it may not answer the purpose of a legal argument. Speaking to you as Scotchmen as well as lawyers, I shall expect your attention to the proofs which I can give you of a steady progress in the agricultural class. I will show you first how the great agriculturists cultivated their lands chiefly by serfs bound to the soil. We shall observe serfdom gradually disappearing, leaving behind it only the system of heavy services done to the *master;* and the gradual conversion of these into money rent marks everywhere a great step in agricultural progress. From the thirteenth century, when the serfs must have formed a large proportion of the population, when gifts of serfs, and sales of serfs, and claims of runaway slaves, are of as frequent occurrence as any transactions connected with land—between that century and the end of the fifteenth, hereditary slavery had ceased among us without any legislative Act, and from 1500 down to 1600, all that sixteenth century, I shall endeavour to present to you a free agricultural class, as it is shown in careful rentals—rentals both of Church lands and of great lay lords,— affording a fair specimen of the relations between landlord and tenant over Scotland.

In that history of landlords and tenants I must say something on the question of rent, or its equivalents, of the agricultural divisions of the soil, oxgate, husband-land, ploughgate, merk-land, penny-land, and our northern designation of *Davach.*

The Lecture which I have headed 'The Vestiges of Early Taxation' serves to call up the subjects of Thomas Thomson's great labour. I trust you will find some progress in the amount of our knowledge since his day; and no man would have rejoiced more than he, if it shall turn out that we have successfully brought the ancient valuation to its common and popular equivalent in the agricultural divisions of land, and have proved that a 40 shilling land of old extent was nothing more nor less than a ploughgate of land.

I will not detain you with more remarks of my own, as it were in apology of our studies, but you will allow me to quote three or four sentences from an author whom you must know if you have sought back into the wells of pure English, as the purest writer between the old heroic times and our slipshod modern style, I mean Lord Bolingbroke.

Bolingbroke is a good authority in this matter; for he was no dabbler in antiquities, and would have been much disgusted with the dirt and dust of an old charter. Hear him whilst he speaks of our own professional studies.

"I might instance," he says, "in other professions the obligation men lie under of applying themselves to certain parts of history, and I can hardly forbear doing it in that of the law, in its nature the noblest and most beneficial to mankind, in its abuse and debasement the most sordid and the most pernicious.

"A lawyer now is nothing more,—I speak of ninety-nine in an hundred at least, to use some of Tully's words,—'nisi leguleius quidam, cautus et acutus, praeco actionum, cantor formularum, auceps syllabarum.' But there have been lawyers that were orators, philosophers, historians; there have been Bacons and Clarendons, my Lord.[1] There will be none such any more till in some better age, true ambition or the love of fame prevails over avarice, and till men find leisure and encouragement to prepare themselves for the exercise of the profession by climbing up to the vantage-ground (so my Lord Bacon calls it) of science; instead of grovelling all their lives below in a mean but gainful application to all the little arts of chicane.

"Till this happen, the profession of the law will scarce deserve to be ranked among the learned professions; and whenever it happens, one of the vantage-grounds to which men must climb is metaphysical, and the other historical knowledge. They must pry into the secret recesses of the human heart, and become well acquainted with the whole moral world, that they may discover the abstract reason

[1] His book was addressed to Clarendon's son.

of all law; and they must trace the laws of particular states, especially of their own, from the first rough sketches to the more perfect draughts; from the first causes or occasions that produced them, through all the effects, good or bad, that they produced."

LECTURE II.

CHARTERS.

WE have no Scotch charter extant so early as the reign of Malcolm Canmore.[1] In the reigns of Canmore's sons who preceded David I. we have a very few grants to religious houses, but none to individuals or laymen. The very oldest writ, in the shape of a charter connected with Scotland, is that of Duncan, the son of Malcolm Canmore, the date of which is about 1094. With David I. really begins our body of Scotch charters, and we have a suffi-

---

[1] A.D. 1056-1093. As to the antiquity of writing with us, the highest authority in England has pronounced that there is no trustworthy record of any single event of English history previous to the arrival of Augustine (A.D. 597). We cannot go quite so far back in Scotland, and perhaps we must limit our assertion of the antiquity of Scotch writing to the ascertained period of the Book of Deer, the margins of which are covered with narratives of the endowment of the little Buchan convent, all written in Gaelic, and without doubt, of the ninth and tenth centuries.

You will find similar narratives or notices in the venerable Register of the Priory of St. Andrews, where gifts of Macbeth and of Lady Macbeth, and of a Pictish king Brude, perhaps traditionary, are engrossed in order before the charters which we now look upon as of the most venerable antiquity.

cient number of *his* preserved either in the originals, or recorded in the registers of religious houses, to give us an accurate idea of their manner and contents.

You will observe that David's charters begin with setting forth his title in the simplest form, "Rex Scottorum,"[1] but then they are addressed to all his subjects in Scotland and in Lothian, to Scotsmen and Englishmen; or like the charter[2] of Melrose, to Bishops, Abbots, Earls, Barons, and good men of his whole kingdom, French and English and Scots; or as in Bruce's charter of Anandale,[3] to all his Barons and men and friends, French and English; or to all the good men of his whole land, French and English and Galwegians;[4] or as in an old charter of Swinton,[5] to his Earls, Barons, Sheriffs, officers, and all his liegemen of his whole land, cleric and laic.

I think it is plain that David King of Scots wrote himself King of the whole population, native and foreign, in Scotland proper, be-north Forth, in Lothian, and in Galloway; and that, although he set forth his title so shortly, he claimed the allegiance of all the inhabitants of these lands, whether Scots, English, French, or Galwegians.

You will find the earliest Scotch deeds without

---

[1] 'National MSS. of Scotland,' Part I. No. 15.   [2] *Ibid.* No. 17.
[3] *Ibid.* 19.   [4] *Ibid.* 20.   [5] *Ibid.* 22.

date—without *anno domini* or *anno regni*. Occasionally, but very rarely, the writer gives a bit of contemporary history to mark the era. The perambulation of bounds and marches between King David and Henry Abbot of Melrose is dated on "Friday, the morrow of the Ascension of our Lord, in the second year after the taking of Stephen of England"[1]—an historical event now almost forgotten. *Postquam arma suscepi*, says one king,—after I assumed arms,—pointing to the king's receiving knighthood. *Post devictum Somerledum*—after the defeat of Somerled, and *post concordiam cum Somerledo*—after the peace made with Somerled, —*post adventum Ducis Saxonie*—after the arrival of the Duke of Saxony,—mark events of the greatest importance in the writer's opinion. It was not till a considerable time after charters had been introduced into Scotland, that the practice began of marking the date by the year from the nativity of our Saviour, which had been used on the Continent, however, somewhat earlier. The Anglo-Saxon charters are, for the most part, devoid of any date; and following them in style and manner, our earliest Scotch charters are to be chronologised or placed in their true era chiefly by the names of the granter,

---

[1] Stephen was taken at the battle of Lincoln, on February 1141, by Maud the Empress (daughter of Henry II. of England, wife of the Emperor Henry IV.)

grantee, and witnesses. It is but an approximation, but in general the names of a bishop or two, or of a great officer of state, joined with the granter, leave little room for error. In a charter of Malcolm the Fourth the date is fixed by a single witness. William, Bishop of Moray, is styled, in addition to his episcopal title, "Legate of the Apostolic See." Now, we know that Bishop William of Moray went on a mission from Malcolm the Fourth to the Pope, and returned with the power and title of Legate in 1160. We know also that he died in 1161, so that single witness brings the time to a point. It is more frequently ascertained from the concurrence of several witnesses, and now, when so many Scotch chartularies have been printed, it is not so difficult as it used to be to find an approximate date for any charter with witnesses named. Of the general chronology of our records, I have only to remind you that in all the charters and documents of David II. dated after his return from England, the *annus domini* is found not to agree with the *annus regni*, the latter falling short of the former by one year.

Some of the charters of David to monasteries and churchmen are elaborately handsome and full of details. Both as to matter and shape, the monkish writers took great pains about their own charters.[1]

[1] *e.g.* The Great Charters of Holyrood and Kelso: National MSS., Part I. Nos. 16 and 32.

But charters to laymen, even of the greatest consequence, and conveying territories of immense extent and jurisdiction all but royal, were often extremely short. Bruce's first charter of Anandale, the first title of that illustrious family in Scotland, consists of ten lines, and is about the size of a modern letter folded for post. His charter of the same territory to be held in free forest is still smaller, and might well go in a modern post letter without folding,[1] and you will observe that all charters in early times are written only on one side. Those little ancient charters contain simple words of gift, and when you can read the hand, which is easier than the writing of some centuries lower down, and can decipher a few simple contractions, there is nothing that requires explanation. I do not mean that these two writs are not worthy of much study from the conveyancer. Observe, the *barony* does not occur in either charter, and it would seem that a grant of forest was the most extensive and most privileged then in use.

But from that time, and during centuries afterwards, charters were increasing in bulk, and the additional matter is often no help to the sense. I propose to take a charter, or rather a composition

---

[1] The writer is not strong in his Latin. He writes *foresto* instead of *foresta*, *vallum* instead of *vallem*, and *venatur* instead of *venetur*. But, after all, our old charter Latin is not so bad as the French, which confounds all grammar.

of many charters, at a time when this verbosity had come to its height, and to explain, as shortly as I can, such difficulties in matter or in language as seem to me to require explanation. With this view we will take the order of the clauses as adopted by Mr. Erskine, and indeed as found in the charters themselves.

I shall not detain you upon the designation and styles of the granters of early charters, although it is worth while noticing how, from the very beginning of our writs, our kings threw themselves free of the absurd magniloquence of the granters of Anglo-Saxon charters, where the petty kings of an English county called themselves *King* and *Basileus*, not only of their own tribes of Saxons, Angles, or Jutes, but of all the surrounding nations—*omnium nationum circumjacentium*. Our king was from the beginning "Rex Scottorum," and never added to his style, whether he acquired an English earldom, or gained a surer footing in Galloway or the Isles, or enlarged his borders in Lothian.

One other remark, and I have done with this point. An assertion of hereditary right in our first received charter has been held to throw a little doubt either upon the hereditary right of the granter, or upon the authenticity of the charter. I allude to the first charter in all Scotch collections, where

Duncan, the son of Malcolm Canmore, styles himself "constans hereditarie rex Scottorum." And I myself at one time thought the phraseology of that assertion a circumstance of suspicion, but I had not then observed that it was a mere copy of the style just before adopted by the English king, William the Conqueror.[1]

Neither shall I detain you long upon the persons or classes to whom early royal charters are addressed.

I mentioned already that David the First addressed them to the different nations over whom he ruled, "To Scots and English, to French and Galwegians, in Scotland (Scotland proper, that is, from Forth to Spey) and Lothian," and he and his successors frequently addressed their charters to the Bishops, Abbots, Earls, Barons, Justiciars, Sheriffs, *Prepositi*, Officers, and to all the good men of his land. One charter is addressed to his Thanes and Drengs in Lothian and Teviotdale.[2]

I do not know that there is much to explain here. These styles were borrowed almost *verbatim* from Anglo-Saxon England. Of *Thanes* I shall

---

[1] National MSS., Part I. No. 1. A very few years before the granting of Duncan's charter, there were laid upon the altar at Durham two charters of gift from the Conqueror to the monks of Durham, the granter styling himself "Willelmus dei gratia Rex Anglorum hereditario jure factus."—Raine's North Durham.

[2] National MSS., Part I. No. 12.

speak hereafter; *Dreng,* a title almost forgotten, was the name of a class somewhat above villenage, but yet not free tenants. The class of the "good-men"—*probi homines,* does not precisely mean men of morality. Like *liberetenentes,* the title of *probi homines* has been a great subject of controversy in England, without much fruit from the strife. Without even opening the argument, which you will find at length in Brady, and the writers of his time, I think English lawyers have now agreed that *probi homines* may be correctly rendered either vassals or subjects.[1]

The common inductive cause for granting charters in feudal times was, of course, *pro servicio suo.* It is often stated that the grant is in reward of service, but most commonly the gift is for service done and to be done, past and future. Along with service is joined homage and fealty—*pro homagio et fidelitate.* Sometimes an old charter runs like a modern conveyance in a marriage-settlement—*pro*

---

[1] With us *probus homo* has a similar meaning. I have myself a series of charters and letters in which the owners of certain lands in Moray are styled "Good-man of Cotts"—"Good-man of Leuchars;" and that designation lasted for a century or two, during which time the lands were held of a subject-superior, the Earl of Huntly. But a time came when (I daresay for political purposes), with the consent of the Earls, these old vassals of theirs were promoted to a crown holding, and then, contemporary with their very first royal charter, they are styled by their neighbours and the notaries no longer "Goodman," but "Laird."

matrimonio contrahendo per Dei gratiam.¹ When the grant was to a religious house, you will find that the motive set forth is the weal of the granter's soul, or of his friends and kindred—*pro salute anime mee et sponse mee*—and it runs sometimes into a bargain for prayers to be said, not only for the soul of the granter but of his father and all his predecessors, and even for the welfare of the souls of all his descendants. Walter Fitzalan, the Steward, gave to the monks of Dunfermline twenty acres and a toft for the soul of King Malcolm and his ancestors, and for the souls of the granter's father and mother and his ancestors, and for his own soul, in free alms, reserving a lodging for himself and his heirs —*salvo hospitagio meo et heredibus meis*.² Robert III. grants to Sir William Inglis the barony of Manor in Peebles for the slaughter of Thomas Struther, Englishman, in a single combat.³ Let us hope that such inductive causes were few on both sides of the Borders!

Next come the subjects granted. You have lands, described by their marches, or by the tenure of the former proprietor, or by the value of the land—*viginti libratas terre*, that is, lands valued at £20 annually; *sex mercatas terre cum dimidia*, lands valued at six and a half merks annually;

---

[1] Registrum Magni Sigilli, p. 59, No. 184.
[2] Registrum de Dunfermelyn.
[3] Robertson's Index.

denariata terre, lands yielding a penny annually; *sex davatas*, six davachs of land; *bovata terre*, an oxgate of land; *virgata terre*, a rood of land—of which words I shall offer some explanation in a subsequent lecture. There are grants too of other subjects, such as the offices of Sheriff, Constable of castles and palaces, Coroner, Thane, and the like. There are grants of fairs—the right of holding a fair; frequently mills are granted. There are grants of fishings very specific, grants of freedom—of emancipation, grant to the men of Galloway of their peculiar laws and liberties,—in short, grants of every description of property, office, and privilege.[1] In one case, where an earldom is granted, the regality of the earldom is reserved. Robert Bruce granted to the monks of Melrose for the weal of his soul, and for the souls of his ancestors and successors kings of Scotland, £100 sterling of annual rents from the farms of Berwick, for finding daily for each monk in the refectory a sufficient dish of rice and milk, or almonds, or peas, or other such dish, which was to be called the *king's dish* for ever, although we see upon the title of the charter that it came to be called the king's pittance —*pitantia*; and the King specially commanded that there should be no reduction of the usual bill of

---

[1] Except, perhaps, the right of sepulture. I do not recollect any separate right of burial in a charter, and yet I suppose that may be, for though often a pertinent of land estate, a right of sepulture may be held by itself, and, it would seem, without writ.

fare, by reason of the addition of this dainty dish.[1] Robert III. when getting near his latter end granted to his Chancellor the Bishop of Aberdeen, a silver cross, in which was contained a part of the wood of the Cross of St. Andrew, and two pictures, one of wool, tapestry of arras, of the offering of the three Kings of Cologne to the blessed Virgin, and another of linen painted with beasts and birds, as also a large missal.[2]

We come now to the *Quaequidem* clause, the clause giving the history of the tenure and setting forth by what right the subject came into the hands of the granter. This clause is, however, too often wanting in our old charters. Where it occurs, it sometimes runs *que perprius fuerunt* A. B. *inimici nostri*—which formerly belonged to A. B. our enemy,—not setting forth any act or judgment of forfeiture. I have observed some charters in Bruce's time, where the lands given by the King had formerly been in the possession of a Balliol or a Comyn, and *that* was sufficient account of their coming into the King's hands. You will find, I think, that the greatest number of the charters of King Robert I. proceed on forfeiture. The fact of a man dwelling in England *contra fidem et pacem regis*, is set forth as a sufficient ground of granting his lands to another.

[1] Liber de Melros.
[2] Registrum Episcopatus Aberdonensis.

In some cases they had fallen to the king by bastardy, or *propter defectum heredum;* but most frequently the charter bears that the lands were resigned by the previous holder purely and simply into the hands of the king. We cannot doubt that in this last case resignation was for the most part made in favour of the new grantee; but resignations expressly *in favorem* had not yet come into fashion.

We come next to the tenure—*modus tenendi*—of the subjects granted by these early charters.

A grant of regality took as much out of the Crown as the sovereign could give. It was, in fact, investing the grantee in the sovereignty of the territory, and it raised up those formidable jurisdictions which too often set the Crown at defiance. You will find it in its fullest and most objectionable shape in the charter by Robert Bruce to his nephew, Thomas Randolph, of the Earldom of Moray, where even the ancient free boroughs of the kingdom are included within the King's grant to his favoured tenant *in capite;* but such inordinate concessions were soon checked by Parliament.

A grant of *comitatus*—of earldom—included a grant *in liberam baroniam*, but all the subjects, pertinents, and jurisdictions conveyed in a grant of earldom or regality were frequently given with more minute specification in the grant of a barony.

Grants *in liberam forestam* having special reference to game and the privileges of what we now call "*sport*," furnish a multitude of points and terms to be explained as we best can, when we come to the chapter of parts and pertinents, but I would venture only one observation here. In so far as I remember, the right of property precedes the right of forest. The king gives an extensive grant of lands—a great barony, in short, to a powerful and faithful vassal, and then afterwards, frequently at a good interval of time, he improves the vassal's tenure by giving him a right of forest over the same bounds. I do not think we ever had in Scotland the fierce forest laws of the Normans; but the *libera foresta* granted to a subject, gave him all the rights which the king enjoyed in his own forests. The specific advantage conferred by a grant in free forest in Scotland, was that it fixed a definite fine—*ne quis secet aut venetur*—against any one cutting the wood or hunting the deer; and the forfeiture was ten pounds, the same as the king's.

Connected with the grant of forest is the right of pannage—*cum pasnagio*, sometimes misspelt *padnagio*—that is, the right of feeding swine in the forest at the season of pannage, when the mast of beech and oak are falling or have fallen.

A right of warren—a grant *in liberam warennam*, is held to be of an inferior jurisdiction, as compared with free forest; but I cannot state the difference. The charter of warren, like that of forest, prohibits cutting of trees, hunting and hawking, and fishing in *lacubus, vivariis,* etc. Perhaps the difference lay in the penalty for trespass.[1]

Take now a grant *in liberam baroniam* in fullest form, and, rejecting as little as we can for mere surplusage and sound, let us see what are the parts, pertinents, and privileges really granted. Remember that a grant *in liberam baroniam,* without more, implied not only the highest and most privileged tenure of land, but also a great jurisdiction over the inhabitants, and all the fees and emoluments that of old made such jurisdictions valued. And now read with me the terms used in a few of these grants to express more specifically the extent of the grant. The grantee is to hold in free barony by all the right marches and bounds: the first charter I refer to says, "as they were in the time of King Alexander of good memory," *in boscis et planis* (sometimes running *in nemore, in virgultis,* or *in saltibus,* followed by *in planis et asperis*)—in woods and plains;

---

[1] The brieve *de libera foresta* in the Bute MS. concludes with the sanction *super nostram plenariam forisfacturam,* while the brieve *de libera warenna* is without those words of sanction; the latter in the Ayr MS., however, contains the same sanction— *super nostram plenariam forisfacturam,* which the Bute MS. attaches only to the *de libera foresta.* I have always considered the Ayr MS. as the most purely Scotch of our ancient collections of styles.

planum probably meaning "manurit" land—arable lands.

In pratis et pascuis, which we translate meadows and pastures, but not very accurately. *Pratum* was a hay meadow.[1] Our old Scotch custom gave lawful travellers a right of pasturing their cattle where they stopped at night, except always within *prata et segetes*—hay-fields and corn-fields I should translate it, except that perhaps the word *field* implies more of cultivation and enclosure than hay husbandry of old required. I find in English charters *pratum* applied to the hay itself, and tenants and bondagers bound to mow and carry the *prata* to the lord's castle.

In viis et semitis—the liberty of roads and paths—in a grant of barony, has reference to a right of exclusion as well as use. A very curious charter, to which I shall have often to return, declares that an inquest had found that there was no road through the barony of Trauereglys except two, namely, one *per longitudinem*, and the other *per latitudinem*. There may be other causes for a specification of roads and paths, which is almost universal in grants of barony and indeed in almost all considerable grants of territory with us,

---

[1] We do not readily accept the etymologies of Sir Edward Coke, who tells us—*dicitur pratum quasi paratum*, because it grows *sponte* without manurance.—Co. Lit., B. 4.

but I have not found that it has been relied upon in any of the late discussions as to the property of the soil upon which public or high roads run.

In moris et maresiis—in moors and marshes—*in aquis et stagnis,* about which I find nothing to remark, except that *aqua* seems to be the running water in distinction from *stagnum,* which is the pond sometimes for fish, sometimes for mill purposes.

In vivariis—in fish-stanks or ponds, but observe, *vivarium* is sometimes used for parks where game is enclosed.[1]

Amongst the common pertinents of a landed estate besides the moors and marshes, we find *cum bruscis et brueriis,* which I take to mean the brushwood or jungle and heaths—the latter from the French word *bruyère.*

Cum petariis et turbariis—with petaries and turbaries (for these are English words as well as Latin) denoting the places where peats and turfs are cut.

---

[1] This word has been fruitful of mistakes in England, which we have not been slow to follow. In old writing "n" and "u" being undistinguishable, it was excusable, in writs relating to lands in the southern counties of England, to read the ambiguous letter "n," because there really were a few grants to the great southern abbeys of vineyards, but where the word occurs in Scotch charters it is safer to print it with a "u," and to translate it "parks," where it seems to apply to dry ground. In far the greater number of instances, however, *in vivariis* means nothing but fishponds.

In a comparatively modern grant,[1] by which the king erected the lands of the Bishopric of Moray into the Barony of Spynie, I find a very full list of these parts and pertinents, though some of them must have been placed there *ob majorem cautelam.* I have noticed the chief of these, and I only remark my omission of coalpits, quarries, stone and lime-stone, and, along with heath, a grant of broom—*cum carbonariis, lapicidiis, lapide et calce, genistis.*

There is a grant there too of pigeons and dove-cots—*cum columbis et columbariis;* and a few years subsequently,[2] William, Bishop of Moray, grants to John MacCulloch the lands of Cadboll, with nearly the same parts, pertinents, and privileges, and with the addition of *wrak, waith, et wair*—that is, the right of wreck and waif and sea-weed—the lands of Cadboll lying along the shore of the Cromarty Firth.

Cum venationibus, aucupationibus, et piscationibus—with huntings, hawkings, and fishings. These were rights implied in a barony though often specified among its parts and pertinents, and forming subjects of more definite grants in charters of forests. The charters to Melrose and the transactions of the monks with some of their neighbours, afford good instances of the arrangements with regard to game. The Lords of Avenel had from the

---

[1] Registrum Moraviense, No. 193. [2] A.D. 1478.

Crown a gift of free forest in Eskdale, and when the Avenels granted the territory to the abbey they reserved the rights of forest and game, there being still some scruple whether such rights and the occupations that flow from them were suitable for religious men. Therefore the lay lords reserved, in express words, their rights to hart and hind, boar and roe, the eyries of two kinds of hawks, as well as the right to the penalty of trespasses within the forest and the amercement of those convicted. The monks were prohibited from hunting *cum moetis et cordis*—that is, with a *meute* or cry of hounds, and (I suppose) nets—such machinery for sport as Horace describes so lovingly.[1] They are prohibited from setting stamps or traps, except only for wolves, and from taking the nests of hawks; even the trees in which the hawks usually built were to be protected, and those in which they had built one year, were not to be felled until it was seen whether they intended to build there again. The Stewarts,

---

[1] At cum tonantis annus hibernus Jovis
    Imbres nivesque comparat,
Aut trudit acris hinc et hinc multa cane
    Apros in obstantis plagas;
Aut amite levi rara tendit retia
    Turdis edacibus dolos,
Pavidumque leporem et advenam laqueo gruem
    Jucunda captat praemia.
Quis non malarum, quas amor curas habet,
    Haec inter obliviscitur!—Epod. ii. 35.

who held a great part of Ayrshire in barony and free forest, granted great territories there to the monks of Melrose, but reserved at first the right of game nearly in the same terms with the Avenels—*hoc enim illorum ordini non convenit*—for *that* was not suitable to the monkish profession. But those Cistercian monks soon got over the scruple about their Rule, and first the Stewarts, and later the Grahams who inherited from Avenel, conferred at length upon them all the rights of game and forest which they had at first reserved.[1]

In molendinis—mills, perhaps one of the oldest adjuncts of a barony,—one of the most grievous oppressions of the peasantry. It is often amplified by the addition *cum multuris et sequelis*—specifying the multure dues of the baron's mill and the *sucken*, as we call the population *thirled* to the mill. These rights are the subject of very frequent transactions. The neighbours fought not only with the miller, who was the universal enemy, but with each other, as to their *roume* and order of service. One curious point of the service of the sucken was the bringing home of the mill-stones. Considering that there were few or no roads, the simplest arrangement was to thrust a beam or a young tree through the hole of the mill-stone, and then for the whole multitude to wheel it along upon its edge—

[1] Liber de Melros, Nos., 39, 41, 72, 72*, 196-8.

an operation of some difficulty and danger in a rough district.

Dugdale tells us of the manor of Newbigging in England, where the tenants were bound to four days' reaping in harvest, two days' ploughing, two of harrowing, one of carrying the hay and repairing the mill-stank, and dragging the mill-stones—*molas attrahere*—and two days' service among the sheep, one for washing, the other shearing; and yet Daines Barrington (whose book on the English Statutes is generally very trustworthy) tells us that mills were never monopolies in England. That is worth inquiry.

It would appear that the smithy—*fabrina, fabrile*—and the brew-house—*brasina*—were held natural pertinents of an estate in land. I cannot tell if there was any ancient common law right or privilege connected with the brew-house. By the tenure under the monks of Kelso, the brewer, or—as I suppose it was even then a lady—the brewster wife, was bound to furnish my lord the abbot with beer at a halfpenny a gallon, while to the outside world it cost twice as much. I find in later charters the *brasina* superseded by the alehouse, which had generally a croft appended to it. I suppose the alehouse was originally the hostelry for travellers. I need not tell you that in later times it became the scene of relaxation and jollity of the neighbouring gentry, who enjoyed there the freedom from restraint which compensated for simple entertainment, but who drank there claret as well as ale.[1]

A very common pertinent of a barony was a salt-work—*salina*—sometimes with the grant of firewood from the neighbouring forest, sometimes simply with five or six acres of land. I am not scientific enough to know the reason, but you will find that a great many of these are granted far from the sea—as far up as the tide flows, of which the Carse of Stirling is one instance, where the water can have retained but little salt. The only ancient *salina* which I know, so well preserved that the structure and *modus operandi* can still be discerned, is on the estate of Duffus, close by the loch of Spynie, where the sea at one time had an entrance, though it is now fresh water.

Such are the most important rights of the baron as lord of the soil. We now come to his rights as feudal superior and lord of the inhabitants.

Cum tenentibus, tenandriis—with tenants and tenandries, seems to give the grantee only the rights of a landlord over a free tenant, though no doubt there were services exacted from the freest tenant

---

[1] The *reddendo* for an alehouse and alehouse croft was often a quantity of tallow, the produce, perhaps, of the kitchen of the little inn. A mill, even in modern rentals, often gives the *reddendo* of a fat pig or a litter of sucklings—*grice*, a word which has given rise to some laughable mistakes at the bar.

by the lord—service in harvest, carriages, labour on the roads of the barony. The clause runs sometimes *cum tenandriis liberetenentium*, and sometimes *cum tenentibus et eorum serviciis.*

Cum homagiis, wardis, releviis do not seem to me to require explanation. Homage was the honorary observance, ward and relief were the common casualties of superiority explained in all books of feudalism, and none of these that I have now mentioned have any reference to the lowest class of rural occupants, which come next.

Cum bondis et bondagiis—with bondmen and their holdings and services. I cannot pretend to distinguish with any accuracy the bondman from the neyf. It is not improbable that the neyf or serf by descent—*nativus de stipite*—was distinguished from the bond-labourer, but we cannot tell to what extent, or in what manner.[1]

Then comes the clause *cum nativis*, or *cum hominibus*—that is, with natives or neyfs, whose name, both here and in England, points to their

---

[1] It is well known how serfdom left its remains still visible till a very recent period in the condition of colliers and salters. There was an attempt in the end of the seventeenth century to extend serfdom to fishers as well as colliers, founding upon a general custom that prevailed in the North, but the Lords found "that the custom was not general, and condemned it as a *corruptela* and unlawful, and tending to introduce slavery, contrary to the principles of the Christian religion and the mildness of our Government."—Fountainhall, Feb. 16, 1698.

being regarded as the remains of the native population obliged by the invaders to become serfs.[1] *Cum nativis et eorum sequelis* means exactly with neyfs and their followers, just as a horse-dealer now sells a mare with her followers. It implies a transfer of the property of the whole descendants of the neyf for ever, and there were various means used to prevent the race escaping from that thraldom. Both here and in England we have books recording all the members of the servile family,[2] indeed of all the descendants of all the serfs of some great lord or religious house. The sons were slaves for ever, they and their descendants—but for the freedom which the privilege of free burghs, or which that grand emancipator, the Church, opened to them. Our lawyers do not point to any distinction between the neyf *in gross*, the out-and-out slave, and the neyf *regardant*—that is, astricted to a certain land; but I have seen transactions for removing slaves from one estate to another, which show, or seem to show, that the difference was known with us also, and that a neyf astricted to the soil might not be moved at the mere will of his lord, even to another estate of

---

[1] A charter of James VI. (8th February 1584) grants the lands of Bandeith in Stirlingshire to Alexander Rannald, son of John Rannald and Elizabeth Alschinder—*veteri nativo et tenenti nostro.*—R. M. S. xxxvj. 193. The tenure was to be in feu-ferme. I suppose the Rannalds before that were kindly tenants and rentallers of the Crown.

[2] Registrum de Dunfermline; Raine's N. Durham.

the same lord. As for the neyf in gross, you will find printed amongst our " National MSS." a deed of sale, by which a Berwickshire laird sells to the priory of Coldingham a serf named Turkill Hog, and his sons and daughters; the whole family fetching the price of three merks. If you think it worth while to look at that deed,[1] you will find expressions showing that the sale was made under urgent necessity, which, with other circumstances, leads me to infer that it might not have been otherwise warrantable, and that the poor serf was protected by law from capricious sales. Mr. Bradshaw showed me lately, during a visit to Cambridge, a MS. of the fourteenth century, of the nature of a stud-book, which had belonged to the Abbey of Spalding in the fens of Lincolnshire. It gives the pedigree, for several generations, of the serfs on the Abbey estates, their marriages and those of their sons, the names of the men whom the daughters married, and notes of the fees paid for these marriages—the *merchet*—which brings me to explain what, with us at least, was the meaning of *merchetae mulierum*. Mercheta is the older form of the *maritagium* or marriage-tax, in the charters of Robert I., and not only the servile class, but the free tenants also paid a *maritagium* on the marriage of their daughters. But I cannot say whether the fine paid for the marriage of a

[1] Part I. No. 54.

serf's daughter was remitted, if the marriage took place between vassals of the same lord. I fear not, but I see no evidence on the subject.

Some learning has been brought to show that, on the Continent, this tax—*mercheta mulierum*—represented an ancient seignorial right—the *jus primae noctis*. I have not looked carefully into the French authorities; but I think there is no evidence of a custom so odious existing in England; and in Scotland, I venture to say that there is nothing to ground a suspicion of such a right. The merchet of women with us was simply the tax paid by the different classes of bondmen and tenants and vassals, when they gave their daughters in marriage, and thus deprived the lord of their services, to which he was entitled *jure sanguinis*.

In England we find in some manors a precise fine fixed, which was to be paid even if any son of a villein took orders in the church, and thus secured emancipation.

I find in the charter erecting the lands of the Bishopric of Moray into the barony of Spynie already referred to, that the clause of *Courts* runs " *cum herizeldis, bludwitis et merchetis mulierum* "—a strange classification, showing, I think, that the scribe did not know what he wrote. But there is no doubt as to the meaning of the words themselves. *Merchetis mulierum* I have explained already. *Heri-*

zeld or heriot is the best horse or ox—the best animal —the best aucht—*optimum averium* of the vassal, which became the property of the lord on his decease. I shall return to Bludwitis, thrust in here so irregularly, when I come to speak of the rights of jurisdiction which a grant of barony conveyed to the lord.

But first let me mention a very old grant, more regular and from a higher authority. In the year 1182, whilst their founder, William the Lion, was still alive, the monks of Arbroath obtained a papal bull confirmatory of all their rights; and truly Pope Lucius the Third, or his Italian chancellor and Italian scribe, must have written and read with great astonishment the words of that grant which they themselves were confirming. The monks are to be free from all toll and custom—*tollonio et consuetudine* —through the whole kingdom and all the ports of Scotland, for all goods and merchandise belonging to themselves and their burgesses; they are to have free court in their land with *sac* and *soc*, with *thol* and *them* and *infangthef*, likewise the ordeal—*examen aquae, ferri calidi et duelli*—and pit and gallows— *furca et fossa*—and the king's firm peace within the bounds of the abbey.

I told you that a barony gave numerous jurisdictions, and I must speak of some of them. Whatever might be the case with the monks of Arbroath in the twelfth century, I am not quite sure that the writers to the Signet, in the age of Robert the Bruce, understood the words *sac* and *soc, toll* and *teme, infangthef* and *outfangthef,* any better than the learned and sagacious Bailie MacWheeble, who paraded those words when he wished to magnify the jurisdiction of his master, the Baron of Bradwardine.[1] They are good Anglo-Saxon, however, and had at one time a definite and well-ascertained meaning.

Sac is the abbreviation of *sacu,* and means *placitum*—a plea, or suit at law, and the jurisdiction or right of judging in litigious suits.

Soc again strictly denotes the district included within such a jurisdiction, just as *socmen* and *socmanni* mean the persons within and subject to it. Sir Edward Coke, who despised such little learning, and yet dabbles in it, is certainly mistaken when he connects soc the jurisdiction, with a plough, and runs poetical upon the interesting qualities of the rural population.[2] Kemble, a better authority in this matter, gives you the meaning which I have followed, and traces *socen* to its origin in the right of *investigating*—cognate, I suppose, to the word *seek*.

---

[1] Such ignorance was not confined to our country. Kemble mentions some Norman charters of English lands which, while they confirm the privileges, frankly state that they—the writers—do not know the meaning of the words they are confirming.—Codex Diplomaticus, vol. i. p. xliii.

[2] Co. Lit., B. 85-6.

Thol has sometimes been supposed to mean exemption from toll or custom—the right to keep your toll-money in your own pocket, and certainly that was one of the exemptions of Arbroath I have just quoted. But in the common case I confess I prefer the interpretation which makes thol—the definite, technical privilege—the right of exacting the duty rather than the right of refusing to pay it. In this way I hold it to mean, and to grant to the holder of the charter, the right to exact custom or customary payment for goods passing through his land.

Them is explained by Kemble as warranty, a word which has a very great variety of meanings in connexion with jurisdictions and form of process of old. When a man found a borgh—*invenit plegium*—to pursue or defend, that was one manner of warranty. There were other sorts of it of larger application. But indeed you cannot read the laws of David I. and William the Lion without seeing an attempt to bind the loose and separate parts of society together in some bond of mutual warranty, such as was known in England under the name of *frank pledge*, and to such a system this old word Them may apply.[1]

---

[1] Something of this nature we can see in use in Scotland, where in the time of William the Lion the law of Claremathen, a name I do not pretend to explain, indicates a system of pledge or warranty as applied to the recovery of stolen goods. The law which is found in our oldest MSS. is now chiefly interesting for its information as to the state of the country, and the attempts to remedy an

INFANGTHEF.   57

But let me repeat that these terms, which came to be words of style and put *ob majorem cautelam* in our Scotch charters, are found in Anglo-Saxon charters centuries before the Conquest, and then no doubt they had definite and well-known meanings. They are found in English charters after the Conquest also, but it would seem that the Anglo-Norman writers who then used them did not understand their meaning, nor were able to handle their grammar.[1]

We may have been somewhat more fortunate from our preserving a more Saxon form of speech, but I do not pretend that the meaning of these jurisdictions was very clearly understood by the writers of our charters. As to the word *Them* it is unsatisfactory to us to find the great Sir Edward Coke guessing and stumbling about its meaning like any of our poor selves. If you have time you may read a page of it in Co. Lit. 116, A., the beginning of a very learned chapter of "Villenage." I have never found any claim of the lord, or resistance to such claim, founded upon the meaning of these specific terms of jurisdiction.

With us in Scotland, *infangthef* is a short way of

insecurity of property which continued to mark the Highlands at least, in spite of the legislature. It is printed as No. 3 of the Laws of King William the Lion.—Acts of the Parliaments of Scotland, vol. i. p. 50.

[1] I should not venture this remark without the authority of Kemble.

expressing the right to judge and punish a thief caught "with the fang" within the grantee's jurisdiction.

Outfangthef, which is much less common, gave the same power over a thief caught beyond the jurisdiction of the lord, he being followed and caught with the fang. I presume it was necessary that he should be by birth or otherwise subject to the baron's jurisdiction. In both these cases the interest of the lord was not from a pure love of justice. Such a grant gave him a right to the amercements, the escheats, all the goods and chattels which the poor thief could forfeit; and it was that money consideration which made all those rights of baronial jurisdiction so much coveted. When, in later times, Parliament complained of our kings' facility in pardoning, possibly the complaint flowed from the stern demand of justice. But the barons might also grudge the loss of fines, escheats, forfeitures, which were theirs by their charters.

Among the points of jurisdiction chiefly deserving of notice was the *furca et fossa*—the right of pit and gallows, the true mark of a true baron in the ancient time, who had *curia vitae et membrorum*—jurisdiction in life and limb. It was not the peculiar taste of our barbarous ancestors: all feudal lords through feudal Europe were equally fond and proud of the right of executing those whom they had first convicted and sentenced to death. The French had the phrase *avec haute et basse justice*, which meant nothing more than *cum furca et fossa*. The gallow-hill is still an object of interest and, I fear, of some pride, near our old baronial mansions; and I know some where the surrounding ground is full of the remains of the poor wretches who died by the baron's law. Perhaps the *fossa*—the *pit*—was for the female thief; for women sentenced to death were, for the most part, drowned, and I have an old Court book of a regality quite low down in date (c. 1640), where the simple form of record in criminal process was to write in the middle of the page of the Court book the name and offence of the accused, with the names of the assize, and upon the margin to inscribe shortly the words "convickit," "hangit," or "drounit." In the rare cases where it was necessary to record an acquittal, the word on the margin is "clengit."

There was nothing peculiar in the form of process used in Barons' Courts who held their baronies *cum placitis et querelis* (sometimes the word *petitiones* occurs). Pleas between man and man were discussed very much as in the higher courts. In criminal cases, where slaughter or theft was alleged, the baron bailie selected from the suitors of the court his fifteen of an assize, before whom was laid the accusation, and an outline of the evidence; all was accompanied by an assertion of the notoriety of the fact,[1] and a strangely iterated assertion—"which thou canst not deny."

The last kind of jurisdiction noted in my *syllabus* is *Bludwites*. It means the jurisdiction in assaults where there is bloodshed, and where the *wite* or fine was to the lord of the court. The fine varied one-third as the wound was above or below the breath.

Such were the common terms descriptive of jurisdictions which gave the baron the power he loved, accompanied with the emolument of fines, escheats, forfeitures, which perhaps he loved no less. For the most part in grants of barony the Crown reserved its own jurisdiction in what are called the "Points of the Crown"—*quatuor puncta coronae*—murder, fire-raising, rape, and robbery, but the jurisdiction in these was sometimes granted. For instance, the charter by Robert Bruce to his nephew, of the great Earldom of Moray, granted these; and the charter by King Robert II. to his son David, Earl Palatine of Strathearn, expressly gave him jurisdiction in those points—*cum feodis et forisfactis et cum placitis quatuor punctorum coronae nostrae*—with fees and forfeitures, and with the pleas of the four points of our Crown.[2]

But it was different when the Sovereign bestowed

---

[1] A form of words not unknown in the High Court of Justiciary in former times.

[2] Registrum Magni Sigilli, p. 85, No. 294, and p. 88, No. 306.

these jurisdictions upon religious houses. The ecclesiastical judge might not try, at least in the common form of human justice, cases of life and death. To him, therefore, was given the higher and more mysterious jurisdiction—the direct appeal to heaven by ordeal. The abbots of all our great monasteries had this high jurisdiction. The Abbot of Scone had a specific grant of the island in the Tay, which flowed past his monastery, for the purpose of there holding courts for the trial of accused persons by water, by hot iron, by duel—*examen aquae, ferri calidi, et duelli.* But such forms of jurisdiction, as they require some explanation, will be better treated in the chapter of *Origines Justiciariae,* where I have tried to gather together some vestiges of the oldest forms of legal procedure.

The *Reddendo* or *Faciendo* clause furnishes a few words and customs that are noteworthy. In Robert the Bruce's time a charter is given of land, to be held for the service of two archers—*servicium duorum architenentium,* and for giving suit in the Lord's Court—*sectam ad curiam nostram;* it was often more definite, as *reddendo tres sectas curiae ad tria nostra placita capitalia.* This *suit* was to make up the necessary gathering required for business, members of assize, witnesses, compurgators, etc. Those holding by such service were suitors—*sectatores curiae;* and you find in all records of old court proceedings the commencement is—*sectis vocatis—curia legitime affirmata,* or when it comes to the time when Scots was used,—"Suits called, the Court lawfully fenced."

The reddendo of service means service in war; *servitium debitum et consuetum* is the common form, or more specifically *servitium in exercitu regis.* *Servitium forinsecum* or *Scoticanum*—service without or within Scotland, corresponded to the old Saxon *utwer* and *inwer.* You will find these Saxon words preserved in a charter of the Abbey of Kelso, A.D. 1190.[1] Sometimes it is more definite. My own forebears held their lands by a charter of Malcolm IV. for rendering *servicium unius militis in castello meo de Elgin.* So Robert II. grants to Patrick Gray a part of the land of Longforgund, *faciendo servitium quantum pertinet ad terciam partem servitii unius militis in exercitu nostro una cum Scotico servitio de dicta terra debito et consueto*—doing therefor the service pertaining to the third part of the service of one knight in our army, together with the Scotch service used and wont for the said land.

We had no tenures by *serjeanty.* The name is not known with us, at least not in the English sense. So we have few, if any, of those curious quaint *reddenda* of English manors which were gathered into a most entertaining volume by Thomas Blount[1] a little while

---

[1] Liber S. Marie de Calchou, No. 252.

[1] He calls his book Fragmenta Antiquitatis, Antient Tenures of Land, and Jocular Customs of some Manors.—1679.

before the Revolution. Blount tells us of divers manors and lands in Cumberland held by the service of *cornage*, that is of blowing a horn when the Scotch were coming. Amongst a multitude of curious and interesting particulars of rural life, he tells us of the Manor of Brayles, where the tenants of the manor must not marry their daughters, nor crown their sons—*nec filios coronare*,—that is, make their sons priests, without license from the lord; and upon this, Mr. Blount observes, that it was a common restraint of villenage tenure, to the end the lord might not lose any of his villeins by their entering into holy orders. Unluckily he does not give the original language of this tenure, but it is plain that those whom he calls tenants were not *free* tenants.

Although the word *rent* perhaps comes from *reddendo*, there is little of actual rent, according to our meaning of the word, specified in those old grants of land; a money rent is a rare case of old, but we find such payments as the following:—An annual rent of four chalders of oatmeal and one pound of pepper. To a religious house we have payments of eight wax candles, each of a pound weight, to be burned around the tomb of Saint Machutus. Then we have ten chalders of good wheat and barley. The land upon which I live myself at Inverleith, which I can trace back by charters into the possession of the Baker of William the Lion, paid, in the time of Robert I., one hundred shillings of *sterlings*. Some fields beside me are still called "Baxter lands." With regard to this word "sterling," it no doubt meant the coinage of the "Easterlings," as it was the currency of the people who went by that name along the shore of the Baltic and in the trade of the north. It gradually narrowed, however, in meaning, until it came to express precisely the silver penny which was the universal medium of commerce in the north of Europe for many centuries; and a sum of money or a weight of silver was specifically fixed to be of good and lawful pennies—*denariorum*, or more commonly, *bonorum et legalium sterlingorum*. As England rose in wealth and trade, the pennies coined by the English Edwards and Henries became the prevailing currency over the north of Europe.

Besides these real payments, we constantly meet with what are so well known as *blench duties*. Here are a few specimens of this class:—

Unum par calcarium deauratorum—a pair of gilt spurs.

Sagittam amplam—a broad arrow. Again—*Tres sagittas latas*—for Lochindorb, the centre of a wide district used for deer-preserve and hunting.

Unum arcum et duodecim sagittas latas—a bow and twelve broad arrows.

Unam falconem rubeam et unum nisum—a red falcon

and an *épervier*, perhaps a tercel—for the thanedom of Glamis.

Unum par cyrothecarum albarum vel duos denarios argenti—a pair of white gloves, or two pennies of money. Sometimes they are *cyrothecae Parisienses*—Paris gloves.

Unum arcum cum uno circulo pro alaudis—perhaps a mirror for flushing larks, as still used in Italy—for the land of New Park (the Royal Park of Stirling).

Unum denarium argenti nomine albae firmae—one penny of silver in the name of blench farm.

Unam libram piperis vel cucumeris—a pound of pepper or cucumber seed.[1]

[1] The Books of Exchequer afford the following valuations of blench fermis, 9 July 1596.

Item, it is statut and ordanit that all schireffis in tym cumming sall pay yeirlie in the Cheker the prices of the blenschefermis eftir following; viz.,—			
Item, ilk pair of gilt spurris,	1 rois nobill.	Item, ane braid arrow heid,	ij s.
Item, for ilk pund of piper,	xxx s.	Item, for ilk braid arrow,	x s.
Item, for ilk pund of cummyn,	xiij s. iiij d.	Item, ane floren of gold,	1 goldin pistolett.
Item, for ilk pair of gluffis,	iiij li.	Item, ane myrrour,	xx li.
Item, for ilk siluer pennie,	x d.	Item, ane halk,	xx li.
Item, ane pair of quhyt spurris,	xx s.	Item, ane halk gluff,	xxx s.
		Item, ane pund of walx,	x s.
		Item, the pryce of ane cowdeche to ane prebendar or chaplane,	xij s.
		j pennie monetae,	j d. vsuall money.
		Ane pund of zinziber,	xxx s.
		j wyld duik,	xiij s. iiij d.
		j pair of dogge colleris,	xl s.

I add a few more *reddendos*.

For the lands of Lochaw, Bruce's charter bound Colin Campbell—the ancestor of the family of Argyll—to find a ship of forty oars for the King's

j garlike heid,	x d.
j grew hund,	x li.
j henne,	x s.
j harie nobill,	
j fudder of hay,	vj li. xiij s. iiij d.
j stane of cheis,	xxx s.
j laid of hay,	xx s.
j pund of gwme,	x s.
j pund of incenss,	iij li. vj s. viij d.
j halk huid,	xiij s. iiij d.
j ganzie [cross-bow],	x s.
Ane sparue halk,	j ros nobil.
j reid mantill,	xl li.

JOANNES SKENE,
Clericus Registri.

TABLE of Conversions of blench duties in use before the Union.

	Scots.
An ox, cow or mart,	£10 0 0
A white plumash feather,	10 0 0
A rose noble of gold,	10 13 4
A pair of gilt spurs,	8 0 0
A stone of wax,	8 0 0
A hawk,	8 0 0
A grew hound,	5 6 8
A boar,	4 0 0
A pound of incense,	3 6 8
A pair of gloves,	3 0 0
A stone of butter,	3 0 0
A sparrow-hawk,	3 0 0
Conies or rabbits, the pair,	0 13 4
A wild duck,	0 13 4
Kain-lime, per boll,	0 12 0
	Scots.
A broad arrow,	£0 10 0
A goose,	0 10 0
Onions, per barrel,	0 10 0
A fresh salmon,	0 10 0
A capon,	0 6 8
A pair of doves,	0 5 0
A pound of wax,	0 10 0
A sheep,	2 0 0
A barrel of salmon,	2 0 0
A bow,	2 0 0
A kid,	2 0 0
A pound of pepper,	1 10 0
A pound of ginger,	1 10 0
A wether,	1 10 0
Cheese, per stone,	1 6 8
A pair of white spurs,	1 0 0
Muttons of Ross, Buchan and Murray,	1 0 0
A stone of meal,	1 0 0
A hawk's hood,	0 13 4
A pound of cummin seed,	0 13 4
A horse shoe,	0 4 0
A hen,	0 4 0
A long carriage,	0 4 0
A cart-load of turfs,	0 4 0
A sheer day's work,	0 4 0
Capons of Ross, Buchan and Murray,	0 3 4
The head of an arrow,	0 3 0
A short carriage,	0 2 0
Poultry of Ross, a piece,	0 1 8
Eggs, per dozen,	0 1 0

service, with sufficient tackle and men, for forty days, besides giving foreign service like the other barons of Argyle.[1]

For Balmaschennan, Forfar, 600 wains of peats *pro duplicatione albefirme.*

For the barony of Muirhouse, Edinburgh, two falcon-hoods.

Abirdalgy and Duplyn, *duabus merulis sive speculis.*

For Gask, *duas capellas*—chaplets—*albarum rosarum.*

For Glensaucht, *duas capellas de lentisco*—mastic.

For Balgony, *unam albam pinnam seu plumam,* lie quhyt pannasche or quhytfeather.

For Birdisfield and Bellisfield, in the barony cf Blantyre, an eighth part of a neck-chain of gold, of the weight of a Harry noble.

For Ewirland, Cramond Regis, *servicium lavacri.*

The Pultrie lands near Dene, Edinburgh, were held *cum officio pultrie Regine* (1545).

Dewar lands in Glendochart were held in virtue of the custody of a relic of St. Fillan.

Sir Andrew Wood of Largo, by charter, 21st August 1513, had the lands of Fawfield and Frostleys for going once a year on pilgrimage with James IV. and his dearest spouse to the Isle of May if required.

---

[1] Anderson's Diplomata. In like manner, Malcolm, son of Turmode Maclode, for 8 davochs and 5 pennylands of Glenelg, paid a reddendo to David II. of a service of one ship of twenty-one oars when required by the King.—Supplement to the Acts of Parliament.

The *reddendo* for the barony of Penicuik was blowing six blasts on a blowing-horn—*in cornu flatili*—on the moor of the burgh of Edinburgh, formerly called Drumselch, at the King's hunt.

As *reddendo* for the barony of Carnwath, two pairs of shoes, each containing half an ell of English cloth, were to be given on Midsummer day to the man who ran fastest from the east end of Carnwath to the Tallow Cross.

I have told you that old charters were very frequently without dates, and, until quite modern times, no charters, even of private individuals, were subscribed by the granters. The deed was completed by affixing the granter's seal, and in Crown charters that solemnity was performed in presence of the Chancellor or Keeper of the Seal, and other officers of the Court and great persons (for you will observe that the persons habitually mentioned as witnesses to Crown charters were always personages of some importance). I have only one other observation, under this head, worthy of being laid before you: that in theory, and I believe in practice, from the earliest times the affixing of the great seal marked the presence of the Sovereign himself. In later times, however—times when conveyancing had become much more complicated, the *signature* or first step of the process was subscribed by the King's own hand, perhaps at a distance from the seals;

but all the subsequent steps, passing through the different seals to the completion of the gift by affixing the great seal, bore the same date with the *signature* subscribed by the King himself. A knowledge of these particulars, trifling as they may appear, has furnished the most satisfactory evidence of forgery in a *cause célèbre* in our own time.

Such is the trifling help that I am able to give you with the mere words of charters. But the curious words are the least part of the interest of some of our old charters. I must mention one to you that seems to embody a complete and lively picture of the country which it concerns, and the state of the population at the time. It is a charter[1] of King David the Second to Sir John Heris, Knight, granting the lands of Trauereglys (now Terregles), in Dumfriesshire, in free barony, with all the common pertinents and jurisdictions; and it specifies certain privileges that seem to have been much valued, and which had just been ascertained by an inquest of the best, oldest and most trustworthy of the whole sheriffdom. We see, by the privileges claimed and ascertained by the verdict of the assize, the disturbed state of the country. One great object was to shut out marauding parties bent upon plunder, and to limit the right of passage, even of the officers of the law. These officers were re-

[1] A.D. 1364.

quired, even when they came carrying a robber to justice, or bringing a robber's head to show the purposes of their expedition; and even they were not allowed to pass through in the night, but provision was made for the safe custody of the robber or the robber's head during the night of their stay. Now let me read to you an extract from the charter, the whole of which, however, is well worthy of your attention. You will find it in the printed volume of the Register of the Great Seal, page 37. After the common and special pertinents of a barony, the King continues in this manner: — together with all the liberties which we have found by an inquest of the sheriffdom of Dumfries to belong to that barony of right and custom; first, that it is held of us in free barony, and that there is no road—*via*— within the barony except two, one through its length, the other across its breadth; and that the barony is free of "sorryn and fachalos,"[1]—unless officers come through it with a robber, or with the

---

[1] I commend these words to your attention. At first I set them down for Celtic and hopeless; but, upon consulting the record itself, I do not find the matter quite so desperate. We have not the original charter. The first of the two words is plainly enough written in the contemporary Register, and printed unexceptionably from that source. Still if it were lawful to conjecture that in the original charter the word *sorryn* of the Register may have been written with a final dash, indicating some indefinite termination, it would not be violent to suggest that *libera de sorryn = libera de sorrynin*—stood for free from sorning. The barony is to be free from that which we know to have been the oppression

head of a robber, and if they, the King's officers, can pass beyond the barony before sun-setting, they shall have nothing for their expenses, and if they cannot pass beyond the barony before sun-setting, they shall have hospitality for that night—*hospicium ad hospitandum;* or otherwise the men of the barony shall receive the robber or the robber's head from the said officers, to keep for that night and deliver again to the officers at sunrise, the said officers lodging where they please. Also that no officer of ours—*sergiandus noster*—nor coroner, ought to do his office within the barony unless he first come to the *chymis* (the chief dwelling-place) of the lord of the barony, and there present his attachments—*attachiamenta sua*—that is, his warrants, to the constable or bailie of the barony against certain persons; and if the bailie acknowledge that they are men of his lord and dwelling within the barony, the bailie shall be security for entering them before the justiciar. And if the bailie does not acknowledge them to be men of his lord, the crowner or crowner's serjeant shall do his office before witnesses of his barony. And if the crowner or

of many parts of Scotland, the masterful quartering of brigands, known technically as *sorning.*

The word printed *fachalos* is in the Register more like *frithalos*, a good Saxon word made up of *Frith*, protection and *los* the termination now written *less*, *e.g.*, god-less, end-less, etc. So that the sense is very near what the old dictionaries make it—*a pace regia exclusus*—an outlaw; and the intention of the charter is seen to be that the land shall be free of sorners and outlaws.

crowner's serjeant shall find one hiding, the lord of the barony shall have his goods, and not we. And if the crowner shall find any one within the barony, and if the bailie of the barony wish to repledge him, our crowner or his officer shall carry that person with his goods to our prison. Also, that the men of that barony are not bound to answer for the support —*ad victualia*—of the guardian of the country,[1] or the justiciar or sheriff. But the men of the barony shall be answerable for service in our army. Also that no crowner nor other officer shall make search—*ranciare*[2]—within the barony, unless he first find a pledge that that house is culpable—*quod ista domus sit culpabilis*. And if any one follows his goods with a blood-hound—*cum odorinseco*—he shall not search without licence of the officer of the barony. Also that the men of the barony shall not be bound to answer any demand of carriage—*carriagio*—except our own (*i.e.* His Majesty's), and *that* only in our passing through the barony to its boundaries. And that there be paid for each horse for four leagues one penny;—and then the charter goes on with the usual jurisdictions.

[1] *Custos patriae*—a title, I think, of a district magistrate, not of the Warden or Guardian of Scotland.

[2] I have not found this word elsewhere in charters, but it is perhaps the word we find in use in the Shetland Islands—*Rancel* or *ransel* — to search through a parish for stolen goods, also to inquire into every kind of misdemeanour.— Edmonston's Glossary in Jamieson's Scottish Dictionary.

Does not the whole charter raise to your mind a savage state of society! Every man jealous of his neighbour—no road or path allowed that way if possible—even the officers of law, who have caught their robber, or who are carrying his bloody head in sign of their employment, must not remain there all night, or must be specially watched. The charter receives much light from the legislation of the reign of David II.

I will mention two other charters, standing together in the Roll of Robert II., which are of more than usual interest and curiosity. The first was brought prominently forward by Lord Hailes in his *Sutherland Case*, and formed, indeed, the most important foundation of his pleading. Thomas Flemyng, Earl of Wigton, had reason to be dissatisfied with his possessions in that earldom. The native population were at feud with him, and their native Chiefs led him an uneasy life. It is plain that the world was against him and funds had failed. In these circumstances he was induced, in his great and urgent necessity, to sell his whole earldom for a certain notable sum of money to Sir Archibald of Douglas, knight, Lord of Galloway " be east the Crie." The charter of sale calls the seller Earl of Wigton, but the King's charter, which confirms it, calls him Thomas Fleming formerly Earl of Wigton. As Lord Hailes says, he resumed the " ancient appellation of the family, and styled himself Thomas Flemyng of Fulwood, *dudum comes de Wigton.*" He grants a charter to the purchaser with the most complete array of parts, pendicles, and jurisdictions, of his ancient earldom, and that charter is confirmed by the King.[1] It seems certain that by the sale of the earldom lands he had, according to the law of that time, parted with the dignity also.

The next charter makes us acquainted with an office scarcely to be found in the law books. In 1372, Robert II. confirms a charter granted by King Alexander, which again ratified a grant made by Niel Earl of Carrick to Roland of Carrick and his heirs, namely, that the said Roland and his heirs shall be the head of all his race—*caput totius progeniei*—in all things pertaining to chiefship—*Kenkynoll*—with the office of baillie of the earldom, and the right of leading the men of the earldom on all occasions under the Earl.[2]

I think I have nearly completed my task as to charter language, but perhaps you will allow me, before leaving this subject, to run over the great officers of State, who appear so frequently in the testing clauses of charters.

The Seneschal—*seneschallus, dapifer*—Steward—

---

[1] Regist. Magni Sigilli, p. 114, No. 5.

[2] This and another charter on the same subject are titled Confirmacio Johannis Kennedy.— Registrum Magni Sigilli, pp. 114 115, Nos. 5, 6.

was perhaps the greatest of the officers of the Crown from the days of David I. to the time when the name of *Steward* was lost in royalty. There is no longer any doubt that the Stewards were originally Fitzalans. When they first appear among us their family had not yet adopted coat-armour, and when they complied with the fashion they took a bearing suggestive of their office—the fess-checquy, in allusion to the chequered table-cloth used for computing the public accounts and all accounts before the introduction of Arabic numerals.

The Constable—*constabularius*,—in theory, commanded the King's army in the field, and under his cognisance came all offences committed within the precincts of the King's Court.

Marischal — *marescallus* — like the Constable dwindled into an office of state and solemnity, though at an early time it must have been an office of importance in the Royal army.

The Justiciar—*justiciarius*—was the head of the law, the Chief-Justice, in early times not confined to criminal matters. From a very early period our kings had two Justiciars, one for Scotland proper—benorth Forth, the other for Lothian. I believe, in theory, they went circuits twice in the year—once on the grass and once on the corn—but it was rare for Scotland to have long enough peace for two yearly circuits.

The Chancellor—*cancellarius*—was usually, but I think not necessarily, Keeper of the Great Seal, and no doubt also, like the Lord Chancellor of England, keeper of his Majesty's conscience—his adviser in all legal matters, his assessor in courts of justice, while the King still held them in person. You will find the Chancellor generally a Churchman, but that was only because the Churchmen had almost a monopoly of legal learning. There are many exceptions, and laymen of the two great families of Gordon and Campbell frequently held the office.

The Chamberlain—*camerarius*—had his name from the royal *camera*, not the bed-chamber but the treasure-chamber of the King. I think the Chamberlain was the Treasurer before any other officer appears with that name. The Chamberlain had a peculiar function, as a sort of moderator and mixed judge, presiding in the Court of the Four Burghs.

The Treasurer—*thesaurarius*—was introduced by James I., and thenceforward the sheriffs and other officers accounting to the Crown rendered their accounts to him, the Chamberlain remaining to superintend only the burghs.[1]

The Comptroller—*computorum rotulator*—was the chief accountant of the domestic expenses of royalty.

---

[1] Of the last three dignitaries, you will find a pretty full list in Crawford's very useful book on the Officers of State.

Lord Privy Seal—*secreti sigilli custos*—introduced by James I.

Lord President of the Council; an office of late introduction, when the King was desirous of multiplying his Officers of State.

The Secretary; an office under different names —*clericus regis—secretarius—clericus noster*—often appearing as assistant to the Chancellor; two officers styled *clerici* sometimes sign Crown-charters next to him.

The Lord Clerk Register—*clericus rotulorum et registri*—by right of office Clerk of the Supreme Court of Parliament, of the King's Council, and of all royal Courts of Judicature.

The King's Advocate—was not so important an officer while Scotland was an independent kingdom. But he was the public prosecutor and adviser and counsel in all Crown cases.

The Justice-Clerk—*clericus justiciarie*—having been at first perhaps an assessor to the High Court, has been beyond time of record the second Judge of Justiciary.

Master of Household—*magister hospitii*—one of the offices introduced by James I.

The Door-ward or Usher—*ostiarius*—the Keeper of the palace door; a very honourable office, giving name to a family of ancient nobility and great power which has left only a tradition of its old grandeur, mixed with some circumstances of superstition that seized the fancy of Scott and led him, as his manner was, to bring back the old historical name of Durward for one of his most charming romances.

The Almoner—*elemosinarius*—the King's Almoner.

I wish now to add a few words touching offices which we find in Celtic Scotland.

Maor is a native Celtic word for an officer, equivalent to our sheriff's officer. We had numerous mairdoms or subdivisions of sheriffdoms, and several mairs of fee, that is, hereditary mairs. The sheriffdom of Angus had four bailliaries,—the quarters of Dundee, Kirriemuir, Brechin, Arbroath —each having a maor to execute the sheriff's mandates.[1]

My friend Mr. Skene has handed me an instructive example of maorship from the Craignish papers. It is a precept of Clare Constat by Colin Campbell,

---

[1] Hereditary maors of Moray are traced for two centuries. The Dunbars, who were great lords in Moray, held as part of their property the office of mairship of the earldom and westshire of the same; along with the whole mair corns, reek hens and other casualties and fees of the lands of Tarress, Balnaferrie, and other lands of the earldom and westshire of the same, lying on both sides of the water of Findhorn—from every parish a stook of bear, a stook of oats, with the cottars' reek hens of every plough yearly, together with the acre of land, houses and biggings within the town of Darnaway, belonging to the office of mairship.— Retours, Elgin and Forres, No. 22.

son natural to Archibald Earl of Argyll, *dominus de Craignische*, for infefting the grantee in the lands of Corworanbeg, and also *de officio Sergiandriae seu maiori, tenandrie seu balliatus de Craignish*—of the office of serjeantry or maorship of the tenandry or bailliary of Craignish—in favour of Donald M'Illechallum vich Donill vich illechallum, dated 18th June 1592.

Maormor—the great maor—is an ancient title among the Celts, found in misty and hardly historical Irish annals, but now made Scotch history by the Book of Deir. The maormors were the greatest officers of great districts, and it is to them, and not to the Thanes, that Shakespeare, in Macbeth, should have made young Malcolm address his speech—" Henceforth be Earls!" The Maormors of Moray, Buchan, Mearns, and Angus, were exactly *Comites* or Counts; and, when the great change took place about the time of Canmore, they became Earls, and some of their descendants are so still.

Another officer well known within the Highland border was the *Toschach*. The name is sometimes written Toscheochdorach, which seems to me, ignorant as I am of Gaelic, to apply to the office rather than to the man. The Gaelic toschach is equivalent to our Scotch thane, and remember that the thane of Scotland is very different from the

English one. With us the thane was the administrator or steward of lands, generally the property of the Crown, but not always so, and in all the cases of which we have evidence, the thane sooner or later became hereditary, and also came to pay a fixed instead of a fluctuating rent.

The following is a curious bit of early Scotch—half Gaelic—conveyancing, and I hope I may count upon your patience when I describe to you the tenures of two thanedoms.

Many years ago I found in the Athol charter-chest a set of titles that much interested me. Robert Stewart of Scotland and Lord of Athol, afterwards Robert II., by an undated charter, but necessarily before 1371, granted to Ewen Thane of Glentilt—*Eugenio Thano de Glentilt*—brother of Ronald of the Isles, the whole thanedom of Glentilt, being three davochs of land, he giving faithful service and paying for the thanedom yearly eleven marks of money. In the middle of the next century, I find a service, in the Court of the Justiciary of the Earl of Athol, of Andrew de Glentilt, as heir to his father, Johannes le Thane de Glentilt. Finlay—*Finlaius*—the Thane of Glentilt, son and heir of Andrew, whom I have just mentioned, sold the lands to Stewart of Fothergill. In making up the titles afterwards (about 1502), John Stewart holds the same lands, by resignation of Finlay, deceased, who is now called Finlay Toschach, Thane of Glentilt; and the descendants of Finlay having, like him, turned their Saxon title of Thane into a Gaelic family designation of Toschach, founded a family called Toschach of Monivaird, still remembered, though I think now extinct, in Athol.

Or, take another very instructive progress of the titles of a thanedom which I found in a charter-room of a family whom I called Cameron, but who, I found, were known by the natives as MacMartin or Mac-Soirle of Letterfinlay in Lochaber.

In 1456, John of Yla, Earl of Ross and Lord of the Isles, grants to his armour-bearer—*armigero nostro* —Somerled, the son of John, the son of Somerled, a davoch of the lands of Glennyves, along with the office which is commonly called *Toscheachdeora,* of all the granter's lands of Lochaber, except the lands pertaining to his foster-child—*alumno nostro,* Lachlan MacLean of Doward; to be held with all pertinents and produce—*cum omnibus pertinenciis et fertilitatibus*—for the lifetime of the grantee, and to his eldest son for five years afterwards—for homage and service, and without mention of other *reddendo.*

Then pass a hundred years, and you have this same family of MacSoirle dealing with another superior. In 1552 I find an agreement in Scots between George Earl of Huntly, Chancellor of

Scotland, and Donald MacAlister MacSoirle of Glennyves: MacSoirle is to resign his lands in the Queen's hands in favour of the Chancellor, who is to grant them again to him in feu-ferm for a *reddendo* of apparently ten merks. There is the usual bond of maintenance on the one hand and service on the other, and Huntly grants a feu-charter, in Latin, as befits the Lord Chancellor, to MacSoirle, by name, *dilecto nostro Donaldo Mac-Alister Mc Tosche*, and his heirs. You observe the descendants of the Thane had acquired the name of *Mac Tosche*, in popular language, in addition to their other clannish designation of MacSoirle—son of Somerled. I gather from this that the Thane of Lochaber, like the Thane of Glentilt, took a surname *Mac-tosche* from his family office of Thane, and that that surname was in the speech of the country derived from Toschach, which as I have already said is the Gaelic equivalent for Thane.

It may be an accidental similarity of *reddendo*, but it seems to me worth observing, that the thanedom of Cawdor, when it became hereditary by gift of Robert Bruce, was to be held as it had been formerly held in the time of King Alexander, but paying a *reddendo in cameram regis* of twelve marks. The thanedom of Glentilt, when it was feudalized, paid to the Steward, Earl of Athol, eleven marks sterling; and the Thanedom of Lochaber, when

Chancellor Gordon turns it into a feudal holding, pays ten marks.[1]

When speaking of this office of Toschach, it will occur to you that the great Highland name of Macintosh means simply the descendants of the Toschach, and may perhaps be Englished sons of the Thane, even by one like myself, who would not willingly touch the "cat without a glove." It is plain, from the progress of charters I have read to you, that the thanes of Glentilt bearing the name of Toschach, were of the blood of the Lords of the Isles. From the second progress it is also plain that the little sept who once held the thanedom of Lochaber, and were known as the clan Soirle of Glennyvis, and took the name of MacTosche, were also descended of the same great parentage. I think neither of these had any connexion with the Macintosh of Clan Chattan.

Mr. Thomson makes the word Thane equivalent to Seneschal; and that word or its translation Steward, truly represents the duties and station

[1] The following list of Thanages may serve to show the districts within which this office was in use:

Aberlemno.	Callendar.	Fettircarne.	Kintore.
Aberluthnot.	Cawdor.	Formartin.	Monyfeith.
Abirkerdor.	Conveth.	Glamis.	Morphie.
Alyth.	Cowie.	Glendouachy.	Newdosk.
Arbuthnot.	Crannyk.	Glenlivet.	Scone.
Belhelvie.	Dingwall.	Glentilt.	Tannadice.
Boyn.	Doune (Banff).	Inverkeilidor.	
	Dounie (Forfar).	Kincardine.	
	Durris.	Kinclevin.	
	Edevy.	Kinross.	

of a thane within his thanedom. Sir Henry Spelman, with such learning as was open to him, expressed his opinion that the Celtic Tosche is equivalent to Thane, and we shall not be far wrong to conclude that Thane in Scotland and Tosche in the Highlands meant a steward or administrator of lands, generally hereditary, and generally held of the Crown.

Ballia is the jurisdiction or territory of a *ballivus*, but as the King addresses all his administrative officers as his *bailies*, *ballia* comes to mean any royal jurisdiction. It is written *ballivatus* in more modern charters.

Coronator—coroner or crowner. The name was derived, I think, from this officer having cognizance in the pleas of the Crown—*placita coronae*. At one time the functions of the crowner were very high, both in England and Scotland, and seem to have been co-extensive with the sheriffdom. I do not know at what period the coroner's duty in England was restricted to what it is at present. The office went early out of use in Scotland.

Last of all, let me speak of *Constabularia*. The Constable or Keeper of the King's Castle had a small territory adjoining the castle, which is often still known as the constabulary in our provincial towns. But for the special reasons that gave the name of *constabularia* to the shires of Haddington and Linlithgow, being subdivisions of the great sheriffdom of Edinburgh, I think Mr. Marwick must look into the more ancient charters of our city; for I have never seen any that explains it.[1]

Charters naturally lead to investiture, which was often given by peculiar and appropriate symbols. I will conclude this lecture with a few of the more ancient or remarkable of these. The most ancient notice of symbols in our preserved charters, is when King Edgar, the elder brother of King David I., granted to St. Cuthbert and the Church of Durham, for the souls of his father and mother, brother and sisters, the whole land of Swintun, as Liulf held it, with twenty-four cattle, for reclaiming the land; this gift he offered on the altar of Coldingham—

---

[1] Here are a few of the offices which you will find frequently mentioned in charters:—A grant of the hereditary office of keeper of the castle of Lochdoun—of keeper of the woods and groves —*nemorum*—of Cockburnspath —of keeper of the wraik and wair of Coldingham—of keeper of the castle of Lochmaben—of keeper of the Hermitage of St. Lawrence, Dumfriesshire — of hereditary keeper *roborarii lie* Park of Holyrood-house—of keeper of the palace of Falkland—of the palace of Linlithgow—of the castle of Doune—of keeper and captain of the castle of Stirling —of keeper of the castle of Dingwall—of the hereditary office of constable of the castles and palaces of Skibo, Scrabster, and Dornoch—of the office of constable and justicer of Brechin—of keeper and constable of Beauly—of constable of the castle of Nairn —of the burgh of Renfrew— of Aberdeen—of Haddington—of the constable of Skibo-mains in Caithness—of coroner and forester of the Garioch—of sergeanty and crownership of Argyll—of coroner of the earldom of Carric —of coroner of the bailiary of Kyle Stewart—of coroner and sheriff of Banff—of coroner and

idem ecclesie super altare optuli in dotem et donavi. In that case I suppose the symbol of the gift was the charter itself. But there is nothing either in this charter or in the confirmation by his brother, Earl David, though he alludes to the offering on the altar of Coldingham, to fix in what manner the investiture was actually given.[1] In the reign of Alexander II., Robert de Vere, Earl of Oxford, granted to the monks of Melrose four acres of arable land in Old Roxburgh, upon Tweedflat, and the investiture was given by offering a wand on the high altar of Melrose—*per unam virgam super magnum altare.* Of the same reign I have seen copies of a charter, of which I should be glad to see the

steward of Annandale—of coroner of the regality of St. Andrews—of coroner of the sheriffdom of Fife—of coroner between the waters of Dee and Nith—of steward, coroner, and forester of Strathern, Balquhidder, and Glenartney—of coroner and mair-of-fee of Renfrew—lastly of the Royal standard-bearer—*officium vexillum lie Banner supremi domini nostri Regis gerendi*—an ancient and honourable distinction. One of the few writs of Wallace, as Guardian, preserved, is a grant to Alexander called Skirmischur, of lands round Dundee, with the constabulary of the castle, for services done in bearing the Royal Banner in the army of Scotland.—National MSS., Part I. p. xiv. James Viscount of Dudhope, Lord Scrymgeour, as heir of the ancient Scrymgeours, was infeft in 1643 in the lands round Dundee, and the office of constabulary and banner-bearer of the King.—Retours, Forfar, 280. The office which the Scrymgeours held since the time of Wallace passed in the next reign into the family of Lauderdale, on the death of John Earl of Dundee without heir-male of his body.

[1] National MSS., Part I. Nos. 4, 12.

original.[1] The charter bears to have been granted in 1227, and it confirms to Alan de Leni the lands of Leni, within the shire of Perth, by resignation in the King's hands, of Margaret de Leni, daughter of Gilbert de Leni, as freely as she held them, by the symbol of a little sword—*virtute gladii parvi*—which King Culen of old gave to Gillespic More, her predecessor, for his singular service. The lands are said to have come by descent to one of the name of Buchanan, and lastly to Buchanan of Arnprior. The descent of the lands may be correctly given, as also a drawing of the little sword, the symbol of investiture, which I have seen, in connexion with one of the copies of the charter; but our critical age will not receive a charter of Alexander II. as proof of a feudal investiture by King Culen. We have many instances where the patriotic forger has escaped some of the readiest modes of detection by ascribing the deed which was to dignify his family or burgh to some traditional king of high antiquity, the falsity of whose charter it may not be so easy to expose.[2] In some of those instances of the perpetuating of an old fable, it is not necessary to doubt

[1] The copy I have used here is from a book of careful transcripts of charters by the late Mr. William Robertson, one of the Deputy-Keepers of the Records, now in the possession of his grandson, George Brown Robertson, Esq.,

Deputy-Keeper of the Records of Scotland.

[2] We have examples of this in early charters of Tain, Montrose, Perth, the bishopric of Aberdeen, and the Abbey of Dunfermline.

the genuineness of the existing charter, nor even to question the *bona fides* of the King or Chancellor who asserts as genuine the old myth.

We feel an interest in the famous Emerald charter of Douglas, for the sake both of the giver and receiver. King Robert Bruce gave to his friend, the good Sir James of Douglas, all his lands in free regality, and invested him with a ring, containing a stone which is called "emeraude," put by the King's own hand on Douglas's finger, which was to be the manner of taking of seisin for his successors.[1] Such symbols of investiture are not unknown in other families. The tradition of the Burnetts asserts an old ivory horn at Crathes to be of this description; and Mr. Joseph Robertson fancied it might be held as the symbol for the keeping of the forest of the Garioch.

In quite another class of royal grants, those regarding offices of jurisdiction, there was a symbolical delivery somewhat akin to the manner of investiture of churchmen in ecclesiastical offices. Down so late as 1st July 1541, Henry Lord Methven, in the Sheriff-Court of Linlithgow, takes seisin of the office of Sheriff, by receiving the rod of office of the said sheriffdom in token of the

---

[1] The original charter is not extant, but a transumpt of a precept for making the Great Seal Charter, attested by Sir John Hamilton of Magdalens, Lord-Clerk Register, is preserved in Lord Home's charter-chest.

judicial office, as use is; and then the noble lord was inducted into actual, corporal, and real possession, by shutting him up in the court-house of the said sheriffdom in sign of his possession.[1]

I am indebted to Mr. George B. Robertson, Deputy-Keeper of the Records, for calling my attention to two series of investitures of churchmen, before and after the Reformation, which are in his custody. In the first, of date 8th April 1557, William, Bishop of Aberdeen, collates Master Robert Carnegie, on the presentation of the Queen, to the chanonry and prebend of the church and rectory of Aberdour, vacant by the resignation of a venerable man Master David Carnegie, by placing his episcopal ring on his finger; and he grants precept to the Dean and Chapter for inducting him in the real, actual, and corporal possession of the said chanonry and prebend of Aberdour, by assigning him a stall in the choir and a place in the chapter. The execution of the precept is attested by a docquet in the usual form, under the hand of Alexander Lindsay, notary-public.

The next investiture shows us a presentation by James VI., 10th September 1588, addressed to John Erskine of Dun, Superintendent or Commissioner of Angus and Mearns, where the King being informed of the qualification, literature, and good

[1] Sheriff-Court Books of Linlithgow.

conversation of Master James Rait, and of his earnest affection to travel in the office of the ministry within the Kirk of God, presents him to the parsonage and vicarage of Kinnettles, vacant by the decease of Master Andrew Davidson, or by demission of Master James Davidson, and requires the Superintendent to try and examinate the qualification and literature of the presentee, and if he be found meet, to admit him to the living, receiving the confession of his faith and his oath of fidelity to the King. The collation runs in the name of John by the mercy of God Superintendent of Angus and the Mearns, who directs Master Alexander Kyninmonth, or any other minister within his jurisdiction—in respect that he, the Superintendent, has tried and examined the presentee, and found him of sufficient qualifications and literature for using of the office of "ane minister"—to give full institution, actual, real, and corporal possession, by delivering the "buik of God in his hands." Hitherto the writs are in the vernacular, but the institution is set forth in a formal Latin instrument, subscribed by a notary-public, declaring how Master Alexander Kyninmonth went to the Church of Kinnettles, and there at its pulpit—*apud suggestum ejusdem*—gave state, seisin, institution, and possession of the said church, manse, glebe, houses, fruits, profits, and teinds to Master James Rait, minister, by tradition of the book of God's Word, and of earth and stone respectively, as use is — *per traditionem verbi dei libri ac terre et lapidis.* It is well known that the symbols of investiture generally bore some reference to the subject. Seisin was taken of the mill by delivery of clap and hopper, of a house by the key, of fishings by net and coble, of patronage by a psalter and the keys of the church, of jurisdiction by the book of court. In the older burgh usages, burghal subjects were transferred by the bailie taking a penny for *in-toll* and a penny for *ut-toll*.[1] Here is the law as it ran in the days of the good King David I. : " Quicunque vendiderit terram suam vel partem terre sue ipse qui vendit erit infra domum et exibit et alius qui emptor est stabit foris et intrabit ; et unus dabit preposito unum denarium pro exitu terre et alius dabit denarium pro introitu suo et sasina."[2] You will find in some of the remaining relics of the now abolished seisins, the bailie, to give precision to the transaction, describes the ox which he took as his fee—a red ox with a white face, or otherwise, as it might be—a kind of symbol which is not yet forgotten or despised when our modern Sheriff, as bailie of her Majesty, takes the "seisin ox" for investing some earl in his hereditary domain.

---

[1] Registrum Episcopatus Glasguensis, No. 237.

[2] Ancient Laws and Customs of the Burghs of Scotland, p. 25, No. 52.

LECTURE III.

PARLIAMENT OF SCOTLAND.

At the period when we have for the first time assistance from history, we find Scotland made up of several distinct nations recently gathered and to some extent united under one sovereign. Scots, Picts, Cumbrians, Strathclyde men, with, I think, a fringe along the eastern sea-board of the same Teutonic settlers who had taken a deeper hold of the fertile plains of England.

For my present purpose I do not wish to go farther back than the era of the Norman Conquest of England, and the very point of time when the Norman William won the sovereignty of all England in a single battle.[1] Observe how Scotland was governed. Our kings were the acknowledged rulers of these several territories. Scotland Proper was the country from Forth to Spey, and from the West to the Eastern Sea. Lothian, a section of Saxon North-

[1] Battle of Hastings, 14th October 1066.

umberland (the most powerful and most literate of the Saxon kingdoms of England) had been but recently subjected to the Kings of the Scots. Cumbria and Galloway in like manner brought their British and Pictish peoples in an uncertain and uneasy subjection. The Scots, properly so called, settled at first on the western shore, the Picts, mostly on the eastern, but had united under monarchs who thus came at the time we are examining to rule all the country we still call Scotland: for it is not necessary for our present purpose to distinguish the temporary settlement of the Norsemen, whose great northern Earldom of Caithness, somewhat later, came under the Scotch kings; nor Moray, which was either in a chronic state of rebellion, or subject quite as much to the Sigurds and Thorfins of the North, as to the Kings of Scotland.

The sovereign of these united or confederate nations, ruling the inhabitants of all that we call Scotland, with some part of English Cumbria, at the era of the Norman Conquest, was Malcolm Canmore, who married at Dunfermline about 1070, a lady of the highest Atheling blood, the Scotch Saint Margaret.

Malcolm Canmore, as we might conclude from his name, was a Celt. We know he was son of the "gentle Duncan"—Shakespeare's Duncan—of the old race of the Gaelic monarchs. We know, too, that he understood and spoke Gaelic; but beyond that excellent accomplishment, he was, like many Highlanders, only half a Celt. His mother was a sister of Siward, Earl of Northumberland, of high Saxon blood, and he owed his crown to the help his Northumbrian cousins gave him against Macbeth.

The first point of historical difference affecting our constitution, as compared with that of England, seems to be that the Royal race with us was not changed in all the revolutions which the country underwent. We had no race of Saxons, Woden-descended heroes, trampling out the last embers of the primeval British line; no Cnuts and Harolds of Danish blood to supplant the Saxons; no Norman lords, at least none coming by right of conquest, and filling the throne of Saxon princes. But, though our reigning family continued unchanged, the upper class of our population was in a state of transition as early as we can pretend to examine it. It was no doubt owing in part to the influence of his noble and pious Saxon wife that the Court of Malcolm Canmore became the refuge of crowds of English exiles, driven from their homes by the oppressive rule of the Normans and the frequent rebellions under the Conqueror and Rufus. In all the revolutions of those reigns—again in the disturbed reign of Stephen, and down even under the early Plantagenet Kings, continuous streams of English found it convenient to take the protection of the Scotch King. At one time they were Normans disgusted with the government; at another, Saxons escaping from the insolence of their new masters. Of whatever race, they were all welcomed according to their desert.

Our kings were never left long in repose. When they had no English wars on their hands, a rising of the Galwegians, or a rebellion of the Moray men in favour of some pretender to the throne, a more daring movement of some Norse Jarl, or an attempt at combination among the Highland clans, found them constant occupation in war, and prepared them to be grateful for such assistance as the Norman knight and the Saxon franklin, both good men at arms, were ready to give for the common recompense of a grant of lands out of the territory of the rebels, with perhaps a fortalice which they were bound to hold for the king against future insurrections.

Now, with the Saxon queen and these Saxon and Norman lords came southern laws and manners, not violently as by right of conquest, but received as the most approved, most civil policy, coming where there was not much to displace of definite law and customs endeared by long use. The Celtic part of our population had indeed only in part gone through that greatest of revolutions where the bond of kinship gives way to local adherence and attachment to the soil. But in all southern Scotland, perhaps I may say all south of Spey, even before the period which we are are now considering, we find hardly any traces remaining of a peculiar Scotch or Celtic law distinguishable from the customs of our Teutonic, our Saxon forefathers—the most popular, the freest of constitutions—modified, I will not say spoiled, by the gradual superinduction of the feudal tenures and customs that already prevailed on the Continent and in England.

But of whatever stock, Pictish, Scotch, Norman, or Saxon, the great lords of Scotland, the officers who surrounded the throne of the successors of Malcolm Canmore, judicial and administrative, did not differ in name or function from those of England and other feudal kingdoms. The Chancellor, Chamberlain, Steward, Constable, the Justiciar, all the great officers of the State and of the law, of the French or of the English Court, were repeated with us. In some of the more remote districts indeed, and especially in the more Celtic districts, some of the great lords, and many of the inferior executors of the law, had Celtic titles, showing the remnants of Gaelic customs and speech, but showing also by their infrequency how rapidly that element was disappearing.

In Malcolm Canmore's time the great districts of

Moray, Buchan, Mar, Mearns, and perhaps Angus, were each ruled by an officer, probably hereditary, called "Maormar;" but these were soon superseded by the Earls—*Comites*—Counts, with their ministers and functionaries. One officer in those districts, Latinized *Judex*, translated into Scotch *doomster*—Demster—may originally have discharged higher functions than the antiquary associates with the Scotch name of Dempster. Some of the inferior executors of the law had Celtic names long preserved, as *Maor* and *Toschach*. The Scotch Thane was known as the administrator of the King's rents, and his descendants preserved the name when it had become only a title of honour, when the land was their own, and the King drew only a fixed reddendo. Next arises the question, Was there in old Scotland anything equivalent to the County Court, or the Court of the Hundred or Tithing, those foundations of the English Constitution, those local gatherings where neighbours took counsel about local affairs or settled differences? I cannot tell. I think there are indications of such assemblies. But it is too much the fashion to draw a marked line of distinction between the Celtic and Teutonic peoples and their customs. Until I see evidence to the contrary, I will believe that the Celtic institutions—always except their longer attachment to a patriarchal form of society—resembled those of the other northern nations, though they have left no code or chronicle, nothing but the circle of grey stones on the heath to record their national customs, their manner and form of proceeding.[1]

We know something of the County Court of England, descendant of the old *mallus* of Germany. We know how the earl and the bishop presided there together, and we can trace much of the most valued institutions of England — trial by jury amongst them — to that source. But in Scotland we cannot get so far back, at least not so accurately. The shape of the earliest Courts with us, of which we have any record, was the Court of the feudal lord, the head court of the barony, drawing its origin and rules from quite a different source.

There is no time when we can say that our kings acted or pretended to act by their own authority absolutely. We cannot point to a time in which they did not set forth in all great matters that they acted by the advice and consent of their people assembled for the purpose of giving that advice and consent.

Let me now give you some dates and references

---

[1] It would be curious if it should turn out that these monuments, which our antiquaries of last century named Druids' circles, were places where the old Celtic people met for deliberation and for administering their common affairs, for legislation, for judgment-giving, as well as for burial, for religious rites and ceremonies and solemn contracts — in short, filling the idea and original purpose of a *church*.

to transactions which will serve to mark the progressive changes of the National Assembly while still only forming itself into the shape and not yet bearing the name of Parliament.

Alexander the First[1] held an Assembly in 1107, where Turgot was chosen Bishop of St. Andrews by the " King, the clergy, and the people."[2] The same King re-founded the Abbey of Scone in 1114 —*proborum virorum consilio*—the queen, Alexander, *nepos regis*, two bishops, six earls and others, witnessing and expressing their consent.[3] The next reign, that of David I.,[4] gives little change to the composition of the National Assembly. A charter to the Abbey of Dunfermline, between 1124 and 1127, is granted by "our royal authority and power, with the assent of my son Henry and Matilda my wife, and with the confirmation and witnessing of the bishops, earls, and barons of my kingdom," concluding with the general assent—*clero etiam acquiescente et populo.*[5] And that style is little changed in the numerous charters of this reign.

Malcolm IV.[6] did not materially change that style. A National Council at Perth in 1160, held on the occasion of a conspiracy against the King, records the presence of *prelati et proceres regni majores,* which.

[1] A.D. 1106-1124.
[2] Chron. Mailros.
[3] Liber de Scon.
[4] A.D. 1124-1153.
[5] Acts of Parliament, vol. i.
[6] A.D. 1153-1165.

I read, the chiefs of the clergy and the lay nobles.[1] He granted several charters, but there is, as I have said, no essential difference in style from those of his grandfather.

William the Lion[2] also uses nearly the style of his grandfather. But now we begin to have the National Assembly called *curia regis*, one of which was held at Perth in 1166, in presence of the King, his bishops, and his good subjects —*episcoporum et proborum hominum suorum*.[3] An Assembly was held at Stirling in 1180, in which laws were enacted by the King with the "common consent of the prelates, earls, barons, and free tenants."[4] In 1188 the King of Scots, with nearly all the bishops and earls and barons of his country, and with an infinite number of his men—*cum infinita hominum suorum multitudine*—held an Assembly, in which the demand made by the King of England for the tithes of Scotland for the Crusades was refused.[5] In 1190, in an Assembly at Edinburgh, the prelates and nobles of Scotland assessed a tax of 10,000 merks in payment of the King's ransom.[6] But I must return to this instance of early taxation.

Hitherto I pass over the mention of "Councils" and "Great Councils"—*concilium* and *magnum con-*

---

[1] Fordun.
[2] A.D. 1165-1214.
[3] Acts of Parliament, vol. i.
[4] Acts of Parliament, vol. i.
[5] Benedictus Abbas.
[6] Fordun.

cilium,—and also meetings of the Magnates of the land—*magnatum, optimatum, procerum, magnatum de concilio*—and such phrases, which give us little definite information of the constituent members of the assembly.[1]

Fordun tells us that Alexander II. was crowned at Scone on the 5th December 1214 (8 *Idus Decembris*, says the Chronicle of Mailros) in the presence of the Earls of Strathern, Atholl, Angus, Menteith and Buchan, together with William Bishop of St. Andrews and others of the Three Estates in great number. The same chronicle says the King held a Parliament in 1215 at Edinburgh, but we must doubt if it went by that name. The word Parliament is first used in England in formal style in 1272, although Matthew Paris speaks of the "Parliamentum Runnymede" in 1215. The style of the King's Court, the full Court of the King—*curia domini Regis, plena curia regis, colloquium regis*, and *plenum colloquium*—runs through this reign and that of Alexander III., who was crowned at Scone in 1249—*coram multitudine presulum prelatorum comitum baronum et militum*.[2] The Letter of the Community of Scotland, written to the King of England, counselling the marriage between his son and Margaret, the

---

[1] In 1211 a Great Council was held at Stirling, where the barons voted 10,000 merks, and the burghs 6000 merks, according to Fordun, but we may reasonably doubt whether the votes were taken in the same Assembly.

[2] Fordun.

Maiden of Norway, runs in the name of the guardians, bishops, earls, abbots, priors, and barons of Scotland.[1] The Parliament of Brigham was perhaps the first national assembly called by that name. It was held on the 17th of March 1289, on occasion of discussing the marriage of Queen Margaret.[2]

John Balliol held a Parliament at Scone in 1292, and another at Stirling in 1293;[3] but the other assemblies of his counsellors and people were not so styled. In an Assembly at Dunfermline in 1295, the Scotch part of the treaty between John Balliol and Philip, King of France, was ratified by the prelates, earls, barons, and other nobles of Scotland, and also " per universitates ac communitates villarum regni Scotie." The deed is sealed on the Scotch part by four bishops, four abbots, four earls, eleven barons, and six burghs, viz., Aberdeen, Perth, Striuelin, Edinburgh, Roxburgh, Berwick.[4]

William Wallace, Knight, Guardian of Scotland and leader of its army, grants his charter to the Constable of Dundee in 1298, in name of the King and by consent of the nobles of the realm.[5] A letter of the same date to Eric, King of Norway, runs in the name of the guardians and all the community of the realm of Scotland.

---

[1] Supplement to the Acts of the Parliaments of Scotland.
[2] Acts of Parliament, vol. i.
[3] Acts of Parliament, vol. i.
[4] *Ibid.*
[5] National MSS., Part I.

The Letter from Torwood to Edward King of England, dated 13th Nov. 1299, runs in the names of William Bishop of St. Andrews, Robert de Bruce Earl of Carric, John Comyn the son, Guardians of the kingdom of Scotland acting for a mighty Prince, John King of Scotland (by the community of the same realm appointed—*per communitatem ejusdem regni constituti*), and for the community of the said kingdom.[1] The letter of the ambassadors of Scotland in France sent to the Government of Scotland, dated at Paris, 25th May 1303, is addressed to venerable and discreet men and their friends, John Comyn, Guardian of the kingdom of Scotland, and the prelates, earls, barons and others, faithful subjects of the same kingdom.[2]

Robert Bruce,[3] two years after his coronation, on the 16th March 1308, held a Parliament—*plenum parliamentum*—at St. Andrews; that Parliament dictated a letter to the King of France, styling themselves the "earls, barons, communities of all the earldoms, and also the barons of all Argyll and Ynchegall, and the inhabitants of all the kingdom of Scotland."[4] The clergy seem to have acted separately.

The name of Parliament was now common, though perhaps not strictly technical. In 1314, a Parliament held at Cambuskenneth, set forth as

---

[1] Acts of Parliament, vol. i.
[2] *Ibid.*
[3] A.D. 1306-1329.
[4] Acts of Parliament, vol. i.

its constituent members the King, prelates, earls, barons, and other nobles of the kingdom of Scotland—*necnon et tota communitas regni.*[1]

On 26th April 1315, in a very solemn meeting in the parish church of Ayr, the bishops, abbots, priors, deans and archdeacons, and other prelates; earls, barons, knights, and others of the community —*de communitate*—of the kingdom, as well cleric as lay, held for deliberating on the defence and security of the kingdom of Scotland, Edward Bruce was declared successor in case of Robert I. dying without heirs-male of his body.[2]

A body of Statutes of Robert's reign, of date 1318, and of which there is an old Scotch version, runs in the name of Robert, "be the grace of God, Kyng of Scottis . . . of the consal and the expres consent of the bischopis, abbotis, priouris, erlis, barounis, and other great men, and with the hale communite of the kynrik there gathered in our ful Parliament haldyn at Scone."[3]

The famous Letter by the Scotch barons to the Pope, dated from the Monastery of Arbroath, 6th April 1320, asserting the independence of Scotland, after a long list of their names, ends with " ceterique barones et liberetenentes ac tota communitas regni Scotie."[4] Finally, in the Parliament at Cambusken-

[1] Acts of Parliament, vol. i.
[2] *Ibid.*
[3] *Ibid.*
[4] National MSS., Part II.

neth, 15th July 1326, held by the King in person, and in the presence of the earls, barons, burgesses, and all other free tenants of his kingdom, the constitution of Scotland was fixed; an annual revenue was assigned to the King, and all taxes and impositions without the authority of Parliament declared illegal.[1]

The Parliament was now complete with the King and its Three Estates—clergy, nobles, and commons,—the latter made up of the smaller barons and the representatives of burghs. All the same doubts and questions arise in our study of the Scotch Parliament that meet us in the infancy of the parliamentary constitution of England. For our purpose it is enough to know that the great national Council, as early as we can watch its existence, consisted of the Sovereign; the bishops and great churchmen; the earls, barons, and great lay lords; and a class here, as in England, set down as *probi homines, libere-tenentes*—immediate vassals of the Crown of inferior station. When David the First's charters, granted in presence of the great Council of the nation, set forth the assent of the bishops and barons, ending with the assertion of general approbation " clero etiam acquiescente et populo," the bishops and prelates might perhaps be taken to speak the assent of the clergy ; but through whom was the assent of

[1] National MSS., Part II.

the people given? The *omnis populus*, as it is given in some instances, had no means of expressing their assent; it is certainly a mere form of words as regards anything actually done in the Assembly. Assuredly there was as yet no idea of representation *de facto*, but it must be held a very important form if it recognises even in theory that the consent of the people was necessary for legislative enactment. It is worth noticing that the constitution of Parliament, defined in a few words at Cambuskenneth, was not peculiar to Scotland. We have it at the same time in Spain (witness the Cortes of Catalonia, Aragon, and Castille); in the States-General of France; in the Parliament of England, licked into shape in the long and most parliamentary reign of Edward III. The elements were the same in all—King, clergy, nobles, burgesses. The difference was, that in the constitutional governments of the Continent the Three Estates fell asunder through continual jealousies; only in our Island did the parliamentary constitution take root and thrive.

David II.,[1] who had been taken prisoner at the battle of Durham in 1346, but not indeed held in rigorous durance, was at length to be ransomed in 1357. At a Council held in Edinburgh, 26th Sept., seven bishops of the kingdom gave an obligation

[1] A.D. 1329-1371.

in name of the whole clergy for the King's ransom
in 100,000 merks sterling. On the same day, thirteen members of the baronage, on behalf of all
the earls, nobles—*procerum*—barons, and the community of the kingdom of Scotland, appointed their
procurators, viz., Patrick Earl of March, Thomas
Earl of Angus, William Earl of Sutherland, Thomas
de Moravia Panetar of Scotland, William de Livingstone and Robert de Erskine, Knights, to bind all
the other earls, nobles, and barons for that ransom
of 100,000 merks sterling.

Nor were the representatives of the burghs
wanting, and I think their names are of sufficient
interest to be enumerated. On the same day,
Alexander Gyliot, Adam Tore, and John Goldsmith
of Edinburgh; John Mercer, John Gill, and Robert
of Gatmilke of Perth; Laurence of Garuok, William Leith, John Crab of Aberdeen; Mr. John of
Somerville and Robert Kid of Dundee; Roger
Phipill and Thomas Johnson of Inverkeithen;
Richard Hendchyld and Richard Skroger of Crail;
Nicholas, rector of the schools, and David Comyn of
Coupar; Laurence Bell and Adam Kirkintilloch of
St. Andrews; Richard of Cadyoch and John Clerk
of Monros; John de Burgo and William Sauser of
Strivelin; John Johnson and William de Saulton of
Linlithgow; Adam de Haddington and Adam de
Congilton of Haddington; Simon Poter and Peter

Waghorne of Dumbarton; Patrick Clark and Patrick Reder of Rutherglen; Andrew Adam and Andrew of Pomfret of Lanark; William of Duncoll and Thomas Lang of Dumfries; Nicholas Johnson and John Williamson of Peebles, aldermen, merchants, and burgesses, appointed Procurators to bind themselves for the fulfilment of the bond. These worthy burgesses affixed the seals of their good burghs to their obligation, and sixteen of those seals remain attached thereto this day.[1]

In the Council held at Scone on 6th November of the same year, an Inquest was ordained to value and assess all property for payment of the ransom as well church as feudal lands—except white sheep, horses broken for use, oxen and household furniture—and enacting that no person be exempt from the tax, of whatever condition.[2] In the same Assembly, for the King's maintenance, it was ordered that all lands, rents, possessions, and customs granted by him should be recalled to the Crown.

Robert the Steward,[3] now passed to the middle of life, was crowned and anointed King of Scots at Scone—*sedente in sede regia super montem de Scon ut est moris.* The Acts of this reign, which excited the greatest interest at the time, were those connected with the settlement of the succession to the

---

[1] Ancient Laws and Customs of the Burghs of Scotland.
[2] Acts of Parliament, vol. i.
[3] A.D. 1371-90.

Crown, but they are now of less consequence and serve only to mark the change made by feudal lawyers in favour of the strict line of male succession. They mark also the manner in which deeds of the greatest importance were published and in a manner stamped with public assent. One of these, preserving many of the seals of those present, sets forth how the foresaid earls, nobles, and others of the Council consented to the settling of the succession to the Crown on John Earl of Carrick, eldest son of Robert II., and how the King made all the people, with the clergy—*omnem populum cum clero*—to be assembled, that in their presence and by their unanimous consent it might be done and published, so that no one pretend ignorance thereof in future. Then the whole multitude of prelates, earls, and barons—*tota multitudo prelatorum comitum et baronum*—and of others both of the clergy and the people, with unanimous will and consenting acclamation—*et clamore consono*—no single one dissenting, affirmed and recognised John, the eldest son, true heir of the King. That was in the year 1371, 27th of March, according to the calculation of the Scotican Church, and the deed is dated at Scone in the time of the coronation. On the 4th of April 1373, the King again holding his Parliament at Scone, and wishing to remove the uncertainty and evils of a succession through females, executed in fact a strict male tailie upon the descendants of both his marriages, and after a fine list of the nobles and knights of Scotland, most of whom sealed the Act, the deed finishes in this way: Immediately thereafter the whole multitude of the clergy and people, being assembled in the church of Scone before the high altar, and the deed having been read and explained—*alta et publica voce expositis*—each person with raised hand, in manner of giving his faith, and in sign of the universal consent of the whole clergy and people, expressed and showed publicly his consent and assent.[1]

To make up for the paucity of constitutional matter in this and the following reign, we have now for the first time original records of proceedings in Parliament written in the vernacular; so that one reads with certain pleasure, or at least with a confidence of truthfulness, the simple memorials of Parliament, —endeavouring to introduce order among much confusion, to establish a systematic coinage—and a sentence like the following, where the poor sick King is treated at least somewhat familiarly:—" Whare it is deliueryt that the misgouuernance of the reaulme and the defaut of the keypyng of the common law sulde be imput to the Kyng and his officeris, and tharfore gife it likeis owre lorde the Kynge til excuse his defautes, he may at his lykynge gerr call

---

[1] These two deeds are preserved in the General Register House.

his officeris, to the qwhilkis he hes giffyn commission, and accuse thaim in presence of his consail. And thair ansuere herde, the consail sal be redy to iuge their defautes, syn na man aw to be condampnyt qwhil he be callit and accusit."[1]

I think I have quoted instances enough to show what were the constituent parts of Parliament. I must be excused for travelling over partly the same ground in collecting the earliest cases where Parliament exercised the right of imposing taxes—the common test, and a very convenient one, of the supreme legislative power vesting in Parliament.

Malcolm IV. gave his sisters in marriage to the Counts of Brittany and Holland, apparently soon after his succession. The marriages were made—*subsidio suorum et auxilio*, says Fordun; and the meaning of the chronicler is, that he obtained the necessary funds for the dowers of the Princesses by the assistance of his barons or feudal vassals, by whose advice the marriages were arranged. The word *auxilium*, which in that sense we translate *aid*, might give the idea of a feudal casualty, and I shall not pretend to distinguish very accurately between such a levy from feudal vassals for the marriage of the lord's sisters and a parliamentary grant. But you will find that there was something parliamentary in it, for a tax was raised from others than feudal vas-

[1] Acts of Parliament, vol. i. 27th January 1398.

sals of the Crown; and the great Churchmen preferred assessing and collecting it themselves within their own bounds. There is evidence to show that the King commanded the Earl of Angus and sundry sheriffs not to enter the lands of the Abbot of Scone for collecting these aids, because the Abbot had obtained a privilege from the King to collect the public aids from his own goods by his own officer—*de pecuniis suis per proprios ministros suos.*[1]

The national Assembly had undoubtedly arrived at the common exercise of its chief and discriminating function—the taxation of the country for the expenses of Government—in the next reign, that of William the Lion. The money for the King's ransom from his English prison was to be raised, and the heavy burden was apparently too great for the feudal vassals. You remember how the thing fell out. In a raid into England in 1174, William the Lion was surprised, overpowered, and taken prisoner by the barons of Yorkshire. The prison was severe, and in his impatience to escape from it, William surrendered the independence of his kingdom by the treaty of Falaise, doing homage to Henry II., and giving up at the same time Roxburgh, Jedburgh, Berwick, Edinburgh, and Stirling—the chief keys and strengths of his kingdom—for the fulfilment of this treaty.

[1] Liber de Scon.

Before the death of Henry II., William's position and character had much strengthened, and when Richard Cœur de Lion, on his accession to the throne, sought every means of raising money for his great Crusade, the Scotch King, by offering a sum of 10,000 merks, obtained the restoration of the national independence in the most ample form of grant, and also the surrender of such of his country's castles as were not already in his hands. It was to meet this debt, this large drain, that the prelates and nobles of Scotland—*prelati et proceres*—I use Fordun's words—met at Edinburgh and raised the sum—*inter se partitam*—not in form and manner assessing the tax; but we know from incidental entries in contemporary writs in the chartularies that it *was* assessed, and levied from others than feudal vassals—the religious and even the Cistercians, who boasted an exemption from all civil burdens, bearing their share of that national tax. You see the national meeting at Edinburgh was divided into only two orders, or arms, as the Catalonians called them. But the citizens were already of importance, especially where money was wanted.

And this brings me to inquire into the early state and constitution of our Scotch burghs—a subject of interest in the history of all nations, but with some circumstances of peculiar interest here. From

H

the very earliest period of our history, free burghs, with certain privileges of trade and other immunities, had existed in Scotland, and from the days of David I. at least, two combinations of these burghs appear, —one, from Aberdeen northwards, including all the burghs beyond the *Munth*, had a confederacy called by the name of "Hanse"—a name so well known afterwards in connexion with the great European combination of free cities; the other, a burghal parliament called *curia quatuor burgorum*, was composed properly of delegates of the burghs of Berwick, Roxburgh, Edinburgh, and Stirling; but when any of these were in the hands of the enemy, the Court included others of the southern burghs for making up the Parliament, which was purely burghal though its president was the High Chamberlain of Scotland. This Parliament of the good towns, which often met at Haddington, was fixed by James II. in 1454 to assemble at Edinburgh.[1] It was of such admitted authority, that it decided all burghal disputes and legislated in burghal questions with sovereign authority.[2]

---

[1] Supplement to the Acts of Parliament.

[2] The English books afford an instance of the general recognition of this Court. In a Parliament held at Newcastle by Edward I. in 1292, in a private suit, depending on the law and customs of Scotch burghs, it was determined that the four burghs should be consulted—*ideo consulendum est cum quatuor burgis contra proximum parliamentum hic, et tunc ad judicium.* And this having been done, judgment on the appeal was given accordingly: "quia compertum est per recordum et veredictum quatuor burgorum quod lex et consuetudo talis est." (Rot. Parl. I. p. 107.)

We can understand that such a confederacy of good towns, having already a recognised judicature and legislature of their own, would be in no haste to make their way into a Parliament of prelates and barons, to divide the responsibility without much share of the honour of legislation. With the burghs, as with the small barons afterwards, seat and vote in Parliament must have been regarded as a burden, and no doubt it was the increase of their wealth and influence that made them sought after. The burghs however came at last to be held as an essential part of Parliament. I would gladly show you the precise occasion on which they took their place and were recognised as one of the Estates of and in the National Council; and although we cannot point to the exact year or meeting of Parliament, we shall come very near it.

I have already shown you the Scotch burghs voting a large share of a national tax, proving their early wealth and importance. When Balliol was negotiating a treaty of marriage for his son Edward with the daughter of the King of France in 1295, the instrument of agreement was ratified by the prelates and barons, and by certain of the burghs of Scotland. The parties consenting and approving are four bishops, four abbots of monasteries, four earls, eleven barons; and the seals of six burghs, Aberdeen, Perth, Striueling, Roxburgh, Edinburgh, and Berwick, are affixed in evidence of consent and approbation—*in signum sui consensus et approbationis*,[1] which may be held as showing at least the position of the burghs in the body politic, and that in a transaction when the voice of the nation was to be expressed, though the treaty does not bear to have been executed in Parliament.

Neither is there any express evidence of the presence of the burghs as a branch of the imperial legislature during the early Parliaments of Bruce, unless we hold as an indication of some change, that the phrase of long use in our old Acts *tota communitas regni* is changed in 1315 for *majores communitatis*. But in the Parliament of that King held at Cambuskenneth on the 15th day of July 1326, when Bruce claimed from his people a revenue to meet the expense of his glorious war and the necessities of the State, which was granted to the monarch by the earls, barons, burgesses and free tenants in full Parliament assembled, the change had taken place—perhaps silently, perhaps gradually, but from henceforth undoubtedly the representatives of the burghs formed the Third Estate, and an essential part of all Parliaments and general councils.[2]

---

[1] Acts of Parliament, vol. i.

[2] Robert himself, though so favourable to the burghs, and apparently so much beholden to them, committed the gravest offences against burghal liberty. You know the very essence of royal burgh tenure is, that the burgh holds immediately of the Crown. But in an extant charter of Bruce, the King granted to Sir Hugh de Ross, son and heir of the Earl of Ross, the whole sheriffdom and burgh of Cromarty

I have already more than once referred to this remarkable Parliament, where we can for the first time ascertain the presence of the representatives of burghs. In it we have the development of what are now considered the fundamental principles of a representative constitution. There is a compact between the King and the Three Estates—a claim of right, redress of grievances—especially abolition of arbitrary taxes—a grant of supplies, and a strict limitation of the grant to its proper purposes. In that notable Act, the Three Estates acknowledge the great merit of the King, and all that he had undergone for restoring the liberties of all. The grievous burdens of the people through arbitrary taxes are pointed out, and that the King had no maintenance without intolerable grievance and burden of the people. *He* undertakes to impose no more illegal *collectæ* and mitigate his legal exactions of *prisæ* and *cariagia*. On the other hand, the Estates grant him

without reserve (National MSS., Part II.); and his famous charter to his nephew, Thomas Ranulph, of the Earldom of Moray, granted him the royal burghs of Elgin, Forres, and Nairn. It declared that they should have the same liberties which they had had in the time of Alexander III. and in Robert's own time, with this difference only, that whereas they formerly held of *us* immediately (says the King), they shall now hold of the said Earl: "hoc solum salvo quod de nobis tenebant sine medio et nunc de eodem comite tenent." (Registrum Moraviense.) It was to remedy this unconstitutional grievance that the Parliament in the time of David II. declared it illegal for the King to interpose any person between him and his vassals.— Acts of Parliament, vol. i.

the tenth penny of all rents during his life, according to the Old Extent of lands and rents in the time of Alexander III. of good memory — a gift which they declare shall be null if the King defeats its application to the public service by any remissions granted beforehand. And because certain of the nobles had liberties and privileges—regalities and high jurisdictions—which impeded the King's officers in levying taxes within their bounds, all such privileged lords undertook to make payment of the tax effeiring to their lands; which failing, the King's sheriffs were to distrain. The concluding words are very remarkable: it is consented and agreed between our Lord the King and the community of his realm —*inter dominum regem et communitatem regni sui*, that on the death of the King the payment of the tenth penny shall stop, and that the thing shall not be drawn into a precedent. The King gave his consent by appending the Great Seal. The other part of the indenture was sealed with the seals of the earls, barons, and other great freeholders —*aliorum majorum liberetenentium*—along with the common seals of the burghs of the kingdom, in their own name and the name of the whole community. The Parliament of Scotland was now complete in all its parts,—consisting of the clergy, barons, and burgesses of the kingdom.

The treaty of Brigeham in 1289 uses the word

Parliament for meetings of the Scotch legislature, but the first Parliament that really called itself by that name in Scotland was that of John Balliol, assembled at Scone, 9th February 1292—seventeen years after it had become the word of style for the legislature of England.

The parliamentary proceedings of David II.'s long reign, though often unconstitutional, are singularly instructive to the historical inquirer, partly perhaps because we find now for the first time regular and consecutive records of Parliament which are still extant and of undoubted authenticity.

In a Parliament held at Scone on the 27th September 1367, the record bears that, after the Three Estates had met, certain persons were elected by the said estates for holding the Parliament —*quedam certe persone electe fuerunt ad parliamentum tenendum*, and the rest were allowed to return home on account of the harvest.[1] So in the Parliament at Perth in March of the following year, the Three Estates, on account of the inconvenience of the season and the dearness of provisions, elected certain persons to hold Parliament, who were divided into two bodies, one for the general affairs of the king and kingdom, and another, a smaller division, for acting as Judges upon appeals—*super judiciis contradictis*.[2] Observe, that though the Parliaments of

[1] Acts of Parliament, vol. i.   [2] *Ibid.* 6th March 1368.

England and Scotland thus far seem to have gone on side by side in constitutional progress, there is this one remarkable difference, that while in England, prior to the reign of Edward I., the judicial power was eliminated from Parliament—her Judges, trained lawyers, administering over the kingdom the settled and venerated principles of the common law—in Scotland duty was done in another manner, and worse, by some selection or committee of Parliament.

In the Parliament held at Perth upon the 18th day of February 1369, the preamble sets forth that there were summoned and called in due and usual manner, the bishops, abbots, priors, earls, barons, and freeholders who hold of our Lord the King in chief, and from each burgh certain burgesses—compearing all those who ought, would and could conveniently attend—but that there were absent certain members, of whom some were lawfully excused, while others absented themselves of contumacy, namely, the Earl of Marr, John of Yle, Gillespic Campbell, and a few of the meaner sort, both clergy and freeholders—*eciam pauci de inferioribus cleri et liberetenentium.* The Record then proceeds : seeing this Parliament was ordained to be held chiefly upon certain points concerning the state of the realm and the King, and the manner of the King's living, and upon certain matters touching common justice, and as it is not and could not be expedient that the whole community — *universalis communitas* — should assist at a deliberation of such a nature, nor yet be kept in waiting — there were elected certain persons by the general and unanimous consent and assent of the Three Estates for the matters which concerned common justice, to wit, for discussing and determining appeals, petitions, and complaints which ought to be determined in Parliament; others were elected for treating and deliberating upon certain special and secret affairs of the King and kingdom before they are brought to the knowledge of the said General Council.

Then follow the names of those elected. For the first committee there were chosen six of the clergy, ten knights, four smaller barons, and seven burgesses. For the second committee or committee of Articles, four were elected of the clergy, and twelve of the great barons, without mention of the smaller barons or burgesses. But there was an addition of " certain other persons whom our Lord the King wished to have there"— a practice borrowed from England. The two committees being thus elected, leave was given to the other members to depart. I will not trouble you with the Statutes of that Parliament, although some of them were of great importance, and one especially spoke in a tone which had not yet been heard in the Parliaments of England.[1]

The foundations were now laid of all that was peculiar in the constitution of the Scotch Parliament. In these arrangements you see the origin of that judicial committee which, under various forms and regulations, became a permanent institution until it terminated in the establishment of a separate and Supreme Court of Justice in civil suits in 1532. Here also we see the adoption of that Committee of the Articles which became an essential and remarkable part of the constitution of Parliament.

James I.[2] returned from his English imprisonment in 1424 full of English constitutional ideas. He wished to relieve the small barons from the burden of attending Parliament, provided they sent two or more "wise men" from each shire to represent them, except Clackmannan and Kinross, which were to send one each; and he enacted that these commissioners of all the shires should choose a wise and expert man, "callit the Common

---

[1] Remembering that it is the year 1369, attend to the words of this short Statute: It is ordained that no justiciar, sheriff, nor other officer of the King execute any mandate addressed to them under whatsoever seal, great or privy seal, small seal or signet, in prejudice of any party, if it be contrary to the statutes or the common form of law—*contra statuta vel communem formam juris;* and if any such mandate be presented to him (that is, any mandate contrary to the statutes or common form of law), he shall indorse it, and return it immediately so indorsed. — Acts of Parliament, vol. i.   [2] A.D. 1406-1437.

Spekar of the Parliament," — a person evidently intended to defend the privileges of the Commons in Parliament; and the Commissioners as well as the Speaker were to have their "costages." While the English representation of counties was imitated in this manner, special precepts, after the manner of the English House of Peers, were to be directed to bishops, abbots, priors, dukes, earls, lords of Parliament and banrents—the last class being equivalent, I think, to the *milites* of the early English legislation. No doubt the separation of the Houses was to follow, but scarcely any of this ordinance took effect. The representative commissioners were not sure of their "costages," and their constituents at home saw no advantage in the measure that could compensate for the expense. That and another attempt at representation failed, and it was not till late in the reign of James VI. that a representation of the smaller barons in counties was effectually carried out. Neither in this reign, nor afterwards, was a Speaker of the Commons known in our Scotch Parliament, though in no legislative assembly could an officer with the original duties of a Speaker have been more wanted.

The Parliamentary history of James II.[1] begins in this manner: "Item, the General Council, that is to say, the clergy, barons, and commissars of burghs;"

[1] A.D. 1437-1460.

and so through the whole reign the Three Estates are set forth as the essentials of Parliament. It is only affirming what had already been law since the Parliament of Cambuskenneth. We have not much of constitutional progress during this reign. The scribe of Parliamentary proceedings vents his temper upon the dulness of the sederunts—*cetera autem presentis Parliamenti sunt nisi Acta tangencia partes;* and true it is that Parliament had relapsed very much into a court of law. To make up, however, for the want of constitutional enactments, we have in this reign some laws affecting, in no common degree, the rural population. James II. is little known to our historians, but I have met him in the transactions of some northern families in documents which show the young King active and enterprising, administering justice in person, and enjoying the sports of the field far down in the north. On one occasion he is found directing in person that an allowance should be made to the poor tenants whose farm labours he interrupted for his sport while hunting on the banks of the Findhorn. I believe that I am not attributing too much to the personal influences of the sovereign in a country like Scotland at that time, and it is pleasant to think that this young generous Prince may have himself directed a Parliamentary enactment of great consequence, to which I must briefly allude.

From the beginning of the fifteenth century a question had been agitated among the lawyers of Europe as to whether the right of a singular successor, for instance a purchaser of land, should prevail against the tenant of the land with a written lease for a term of years. You see it is a great agrarian question, and it was settled in opposite ways in the different Continental schools of law. You will find it in Heineccius, who gives the Dutch form of the dispute—whether

Koop geht for heuren,

or,

Heuren geht for koop.

No doubt the sound of the controversy had reached Scotland, and this first question of tenant-right was settled by an Act of seven lines,[1] which ordains, " For the safety and favour of the puir pepil that labouris the grunde, that all tenants having tacks for a term of years, shall enjoy their tacks to the ish of their terms, suppose the lords sell or analy their lands." Lord Kames has recorded how generation after generation of Scotch lawyers tried to defeat this beneficent provision, and how at last the equitable principle prevailed.

The scanty proceedings recorded in Parliament show the continued feeling of the burden of Parliamentary service. At the same time the judicial duties became constantly more burdensome, and

---

[1] Acts of Parliament, 1449, c. 6, vol. ii. p. 35.

while the greater proportion of the *domini electi ad querelas*—the Judicial Committee, consisted of churchmen and officers of State, it surprises us more to find the sederunts sprinkled with a fair proportion of lay barons and commissioners of burghs.

In this reign our Parliamentary records show some care to preserve the names of the persons present in Parliament. I have found in a private charter a document containing a list of members a little older than the sederunts entered in the formal proceedings of Parliament. It is a charter by the King, granted in his Parliament of the Three Estates at Edinburgh on 21st July 1454.[1] The sederunt consists of the King, James II. by the grace of God, the bishops of St. Andrews, Glasgow, Dunkeld, Moray, and Galloway—*nobilibus et prepotentibus dominis*—William Earl of Orkney Lord of St. Clare, Chancellor of Scotland, James Earl of Moray, George Earl of Caithness, James of Levingstoun, Great Chamberlain of Scotland, William Lord Somyrvile, Thomas Lord Erskyn, Patrick Lord the Grahame, Alexander Lord Montgomery, Patrick Lord Glammys, Andrew Lord the Gray, George Lord Lesly, John Lord Lindesay of Byris, Robert Lord Fleming, Robert Lord Boyd, William Lord Borthwik, Alan

---

[1] I copied it from the original in the Athole charter-chest in 1829, in company with the late Mr George Smythe. I fear the original is now missing.

Lord Cathkert, Patrick Lord Halys, and Robert Lord Lyle, as well as many others of the prelates, nobles—*proceribus*—and commissioners of burghs, assembled in the said Parliament.

I must be allowed to quote one Act of a Parliament of the reign of James III.,[1] chiefly to show how lightly the rural legislators threw away the power of Parliament when they were tired of the labours of it—little thinking that they were making a precedent which, in some captious ages, might be quoted as a deliberate change of the constitution. The whole power of Parliament is intrusted to a committee chosen 4th May 1471, consisting of thirty-four: eight for the clergy, seventeen for the barons, nine for the burghs, " and the maist parte of thame and al uther lordis, prelatis, barons, and commissaris that plese thame to cal to tham, sal have the ful power and strentht of the hale thre estatis of this realme beand gaderit in this present Parliament, to avise, determyn, tret, and conclude eftir as thai fynde in thar wysdomys the materis disposit apon al materis concerning the weilfair of our souerane Lord, that ar now opynnit in this present Parliament and unendit and uthir materis that sal occur for the tyme for the weilfair of our souerane Lorde and the commone gud of the realme."

The following Act of Parliament gives us a

[1] A.D. 1460-1488.   [2] Acts of Parliament, vol. ii. c. 12, p. 100.

valuable hint both of the purposes for which Parliament was assembled and of the parliamentary feeling of the time :—" Our souueran has, with the avise of his hale thre estatis, continewit his parliment to the xj day of Januar nixt to cum, with continuation of dais, and commandis and chargis generaly, that all prelatis, bischopis, abbotis, prioris, erlis, baronis, frehaldaris, commissaris of borowis, and all that aw presens in our souueran lordis parliament, that thai comper befor his hienes in Edinburgh, the said day, with continuation of dais to avise, trete, and conclude apoun thir materis vndir writtin; that is to say, apoun the mariage of our souueran lord, the mariage of our lord the prince, and the lord marques, the matter of the treux betuix this realme and the realme of Ingland, the mater of the castell and toun of Berwic, the mater of our souuerane lordis chapel, anent Coldingham, the process of forfaltour of the lard of Drummelyour and Edward Hunter, and generaly apoun all uther materis concerning our soueran lord and the gude of the realme: and als our souueran lord has declarit that whatsumeuer prelait or lord that beis absent the said day, sall nocht alanerly be punyst of the raising of the unlaw, bot alsa uther wais as accordis to thaim that dissobeis his commandment and incurris his indignacioun and displesance."[1]

[1] Acts of Parliament, 1487, vol. ii. p. 180.

Amongst a body of enactments evidently intended for the benefit of the burghs in the reign of James IV., it is declared that the commissioners and head men of burghs be warned when taxes or contributions are given that they may vote as one of the Three Estates of the realm.[1] In a similar cluster of burgh legislation, so late as the time of Mary, the Queen and Parliament being of " will rather to augment the privileges of burghs than to diminish them," enacted that nothing shall be concluded upon peace and war, or general taxations, without five or six of the principal provosts, aldermen, and bailies of burghs being warned thereto.[2]

It was in the reign of James IV.—the most accomplished of our Scotch kings, Ariosto's hero—that the remarkable Act was passed ordaining that all barons and freeholders send their sons to grammar schools at eight or nine years of age, and keep them there till they have " perfect Latin," and thereafter to the schools of " art and jure " for three years.[3] That Act was passed in 1496. In 1579 an Act was passed ordaining that sang-schools be provided in burghs for the instruction of the youth in music.[4] In 1621 there is an Act exempting colleges and schools from payment of a

---

[1] Acts of Parliament, 1503, c. 39, vol. ii. 245.
[2] *Ib.* 1563, c. 20, vol. ii. 543.
[3] *Ib.* 1496, c. 3, ii. 238.
[4] *Ib.* 1579, c. 58, vol. iii. 174.

taxation.[1] In 1633 the Parliament of Charles i. great-great-grandson of James iv.—a Parliament of Scotch barons and burgesses—ratified an Act of the Privy Council, dated 1616, declaring that every " plough or husband-land, according to the worth," should be taxed for the maintenance and establishment of parish schools.[2] I do not pretend to have made extensive search upon the subject, but I think there is no similar law so early in any other country, and I call your attention to these statutes to vindicate in some degree the parliamentary intelligence of Scotland. The first—that in favour of the poor tenants—was almost defeated by the lawyers of the day, but at length it did prevail. The other Acts may not indeed have produced great results in education, but they show that some minds were at work with liberal forecast for the welfare of the country, at a time when it is commonly supposed that all public men and courtiers were alike selfish and factious.

The beginning of James the Fifth's reign,[3] after Albany was secluded from power, was under the Queen—Margaret of England, who was not a prudent or successful administrator of her son's kingdom. Parliament was now in its full proportions. In the General Council held at Perth, after the fatal Field

---

[1] Acts of Parliament, 1621, c. 2, vol. iv. 600.
[2] *Ib.* 1633, c. 5, vol. v. 21.
[3] A.D. 1513-1542.

of Flodden, which numbered eighteen for the clergy —of whom six were bishops; thirty-four for the barons—of whom ten were earls and ten of the rank of knights, there is hardly any representation of the burgesses, but then no tax was imposed.[1]

In the Parliament held at Edinburgh, November 1516, which confirmed the sentence of divorce of Albany from his wife Catherine Sinclair, there is recorded the presence of the prelates, barons and commissars of burghs "representing the thrie estatis of the realme;"[2] and in the Parliament held at Edinburgh, 16th November 1524,[3] in which the King himself, now about twelve years old, presided, there were present for the clergy seventeen — of whom eight were bishops and the rest lords of houses of regulars; for the barons fifteen, of whom seven were earls and eight commissioners of burghs. Two days after the meeting of Parliament, they proceeded to the election of Lords of Articles, of whom four were chosen from the clergy, who were all bishops; four from the barons, all earls; and four from the commissioners of burghs. Next were chosen the members of the Judicial Committee—*domini ad causas*—of whom six were for the clergy; six for the barons—all great barons; and four of the commissioners of burghs, some

---

[1] Acts of Parliament, 1513, vol. ii. p. 281.
[2] *Ibid.* vol. ii. p. 283.
[3] *Ib.* p. 285.

of whom, however, seem to have been churchmen. Lastly, there were chosen on the Secret Council two bishops and two great lords, with the Queen's grace to direct all matters, and it was declared that nothing be done without their advice thereto. In that Parliament John Duke of Albany is declared to have lost his office of tutory, and the boy King is now to govern his realm, lieges and subjects in time to come by the advice of the Queen-Mother and Lords of his Council; and the Queen is to have the keeping of his person. It was a reforming Parliament, and the greatest of the reforms projected was that "there be chosen certain famous lords and persons of the Three Estates that have best knowledge and experience, who shall sit upon the Session, and begin the same incontinent, and thereafter continue and minister justice evenly to all parties, both poor and rich, without feud, favour, or affection, keeping the order of the table, notwithstanding any request of the King or Queen." There is a similar measure for the constant administration of justice *in criminalibus*, and for police throughout the realm. There are provisions for inbringing of the King's property and the Queen's dower. After that auspicious Parliament, the next, which was held at Edinburgh, in February 1524, gives us an early indication of dissension in Parliament and the cause thereof. The

Parliament had been summoned to meet on 15th February;[1] and then assembled, apparently, only the Bishop of Sodor, Lord Forbes, William Scott of Balwery, Mr. John Campbell of Lundie, John Stirling of Keir, and James Colville of Ochiltree, appointed by special commission of the King to hold Parliament, along with Andrew Dalmahoy, sergeant, and John Anderson, doomster. The suits being called and the Court fenced, the said Commissioners created and appointed William Forbes of Corsinda, deputy of the Earl Marischal, John Sterling of Keir, deputy of the Lord Constable, for exercising their offices in Parliament. The sederunt consisted of fifteen of the clergy, of whom six were bishops; nineteen of the barons, of whom eleven were earls; and four commissioners of burghs.

On the 25th February—that is, ten days after the formal opening of Parliament — the Three Estates chose the Lords of Articles; and we have them on record—six for the clergy; six for the barons; and six for the burghs; and no sooner are the elections recorded than the Register of Parliament is crowded with protests against elections. The Queen, as of right, led the way; and no doubt the sister of Henry VIII. made herself heard in that turbulent assembly, protesting that she desired always

[1] Acts of Parliament, vol. ii. p. 288.

unity and concord amongst all the lords, and no differences to be amongst them; and if they did otherwise it should be laid to their charge, and not to hers.

On the Queen's side, the Abbot of Scone protested, that since he had sworn to take the Queen's part, he would not go against his oath; and the Earl of Arran, and Gawin Archbishop of Glasgow, protested "siclik." It does not appear very parliamentary in our view; but, on the other side, we do not find more of constitutionalism. The Bishop of Ross protested against everything that should be done in this Parliament in prejudice to the King and country, and in that protest all the Lords of Articles joined.

The Earl of Eglinton, the Earl of Arran again, and the bishop-elect of Ross, each protested that the Lords of Articles had not been duly elected, and that those should be Lords of the Articles whom they themselves had severally voted for. It was a strange shape of a national Parliament; and yet, in this assembly, so full of jarring elements, the Lords of Articles went on to elect for the Secret Council, "to steir, execute, and put furth the King's authority," four bishops for the spirituality, and four lords for the temporalty of the party opposed to the Queen.

In the next Parliament, held at Edinburgh in

July 1525, the young King being again present, we find appearing for the clergy twenty persons, of whom eight were bishops and ten abbots, with the dean of Glasgow and the secretary Mr. Patrick Hepburne; for the barons, twenty-four persons, of whom ten were earls, nine lords and five smaller barons; and for the burghs, eight commissioners. It is worth noting that the clerks who wrote down the sederunt have now got a formal style of separating the barons into three classes, first, the earls and great barons; secondly, the lords—meaning nobles of second class; and thirdly, the smaller barons, or commisssioners for them, who about this time, even in Scotland, are called "squires," but whom we do not hesitate to call *Lairds*, though they included men of such consequence as the Laird of Luss and the Thane of Cawdor. Hitherto, I think, there are no Officers of State sitting in Parliament on that title; but we have, amongst the commissioners of burghs, Mr. Adam Otterburne, a member, I think, for Edinburgh, who was then King's advocate, and Mr. Patrick Hepburne who was secretary. That Parliament contained about an average number for the time. The attendance of the lesser barons and of the burgh members was small, and we cannot but observe, that in an Assembly whose proceedings must have almost amounted to a riot, the Parliament did yet enact some careful and well-considered laws.

Notwithstanding the Act of James I. to which I have already referred, no representatives of the lesser barons were actually returned to Parliament; and Acts were passed for more than a century after, to relieve the small barons of parliamentary attendance, successively raising the limit below which they should not be obliged to give personal presence. The project of representation was renewed in 1567, when it was ordered that the barons of each shire should elect commissioners to represent them in Parliament, and that the barons be stented for their expenses.[1] In 1585 the principle of representation is further elaborated, when the Act[2] taking notice how necessary it is that the King and Estates should be well informed of the needs of all subjects,

---

[1] Item of law and reason the baronis of this realme aucht to haif voit in parliament as ane part of the nobilitie and for sauftie of nowmer at ilk parliament that ane precept of parliament be direct to the sheriff of the schire and his deputis chargeing thame to direct thair precept chargeing the baronis of his schire be oppin proclamatioun to compeir within the tolbuytht thairof And thair to cheise ane or twa of the maist qualifiit and wyis baronis within the schire to be commissaris for the haill schire, and that the sheref or his deputis tak foure or sex baronis, being present for the tyme and extent the baronis of the hale schire alsweill thame that beis absent as present to mak the saidis Commissaris expenses.—Acts of Parliament, 1567, c. 33, vol. iii. p. 40.

[2] *Ibid.* 1585, c. 74, vol. ii. p. 422.

specially the commons of the realm, appoints that all freeholders of the King under the degree of prelates and lords of Parliament, elect commissioners to Parliament annually for each shire, but that none have vote but such as have forty-shilling land in free tenandry held of the King, and have their usual dwelling within the shire. Lastly, in 1587, the King ratifies in plain Parliament the preceding Acts, ordains Commissioners to be elected at the first head court after Michaelmas yearly, and their names to be notified to the director of the Chancellary by the Commissioners of the preceding year. The Act also declares that the Commissioners authorized with sufficient commissions, which must be sealed and subscribed by at least six of the barons and freeholders of the shire, shall be equal in number to the Commissioners of burghs on the Articles, and have vote in Parliaments and General Councils in time coming.[1] From the period of this last Act at least, the representatives of the small barons or freeholders formed a considerable proportion of every Parliament, where they were classed and entered as a separate estate, though by the theory of the constitution as received by our old lawyers they formed a portion of the baronage.

The remainder of the parliamentary history of Scotland during its separate national existence is

[1] Acts of Parliament, 1587, c. 120, vol. iii. p. 509.

to be learned from the popular historians. The period of Queen Mary—which is the period also of the Reformation—has been written by our ablest writers, and from all points of view. The reign of James VI. may be said to have been written by himself. After his accession to the English throne, the King persuaded himself that he had reigned absolutely and despotically in Scotland. But that was not so. His real despotism began when he was able to use the wealth and power of the English throne as left to him by Queen Elizabeth and her able servants, in reducing the endless factions and conspiracies of the poorer country. From James's time the history of Scotland became necessarily involved with that of England, and English historians are thenceforward the authorities for Scotch events and changes. Upon the accession of Charles I. the general discontent, as well as the feeling of the power of Parliament, had spread from England, and during that reign the fulness of the sederunts contrasts remarkably with the latter part of James's reign.

The chief event deserving the name of a constitutional change took place in a time which is not regarded as a constitutional period. Cromwell was the first statesman who brought forward a well-considered scheme of the parliamentary representation of the three nations, and he also fixed the proportion between the county and burgh representation of Scotland. Under his direction the whole number of members who were to represent Scotland in the united Parliament were thirty; for the counties twenty, and for the burghs ten. The shires and burghs of Scotland were then for the first time grouped.

In Oliver's second Parliament of the three nations, which met 27th July 1654, four hundred members were summoned for England, thirty for Scotland, and thirty for Ireland. There were twenty members sent from Scotland to represent the shires, of which the smaller and less populous were grouped. Sutherland, Ross, and Cromarty returned one member; Forfar and Kincardine, one member; Fife and Kinross, one member; Linlithgow, Stirling, and Clackmannan, one member; Dumbarton, Argyle, and Bute, one member; Ayr and Renfrew, one member; Selkirk and Peebles, one member; Orkney, Shetland, and Caithness, one member; Elgin and Nairn, one member.

There were ten members sent to represent the burghs:—Edinburgh returned two members; the Inverness group of burghs, namely, Dornoch, Tain, Inverness, Dingwall, Nairn, Elgin, and Forres, one member; the Aberdeen burghs, namely, Banff, Cullen, and Aberdeen, one member; the Forfar burghs, namely, Forfar, Dundee, Arbroath, Montrose, and

Brechin, one member; the Stirling burghs, namely, Linlithgow, Queensferry, Perth, Culross, and Stirling, one member; the Fife burghs, namely, St. Andrews, Dysart, Kirkcaldy, Cupar, Anstruther-Easter, Pittenweem, Crail, Dunfermline, Kinghorn, Anstruther-Wester, Inverkeithing, Kilrenny, and Burntisland, one member; the Glasgow burghs, namely, Lanark, Glasgow, Rutherglen, Rothesay, Renfrew, Ayr, Irvine, and Dumbarton, one member; the Dumfries burghs, namely, Dumfries, Sanquhar, Lochmaben, Annan, Wigton, Kirkcudbright, Whithorn, and Galloway, one member; the Lauder burghs, namely, Peebles, Selkirk, Jedburgh, Lauder, North Berwick, Dunbar, and Haddington, one member.

The grouping of the burghs, the election of deputies for the shires and burghs who should take part in the measures for a Union and represent Scotland, form the subject of a few pages of an Appendix lately made to the Acts of Parliament, headed, "The Government of Scotland during the Commonwealth."[1] Of course, during the Commonwealth, there was but one House of Parliament, of which Peers were sometimes members. A large proportion of the members sent to represent Scotland, were either officers of the English army, or officials of Cromwell's Scotch Government.

[1] Vol. vi. Part ii.

The clergy, as one of the Estates in Parliament, are sometimes called *Prelati*, and at other times a list of their sederunt leaves the impression that there was some representation in their members; but all that is very uncertain. The bishops, and also the heads of the regular religious houses, were undoubtedly required to attend, and came within the term *prelates;* but so did all the clergy whose benefices were above a certain amount—perhaps forty pounds. Many other clergymen of inferior station and income appear in the lists of sederunts of Parliament, whose title I do not pretend to explain. The bishops disappeared from Parliament after the famous Glasgow assembly of 1638, and did not appear again till the Restoration; from which time till the Revolution the bishops alone filled the place of the first estate—the clergy. For some time after the Reformation, abbots and priors, nominally heads of regular houses, continue to sit amongst the clergy; but in a short time the name and title cease to describe the "Lords of erection," who, in feeling and interest, were in no way distinguished from the lay barons.

At first each of the royal burghs was required to send at least two representatives to Parliament, and, though the number actually attending was in general small, it was not till 1619 that they were relieved of a part of the burden. From that time, by an Act of the Convention of Burghs passed, it would seem, without the sanction of Parliament, one member only was to be returned for each burgh except Edinburgh, which continued to send two representatives.

After the Restoration, the forms of Parliament were fixed by an Act dated 13th May 1662, which is referred to as authoritative during that reign. It prescribes fines for absence, and also for coming late, and enacts that none be admitted but the "ordinar" members of Parliament, that is, the archbishops and bishops, noblemen, officers of State, commissioners from shires and burghs, the Clerk Register, and the deputes and servants employed by him to serve in the House. Admittance, however, without vote or voice, is allowed to the eldest sons of noblemen, to the senators of the College of Justice, to the Marischal, to the Lyon's ushers, to the justice deputes, to the King's agent, to one servant of the Lord Chancellor, two of the Constable, two of the Marischal, and to one of the Advocate.

The nobility and clergy occupied the "benches," the officers of State sat upon the steps of the throne, the commissioners of shires and burghs upon the "furmes" appointed for them, the eldest sons of noblemen upon the lower benches of the lower steps of the throne, also called benches. The Lords of Session sat at a table between the throne and the commissioners for burghs, none being allowed to sit at the clerk's table save the Clerk Register and those employed by him in the service of the House. Any others allowed to enter must sit at the far end of the seats of the commissioners from shires and burghs.

It was ordered that in all debates no member offer to interrupt another nor direct his "discourse" to any but the Lord Chancellor or President; that all reflections be forborne; that no man offer at one diet and in one business, to speak oftener than twice; finally, that no member of Parliament leave the House until the meeting be dissolved.[1]

The Parliament in theory sat all together—the Three Estates in one chamber—and no doubt there was at every meeting of Parliament a solemn and very gorgeous assemblage of all the members. In later days the members met in the King's palace at Holyrood; and the *riding of Parliament* from Holyrood to the Tolbooth was the great solemnity and show of the season. That was the occasion—I speak of those latter times from James vi. downwards—of disputes and protests concerning precedency and right of place and vote in Parliament, a subject occupying more than any other the attention of our nobility and their lawyers for a century or two. But whatever were the theory, it is certain that from

[1] Acts of Parliament, 1662, vol. vii. 371.

the time of David II. till the great Rebellion in England had roused some parliamentary feeling in Scotland, our Parliament really cannot be said to have sat at all. It assembled only to adjourn, and met again finally only to receive and adopt the reports of its committees. During all these centuries —from the fourteenth to the beginning of the seventeenth century—I am not aware that an Article—as we should say now a *Bill*—was brought in and discussed, opposed, supported, voted upon, in Parliament—I mean in open and plain Parliament. It seems to me that the accident of the Three Estates meeting in one chamber, as the Three Estates had met in England of old, was but a small part of the cause which destroyed freedom of discussion and prevented the growth of what may be called parliamentary feeling in Scotland for centuries. The time was not parliamentary. No one thought of making a party in Parliament. No one looked *there* for redress of grievances. During all that time—for three centuries—when a party were displeased with the conduct of the existing Government, they did not attack its favourite measure or minister in Parliament, nor try to pass a vote of want of confidence in the Government. The leaders of the Opposition in Scotland took another way of righting themselves—they laid a trap for the young King, and carried him off to Stirling or St. Andrews, as the case might be, surrounded him with their armed followers, Douglases or Ruthvens, Homes or Hamiltons, and then summoned a Parliament of their own friends, which they took care to declare a *free Parliament*. In that Parliament they proceeded to carry on the Government, and always in the first place to pass a long series of forfeitures of the estates of the opposite party.[1]

I do not remember anything at all peculiar in the peerage tenures of Scotland, except the creation of peerages for life. These existed from an early period with us. Walter Steward, Earl of Athole, second son of Robert II., had a grant of the earldom palatine of Stratherne *for life*.[2] David Lindsay, Earl of Crawford, who had lost by a parliamentary forfeiture the hereditary dukedom of Montrose, was restored to the King's favour, and had a grant of the same dukedom *pro toto tempore vitæ suæ*.[3] James III.'s second son, James Duke of Ross, Chancellor of Scotland and Archbishop of St. Andrews, resigned the estates he had received of the royal patrimony, reserving only the messuages which gave him his title of honour *ad vitam*.[4] Remember he was in orders. William Lord Douglas, married to Anne Duchess of

---

[1] The Raid of Ruthven and others are well known. The Gowry attack on King James VI. at Perth, in 1600, seems to have been an unsuccessful raid of the same character.

[2] Earldom of Stratherne, 23d July 1427.

[3] Dukedom of Montrose, 1489.

[4] Dukedom of Ross, 1503.

Hamilton, was created Duke of Hamilton *for life*.[1] Sir Walter Scott of Haychester, on his marriage with Mary Countess of Buccleuch, was created Earl of Tarras *for his life only*.[2] Francis Abercromby, husband of Anne Baroness Sempill, was created Lord Glassford *for his life only*.[3]

While these examples show the competency and the convenience of life peerages, they mark also that they were not the rule but the exception. No soldier nor lawyer, no public officer for service to the State, was rewarded with a life peerage, which was only bestowed to suit the private arrangements of great families already noble.

In the Scotch Parliament the great Officers of State sat in right of their offices. Their number had given rise to such discontent that in 1617 it was limited to eight. This was certainly a very convenient practice, and might well be used as an example in our British Parliament, where every impediment seems to be thrown in the way of ministers of the Crown holding seats—to the great interruption of public business.

The Committee of the Articles was at first, and might have continued, a convenient machinery for preparing business; but its purpose was perverted so as to control the deliberations of Parliament, and

---

[1] Dukedom of Hamilton, 12th October 1660.
[2] Earl Tarras, 4th Sept. 1660.
[3] Lord Glassford, 25th July 1685.

then followed the most shameless abuse and open fraud in the elections of the Lords of the Articles. So careless were our forefathers of their parliamentary privileges, that the Committee of Articles appointed in 1535 were authorized to make Acts with the whole power of Parliament, and they used that power by even imposing a tax. In later and even worse times the election of the Lords of Articles became the great job and juggle of the session. It went through many phases and culminated at last under Charles I.,[1] when it was fixed that the bishops should choose eight lay peers, these lay peers elect eight bishops, and these sixteen elected eight commissioners of shires and eight of burghs. That brought the Parliament to its last degradation—meeting only on two days of the session, the first and the last—the first to choose the Lords of the Articles, and the last to give their sanction to what they proposed. At the beginning of the Civil War, the Lords of the Articles were abolished; and although the committee was revived in the same form after the Restoration, its power and that of Parliament itself was soon suppressed, when an Act was passed "That whatever the King and Council should order respecting all ecclesiastical matters, meetings, and persons, should have the force of law." The remainder of the reign of Charles II.

[1] A.D. 1633.

and of that of James VII. knew no government but the sword. I have already told you that the Three Estates sat in one chamber—the King often present, overawing in part all the Estates—and that there was no Speaker to guard the liberties of the Commons, who were of small account in that assembly.

Such were some of the defects or peculiarities of the Parliament of Scotland in its shape and form of proceeding, but there were defects in the constitution of the country of still greater influence. The King's prerogative of revoking all grants made during his minority was a tremendous engine for unsettling the tenure and right of property in Scotland. The terror of Revocation indeed seems to have done much to hasten the fate of Queen Mary and that of Charles I. Mixed up with the prerogative of Revocation was the Statute of Annexation, which declared all grants of Crown lands of a certain class to be incurably null and void. Not the least considerable of the defects of the constitution of Scotland, was the excessive number of regalities and private jurisdictions among us. These heritable jurisdictions, perhaps more fatal to political liberty than to justice between man and man, destroyed the independence of the Commons. They were not confined to offices connected with land; the Justice-General, the Lord

High Constable, hereditary sheriffs of counties, each jealously defended his own jurisdiction against all the others and against the Crown. The public prosecutor, the State tax-gatherer, could not set his foot within a well-chartered jurisdiction of regality. All Scotsmen know that the Act of Union did not deal with those heritable jurisdictions. They continued to distress the country for forty years, and were at last removed by the Act 20 George II. c. 43, after the suppression of the rising in 1745. It is well known that the union of the two kingdoms, at first so unpopular, seemed for half a century to have failed in the desired effect of promoting the prosperity of Scotland. Men who have studied the modern history of our country sometimes point to the abolition of heritable jurisdictions as the event which crowned the Union, and put an end to the principles which had so nearly triumphed in '45.

Before the Reformation, the Church, by excommunications, of her own authority, might legally strip a subject of all his civil rights in Scotland—a power which was reserved in England to the plainly unconstitutional Courts of Star-Chamber and High Commission.

In everything the freedom of the subject was less protected with us than in England. We had no *habeas corpus* nor anything equivalent to it. The practice of judicial torture continued with us after it had virtually ceased in England, but only for a short time; and the power of putting the dead to trial for treason, borrowed from the law of Rome, was not abolished till after the Union.

Of the treason law of England, imported by the Act of Union, our lawyers used to speak with admiration, perhaps more than it deserved. No doubt the definition of what shall be deemed treason was a great step[1]—a great improvement upon our vague law, which permitted *lesing making*, and everything that a King's Advocate chose to call the *crimen læsæ Majestatis*, to amount to that crime. On the other hand, we had not, till the Union, invented the refined cruelty of punishing the posterity of traitors—what the English call the "corruption of blood." These were some of the defects in Parliament and in our national institutions, and we must acknowledge that there was not constitutional feeling enough in Scotland to remedy or counteract them till they were all swept away by the fortunate Union with the freer nation.

You will find a few styles for summoning a Parliament, of proxies in Parliament, and other parliamentary writs, prefixed to the first volume of the Acts of the Parliaments of Scotland. The style of mandate to the sheriffs under one of the early Jameses runs—" We command you to summon all bishops, abbots, priors, earls, barons, and other free

[1] 25 Ed. III. 1350.

tenants of your sheriffdom, and from each burgh three or four of the most sufficient burgesses to compear before us in our said Parliament with the other prelates, nobles, and commissioners of burghs, to treat, agree, and determine, concerning the welfare of our kingdom and of the republic." Since those styles were printed, I found in the Burgh Charter-Chest of Stirling a letter of James VI., folded and addressed simply like a common letter of correspondence, and dated at Holyrood, 1st April 1589, desiring the magistrates to send their commissioners "instructit with their best advice anent the premisses," namely, his marriage, the quieting of the State, etc. The Parliament is summoned for the 24th of April, or twenty-three days after the date of the letter.

As in England, from an early time — I cannot say how early — the Commissioners for the shires and burghs were paid for their attendance. The amount was long uncertain and variable; but by Act 1661, c. 35, it was fixed at five pound Scots for each day of attendance and of journey to and fro. For the Commissioners of the shires the expenses were far greater than the allowance covered. The clothes, long ago, of a gentleman going to Court and Parliament cost many of them a year's rent; and the foot-mantle and horse trappings for "riding the Parliament"— that is, for the display from Holyrood to the Tolbooth—were as gorgeous as a love of personal finery and a noble emulation could suggest.[1]

---

[1] I am indebted to my friend Captain E. Dunbar for the following accounts of Parliamentary expenses, which he found, I think, in the Hempriggs Charter-chest:—

The Laird of McIntosh his depursements for the shyr of Invernes at the Parliament in anno 1681.

Item, for 52 sitting dayes in Parliament and 16 days comeing and going, at 5 lb. Scotts per day, is . .	£340	0	0
Item, mor for ane consultation with the Lord Advocate,	36	5	0
Item, mor to Mr. David Thores and his servants, .	21	15	0
Item, mor given in with the commission to the Clerk-Register, . .	13	6	8
Item, mor for the testificat of the dyettis of the Parliament sitting, .	14	10	0
Item, mor to Mr. Thomas Gordon for keeping the counsell in mynd from dissjoyning of the shyr of Invernes with that of Ross in the excyse, . . .	8	14	0

Item, his expenses for his foot-mantle and furnitur thereof and other expens for the shyr of Inverness at the Parliament in anno 1685.

Item, for 10 ells fyn black velvat at 16 lb. ell, is .	£160	0	0
Item, for 5½ ells broad black kyligo,	6	15	0
Item, for silk and working the knapes and frenzies, . . .	26	0	0
Item, to David Denoon for makeing the foot-mantle and mounteing the same, . .	24	0	0
Item, for his part given in to the Clerk Register, with the Commission, . . .	20	0	0
Item, for 55 sitting dayes in Parliament, and 16 dayes coming and goeing at £5 scotts per day, . .	365	0	0
Item, for the testificat of the dyetts of the Parliament sitting, . .	13	6	8

It is to be remembered that the Laird of McIn-

I have sought in old charter-chests for such payments of parliamentary expenses; and among them all—and they are not of infrequent occurrence—I have found none of earlier date than 1587. Now, I cannot help connecting the practice which then began—of making payments to Commissioners for attending Parliament—with the custom which began about that time, of representatives of the smaller barons—the freeholders—taking their place in Parliament. The poor laird who had found his desire to serve his country in Parliament not strong enough to prevail against the burden of a journey to Edinburgh, with some expenses in the capital, found he could go as the paid representative of his neighbour lairds without such serious inconvenience; and hence the appearance of Commissioners for the barons, along with the Commissioners of burghs.[1]

In the language of its Acts, the Parliament of Scotland has kept apart from England since an early period. At first the statutes of both countries were in Latin, the only clerkly language. The first statute of the Parliament of England in French

tosh, when the Parliament first sat, after calling the rolls of Parliament, did protest for the shyre's precedency, and depursed ane gau- nie as other shyres did, being . . 13 6 8

———

The soume of all is £1051 19 0

L. McIntoshe,
of Torcastell.

[1] Act. Parl. vol. iv. 1593, p. 6.

is the *Statutum de Scaccario*, 51 Henry III. 1266—two hundred years after the Normans ruled in England; and the Statutes continue French till the time of Richard III., in 1483. In Scotland we never had French used in Acts of Parliament. They were framed in Latin till the end of the fourteenth century. The first time when the parliamentary proceedings are in Scots is in the Council General of Robert III. 1398; and of that Parliament fortunately we have an original record, well preserved—a fine specimen of our early written language.

I do not suppose that any cruelty or injustice was ever premeditated by the legislature or the Government—that there was any intention to favour the rich at the expense of the poor, but there are things in the history of our law that I cannot help censuring—the more because I believe the evil was for the most part attributable to the straining of the law by lawyers. The books tell us what impediments the humane law in favour of the " puir pepil that labours the grunde " had to encounter from the practising lawyers of the day.[1] I think as little humanity has been shown in the divisions of commons. Looking over our country, the land held in common was of vast extent. In truth the arable—the cultivated land of Scotland, the land early appro-

[1] Kames and Walter Ross.

priated and held by charter, is a narrow strip on the river bank or beside the sea. The inland, the upland, the moor, the mountain, were really not occupied at all for agricultural purposes, or served only to keep the poor and their cattle from starving. They were not thought of when charters were made and lands feudalized. Now, as cultivation increased, the tendency in the agricultural mind was to occupy these wide commons, and our lawyers lent themselves to appropriate the poor man's grazing ground to the neighbouring baron. They pointed to his charter with its clause of parts and pertinents, with its general clause of mosses and moors—clauses taken from the style book, not with any reference to the territory conveyed in that charter; and although the charter was hundreds of years old, and the lord had never possessed any of the common, when it came to be divided, the lord got the whole that was allocated to the estate, and the poor cottar none. The poor had no lawyers! Something of the same kind, I think, is taking place now by lawyers extending the meaning of words used in charters. I am afraid the grant *cum piscariis* has been pushed lately beyond its original meaning; and the question still so fresh, of the right to sea-shore has been determined somewhat harshly against the poor fisher seeking for bait, while the interest of the Crown has been made a pretext to annoy both the proprietor of the soil and the poor commons, who used to be considered the proper enjoyers of the Crown property.

These are perhaps the necessary, or at least the natural consequences of increasing wealth and population, whilst the soil does not increase; and I must go back for my great grievance to the time when wide territories that had long been held without charter first were sought to be held by parchment tenure. That was not a mere change in law and land tenures—it was part of a great revolution in society. Mr. Maine lays it down, and truly, that the greatest revolution in the history of any people is when the patriarchal or tribe association is changed into the connexion arising from land—the territorial, if you will—the patriotic bond, instead of the patriarchal. The misfortune was, that in Scotland all such changes told against the poor. A clan in the Highlands before the fifteenth century lived in patriarchal fashion. The clansmen looked to the chief as their leader and father, but what we should call the common people of the clan held their crofts and pastures from father to son, from generation to generation, by a right as indefeasible as the chief's. No doubt the clansmen followed their chief to battle; no doubt they did service in peace —ploughing and reaping the lands around his castle as well as their own; but it was a free service, and *some* land they had of their own. The power of the chief, from its very nature, depended on the good will of the whole tribe—for who was to enforce a tyrannical order? But a time came when lawyers discovered that the lands of the tribe could not be held or vindicated, or perhaps could not have money raised upon them without writ, and then came the feudal investiture. The Crown-charter was taken, of course, to the chief who got the whole land of the tribe in barony. And in the charters of the lands of a great clan the Crown-charter bestowed upon the chief all the rights of jurisdiction, civil and criminal, with pit and gallows, instead of his old patriarchal authority. It was an immense advantage, speaking merely commercially, to the lord. He could now raise money upon the security of his seisin, could provide for his family, could, if need be, sell the lands which he had thus acquired in property. But it was not so advantageous for the poor clansmen, who had never thought of writings to bind their patriarchal head, and who now found themselves with no title of property, often without any written leases or rentals. They became altogether dependent on the will of the laird, and fell a long way below the position which they had held before the lands were feudalized. That, I think, was the most flagrant injustice inflicted by lawyers carrying out to the letter the doctrines of feudalism, which they assumed were the same with the old patriarchal occupation.

Other and smaller rights of the people have been encroached upon by lawyers stretching a written title beyond its meaning. Amongst these perhaps some of us may hold the law as now settled in the matter of trout-fishing. Craig, a great feudalist, allows an exclusive right of the feudal proprietor in all fishing, even trout-fishing, where practised *lucri causa*, but distinguishes the trout-fishing which is pursued only for recreation; this distinction, however, has been lost sight of in modern times, and the most innocent and cheapest of sports wrested from the poor. One popular question was fortunate enough to come into Court only after the modern restoration of jury trials, and after the minds of our educated classes had come to appreciate the poor man, and I think there is now no danger of the people being deprived of their old rights of *road* and *way*. Let us hope that these rights may be vindicated with moderation and without encroaching on the rights of property. In England the paths to villages and churches, with styles through the hedges, contrast with the stone walls and the threatening placards that confine the wanderer through Scotland to the dusty high-road.

Who were the leading men who did the real business of Parliament in that mixed assemblage of clergy and laity, barons and burgesses, we cannot even guess. Lord Hailes, in one of his reports, tells us that the Acts of the Parliament 1621 were drawn by the President, Lord Haddington, but it can hardly have been customary for an Officer of State in so laborious a situation to frame and digest the laws enacted in Parliament. We have not the pleasant memoranda and notes of proceedings in Parliament till a late date, but the Acts to which I have referred show that there must have been in that assemblage, strangely constituted as it was, men of great wisdom and goodness, who must have led the opinion of Parliament, and probably framed those brief, terse statutes which shame the legislation of a later wordy age.

Last of all, let me mention that great peaceful, silent revolution which has never found its way into the pages of our historians. The servile labour of the agricultural class, which had prevailed all over Europe, died out first in Scotland! The last claim of *neyfship* or serfdom proved in a Scotch Court was in 1364. In that or the following century the *institution* must have died out; and when *our* case of the negro claiming freedom came to be judged, the fifteen judges of Scotland had forgotten that our law ever admitted of slavery.[1]

Not so in the English case where the same

[1] Knight's Case, Jan. 15, 1778.

point was tried. The justices of the King's Bench —Sir John Holt among them—held that "one may be a villeyn in England." Justice Powell said, "The villein is an inheritance, but the law says nothing of a negro."[1] And all English lawyers who still took Sir Edward Coke's law for law and history, not to say gospel, and who denied that his law could ever become obsolete, must have approved that opinion. But, spite of Sir Edward Coke and the Court of King's Bench, neyfship *had* died out in England. I think it is now admitted that there were no neyfs in England after Queen Elizabeth's reign. Serfs and serfdom continued in France down to the great French Revolution, and even later in Germany.[2]

[1] Smith *v.* Browne, 2 Salk 666.

[2] De Tocqueville, *L'Ancien Régime et la Révolution.*

LECTURE IV.

THE OLD CHURCH.

In order to lay before you a useful outline of the Church in Scotland as it was before the Reformation, my present lecture will be extremely elementary, and to those of you who have studied the subject with good help will appear superficial; but to others, and perhaps the larger number, it may serve to open a new path and furnish such knowledge of our old Church establishment as you will not find in print.

The greatest mistake in church history, and yet with us the most common, is to confound the regular and secular clergy—the parson with the monk—the cathedral with the monastery. The regular clergy—regular means living *secundum regulam*, that is, under the rule of some religious order and in a monastery or house of religion where that rule was enforced—are to be divided into monks and friars. The monks were of far greater importance than the friars. Your time will not permit me, nor is it necessary, to enumerate the monasteries of Scotland, but I must warn you against the vulgar error of throwing all houses of monks into one class.

Monks and monasteries had existed in the Christian Church from remote antiquity. St. Benedict founded his great order in the sixth century at Monte Cassino, in the kingdom of Naples, which branched off into Cluniac — Tyronensian — Cistercian — Valliscaulium. The Culdees were monks of Irish origin, some houses of their order remaining in Ireland till the Reformation. They were professed followers of St. Columba, but it is a mistake to call all Columbites Culdees. The Culdees had become lax in their observance of rule and had married and appropriated the possession of the monasteries to their own families. In some cases the superior threw off all Church ties, and, having taken his place in the country as a temporal baron, handed down the territory of his monastery to his family as hereditary property.[1]

Sir James Dalrymple and other zealous Presbyterians of last century, finding that the Culdees had broken the rule and their vow, were willing to

---

[1] The Abernethies handed down to their family the property and even the name of their secularized monastery; in like manner did the M'Nabs and some families of Abbe connected with the Culdees of Brechin.

receive them as an anti-monastic body. They found or imagined that they found something of primitive apostolic manners in the lapsarian Culdees, and actually adopted them as Presbyterian brethren. But the Culdees would not have accepted such fellowship. They were undoubtedly Prelatists and Episcopalians as well as Romanists, however erring. They were the council and chapter of election of the Bishop of St. Andrews originally, that is, before the summary ejection of King David; and they continued to be the chapter of election of the bishops of Brechin for a century afterwards—indeed to a time within the period of record. Monasteries of their order had also existed at Dunkeld, Scone, St. Serf's Isle in Lochleven, and Monymusk in Mar.

The Canons Regular of the rule of St. Augustine (A.D. 1050) differed from monks in nothing but name. They were favourites of David I., and in most places were chosen to take the place of Culdees as chapters of cathedrals. There were great houses of the Canons Regular of St. Augustine at St. Andrews, Holyrood, Scone, Cambuskenneth, Jedburgh. The head of each of these great houses was an abbot, except at St. Andrews where the head of the house had the style of prior. St. Andrews was founded by Alexander I. This priory of canons, forming the Chapter of the Bishopric of St. Andrews, soon took its place as the first in rank of the religious houses of Scotland; and its prior, with the ring and mitre of a bishop, had rank and place in Parliament above the abbots and all other prelates of the regular Church. They had property, not only throughout their own diocese, which extended almost from the English border to Aberdeen, but also in Mar and beyond the Grampians. The Register of this house, first of Culdees, then of Augustinian canons, is invaluable to the early historian of our country, and especially to the student of Church history. The Abbey of Scone was long connected with the coronation of our kings, and though historically venerable, had no great possessions. The *fatal chair*, which, alas! the learning of Mr. Skene has reduced to a common red sandstone of the district, gives a mysterious importance to this place in the mythical period of Scotch history.

The Benedictine monks of the original unreformed rule of St. Bernard had a noble monastery at Dunfermline, which, from several circumstances, was one of the most interesting of our old abbeys. Its collected charters help largely to show us the origin and pedigree of our ancient monarchs. This Benedictine house was founded by the saintly Margaret, and it long continued to be a royal house—many of the princes of the Royal family of Scotland choosing it as their burial-place. Some of the English chroniclers speak of the buildings of the abbey as magnificent and spacious enough to receive the Courts and followers of two kings. The monks possessed great territories round the abbey and town of Dunfermline; also a large strip of the shore of Fife opposite to Lothian, including Kinghorn, Kirkcaldy, Burntisland; and on this side of the Firth, Musselburgh and Inveresk. I observe that perhaps the earliest disputes about coal-levels were between the monks of Dunfermline, who had coal upon their lands of Inveresk, and the monks of Newbattle, who had coal on the higher level round their abbey and Dalkeith. Pinkie—I daresay you know the fine old house—was the dwelling of the abbots when they chose to live in Lothian and near the Court.

The Benedictines of Tyrone had the two great and wealthy monasteries of Kelso and Arbroath.

Kelso, the first of the sainted David's monasteries, was, I think, the richest abbey in Scotland. Its founder first placed it at Selkirk—which, from its name, must have been an early religious house —but the French monks, of the order of St. Benedict, were dissatisfied with the position so high on the banks of the Ettrick; and upon David's accession he removed it from Selkirk, "a place unsuitable for an abbey," and established it at the "church of the Blessed Virgin, on the banks of Tweed, beside Roxburgh, in the place called Calkou." Their territories of Molle, Sprouston, Home, Lamden, Greenlaw, Keith, Mackerstoun, Maccuswell and Gordon, were chiefly on the Tweed and Teviot and in the Merse. We are indebted to the monks of Kelso for our earliest accurate knowledge regarding the occupation of land, its tenancy and cultivation. A fine rental of this abbey is preserved so early as 1290. A cell of Kelso was Lesmahago—the church of St. Machutus—famous for its sanctuary.

There is still preserved at Floors a very venerable specimen of the accomplishments of the monks of Kelso—the great charter of Malcolm IV., granted to the abbey in 1159, and which has been photographed by Sir Henry James for the Scotch collection of National MSS. The Abbey of Kelso was perhaps second in importance to the Priory of St. Andrews; and the abbot of Kelso takes place in Parliament and Council next to the prior of St. Andrews.

Arbroath Abbey, the great religious house of Angus, and the greatest north of the Tay, if not of the Forth, had lands through the whole county of Angus, and churches through all the north. In a single reign, that of its founder, William the Lion, there were bestowed upon Arbroath, besides a goodly roll of lands and baronies, forests and fishings, thirty-four parish churches. It was to this abbey that the custody of the *Brecbennach*, the sacred banner of St. Columba, was intrusted.

The Cluniac Benedictines had the Abbey of Paisley, a foundation of the Stuarts before they bore the name, when that great Norman family were but lately settled in Scotland, whither they brought with them a colony of monks, who served to connect them with their original seats in England and Wales. The abbey had lands round Paisley, in Lochwinnoch, Kilpatrick, Monktown, Dalmollan, and Inverwick on the east coast. The chartulary of Paisley is interesting as containing the earliest record extant of a form of ecclesiastical procedure of which I must speak hereafter; and secondly, as supplying the materials which enabled George Chalmers to prove the descent of the Royal Stewarts from the Norman Fitzalans, instead of from Hector Boece's imaginary pedigree of Banquo's thanes of Lochaber. The Cistercians, the greatest and perhaps the most useful branch of the Benedictine stock, had many houses among us. I will only name Melrose, Newbattle, Coupar-Angus.

The historical Melrose, like others of our monasteries, was founded upon an ancient prehistoric religious house. The territory of the abbey was much scattered. The monks had lands upon their own river and round their monastery, and at Berwick, Peebles, Roxburgh, besides great districts in Teviotdale. They had, too, immense grants of pastures in Eskdale, Kyle and Carrick, Haddington and the

Lammermoors, and were the growers of the finest wool shipped from Scotland. In their chartulary we find everywhere strict rules for the protection of agriculture, and evidence of the good husbandry of the abbey. The monks had wheaten bread on holidays. We are indebted to this religious house for our finest collection of original writs and seals —the writs comprising more than 100 royal charters from David I. to Robert Bruce, and the seals collecting the Church and baronial heraldry of Scotland from the introduction of heraldic bearings. You will also find in the chartulary much information regarding our ancient laws and forms of legal procedure; and not the least interesting document in the collection is the deathbed letter of Robert Bruce, bequeathing to his son the care and protection of that favoured house, where he destined his own heart to be buried.

Newbattle Abbey was founded by the great benefactor of Scotch churches, David I., in 1140. Like Kelso, it was an extensive sheep-owner, and though not one of the most richly endowed monasteries in Scotland, it possessed great estates in Edinburgh, Haddington, Linlithgow, Peebles, and Stirling. The monks of Newbattle were probably the first workers of coal in Scotland; digging the coal from rude surface pits before mining was used. The Cistercians enjoyed a general exemption from payment of national taxes—a privilege confirmed by many Popes. I do not know how it was in other countries, but in Scotland I find the rich order ever asserting their right to be exempted from paying taxes; still, however, paying under the most careful protests that their doing so should be no precedent for future imposition.

The Knights Templars, a military monastic order taking its name from the Temple of Jerusalem which they were bound to defend as well as succour pilgrims, spread over all Europe after the loss of the Holy City, and acquired many settlements in Scotland. The suppression of the Templars took place in 1312, when their houses and property passed, for the most part, to the Knights of St. John of Jerusalem, who held a great number of houses with small forts and small estates scattered everywhere. Their chief house or preceptory was at Torphichen, the Preceptor of which was generally styled Lord of St. John of Jerusalem. The family of Sandilands of Calder, at the Reformation, obtained a charter erecting the lands of the Order in Scotland into a temporal lordship in their favour, with the title of Lord Torphichen.

All these orders which I have mentioned, monks, Austin canons, military monks—I mean the Templars and Knights of St. John—and some others of less importance, were entitled to acquire property, not only in the houses and establishments for their own residence, but in lands and heritages of every kind. And undoubtedly they used their right; for a very large proportion of the soil of Scotland—it must be remembered too, the richest and best managed—belonged to them at the era of the Reformation.

The heads of the numerous monasteries sat in Parliament as prelates, many of them wearing the mitre and insignia of bishops, and taking rank next to the earls as members of the National Assembly.

I have not time to describe the different officers of the monastery, but I must warn you that their names do not always express the duties of the office. Next to the abbot came the prior and sub-prior, whose rank is expressed in their names. The cellarer had other duties besides those of the cellar, being often the accountant of the house as well as its cashier. The porter had a higher duty than his name implies. He was the distributor of the alms of the convent; for the poor were supplied and alms distributed *ad portam monasterii*.

The other great division of the Regulars—the clergy living, as I have said, under a definite rule—were the Friars, who came among us at a later period. They were in truth a much later brood of the great Church militant of Rome, and reached Scotland in the good time of our Alexanders, in the thirteenth century. The friars professed poverty, practised mendicancy, and could not by law acquire or hold land or heritage, except their church and place of dwelling—a rule, however, which was extended to include spacious and often tasteful gardens. They were active beggars, and some of them were renowned as popular preachers a little before the Reformation. Contrary to the custom of monks, their settlements were always in towns, among the busy haunts of men. They had no vows of seclusion or solitude.

I will now mention the names of the chief orders of these brethren. The Dominicans, instituted at Toulouse in 1215 by St. Dominic—honoured by having the power of the inquisition intrusted to their hands—were known generally as *fratres prædicatores*—friars preachers (preaching being part of their rule), or black friars from their dress. Their house at Edinburgh was very spacious, and frequently used for great national assemblies of the Church. I think their house and gardens at Glasgow were used for the foundation of the University.

The Franciscans, named from their founder St. Francis of Assisi, who instituted the order in the Papal States in 1210, were known as Minorites or friars minor, or grey friars from their habit. In old writs their superiors named are often described as *custodes*—wardens.

The Carmelites, named from Mount Carmel where they were first established by Berthold Count of Limoges in 1165, were known as white friars from their dress.

There were few nunneries in Scotland, and none of great extent or consequence. They were classed according to their Rule like the monks. Those whose transactions I have most frequently seen recorded are the Cistercian nuns of Coldstream, Haddington, and North Berwick—the last of which came to be a sort of appanage of the family of Home—and Elcho in the Carse of Gowrie. We have honourable cause for remembering the Augustinian nuns of the Sciennes, near Edinburgh, which was excepted from the general denunciation by our great satirist at the Reformation. In his satire of the Papingo, Lindsay makes "Chastity" flee to the nunnery of the Sciennes:—

> "There has she fund ane convent yet unthrall
> To Dame Sensuale, nor with riches abusit,
> So quietlye those ladyis bene inclusit."

A little house at Aberdour, across our firth, belonged to the nuns of St. Clare, a branch of Franciscans, of whom I have seen some charters; and there are also some records preserved of the Cistercian nunnery of Manuel on the Avon.

Hospitals, often very slenderly endowed, were very numerous. At the gates of towns, at the river-side where a boat was placed—beside the ferry, on the mountain pass—were hospitals for the reception of the poor and pilgrims, for the safety of travellers, for the sick, especially for those afflicted with the scourge of leprosy. They are called *hospitale*—spital—*domus Dei*—*maison Dieu*—Lazar-house—*domus leprosorum*. The foundation consisted generally of a maintenance for two or three brethren, who devoted themselves to the service of the sick and poor.

The government of the old Church was strictly episcopal. Each diocese was subjected in spiritual matters to its own bishop by a law at least as definite as that which gave authority to the civil magistrate in his own province. Of the higher organization of Church councils, provincial councils, general or national councils, I shall not say anything here, as the late Joseph Robertson has filled that blank in the history of Scotland with his *Statuta Ecclesiæ Scoticanæ*.

In Catholic times—I mean for about four centuries before the Reformation—there were thirteen bishops and bishoprics in Scotland.

I. The Bishop of St. Andrews, once known as *Episcopus Scotorum*, and for a long time considered the first in rank, was made Archbishop of St. Andrews by Papal authority in 1474. The Chapter of St. Andrews consisted of regulars, at first

Culdees, and later, canons of St. Augustine. The diocese was divided by the Firth of Forth into the archdeaconries of St. Andrews Proper and Lothian—the former comprehending the rural deaneries of Fife, Fothrif, Gowrie, Angus, Mearns; and Lothian, consisting of the rural deaneries of Lothian or Haddington, Linlithgow, and the Merse. The suffragans of St. Andrews were eight, which I will mention in the order of their supposed antiquity:—

1. Dunkeld was a bishopric of very early foundation, and held in reverence for possessing the bones of St. Columba. It possessed property and jurisdiction from the Firth of Forth across the Island—including Iona. By the original foundation the chapter consisted of Culdees, but latterly of secular or parochial clergy.[1] It was divided into the rural deaneries of Atholl and Drumalbane; Angus; Fife, Fothrif and Stratherne; South of the Forth. This bishopric and its possessions followed Columba from Icolmkill to Inchcolm—*Insula Sancti Columbæ.*

2. The bishopric of Aberdeen, founded in the twelfth century at the mouth of the Don, now called Old Aberdeen, consisted at first of three rural deaneries: Mar, Buchan, Garviauch; latterly five: Aberdeen, Mar, Garviauch, Buchan, Boyne.

3. The bishopric of Moray, founded before the

[1] Abbot Milne, first President of the Court of Session, wrote its history.

time of David I., extended from sea to sea. At first the diocese had no defined bishop's seat, but after being successively changed to Birny, Kineddor and Spynie, it was at last permanently fixed in the church of the Holy Trinity beside Elgin in 1224. The diocese was divided into four rural deaneries: Elgin, Inverness, Strathspey, Strathbogy.

4. Brechin, an abbey of Culdees originally, was erected into a little bishopric by David I. in the middle of the twelfth century.

5. The bishopric of Dunblane or Stratherne had at one time a chapter of Regulars. It was the only bishopric in Scotland founded by a subject, of which the Earls of Stratherne long continued patrons.

6. The bishopric of Ross, or as it is sometimes called, Rosemarknie from its see, was founded or restored by David I. early in the twelfth century.

7. The bishopric of Caithness, which included the whole northern peninsula, anciently the earldom of Caithness, now Sutherland and Caithness, had its see at Dornoch. The date of its foundation is not known, but it existed in the beginning of the twelfth century.

8. The bishopric of the Orkney Islands, including Zetland, was originally a Norwegian diocese, and continued subject to the Archbishops of Drontheim till the definite transference of the sovereignty of those isles was made to Scotland under James III.

in 1468, when the ecclesiastical jurisdiction followed. The cathedral, as everybody knows, was the Church of St. Magnus at Kirkwall.

Next turn to the province of Glasgow:

II. The Church of Kentigern of mythical antiquity at Glasgow, and certainly a very ancient bishopric, became the see of an archbishop by papal grant in the year 1491, seventeen years later than St. Andrews.

Glasgow was divided into two archdeaconries, Glasgow proper and Teviotdale; the former comprehending the rural deaneries of Rutherglen, Lennox, Lanark, Kyle and Cuninghame, Carrick. Teviotdale included the deaneries of Teviotdale, Peebles, Nithsdale, Anandale. The suffragans of the western Archbishopric were three :—

1. The bishopric of Galloway, the very ancient foundation of the Scotch apostle St. Ninian, had a chapter of Regulars, and was divided into three deaneries, the names of which are now almost forgotten: Desnes, Farnes, Rinnes. The last is still a popularly known district.

2. Argyle, the bishops of which were called also the bishops of Lismore, from their see in that island, was cut out of the ancient diocese of Dunkeld in the end of the twelfth century; the Bishop of Dunkeld reserving to himself his episcopal connexion with the island of Iona

alone. It contained four deaneries: Cantyre, Glassary, Lorne, Morven.

3. The bishopric of the Isles has gone through many changes; of old the *episcopus insularum* was Bishop of Man and all the Western Isles, including Bute and Arran, and I think Cantyre, which was popularly reputed and called an island. This bishopric was a suffragan of the see of Drontheim in Norway. More lately the Southern Isles (Sudrey) were combined with Man, giving rise to the modern title of "Sodor and Man"—still the name of an English bishopric—but last of all the Hebrides or Western Islands, including Bute and Arran, formed a diocese by themselves, the bishop of which was a suffragan of Glasgow. In this last stage, the see was fixed at the church of Iona, which had long passed away from the Columbites, and was revived as a house of Cluniac monks about the time of William the Lion.[1] All the remaining buildings of Iona are subsequent to the Cluniac establishment there.

The right of appointing bishops lay of old in the chapter or council of the bishop. The royal wish must always have influenced, but only of late years when the rank and wealth of bishoprics had much

[1] The preceding division of bishoprics into deaneries is taken from a chapter of old geography in "Scotland in the Middle Ages," being, I believe, the only printed work where such a division is to be found.

increased, was it expressed in the peremptory form still known in England as *congé d'élire*—granting permission to elect a person designated by the sovereign. The King had a more formidable rival in the appointment of bishops. The Pope, under various pretexts, was continually endeavouring to engross the patronage of our bishoprics; and, when it came to be virtually admitted that an election or presentation was not effectual till confirmed by Rome, that object was not far from gained. The Pope had another hold, for it was laid down as law, and received as such at Rome, that the Pope had the absolute disposition of the benefice of every churchman who died at Rome. Whether by reason of confirmation or by direct grants, the drain of money to Rome was enormous. The rapacity of the Roman officials was however quite unconcealed and open.

The *capitulum*, chapter or council of a cathedral, by law the electing body of the bishop—the little Parliament of the cathedral and diocese, whose consent was necessary to all important acts of the bishop—consisted sometimes of certain secular or parochial clergymen holding benefices within the diocese, sometimes of a body of regulars, monks or canons. I have already mentioned the bishoprics that we know to have had such chapters of regulars, but other dioceses may have had such regular chapters at a time beyond the reach of record. The constitution of our cathedrals was often borrowed from some English authority. Thus Glasgow sent to ascertain the usages of Sarum, and Moray formed its own chapter constitution after the model of Lincoln; and these were imitated by others.

The canons or prebendaries of a cathedral were of no certain number. We find them from ten to twenty, according to endowments. Some of them were simple canons, deriving their style and title from the benefice or prebend—*prebenda*, the living. Others, again, held offices in the cathedral, and sat in the chapter-house and the choir, in the stalls appropriated for their several dignities. I will name some of the dignified canons—the dignitaries of the cathedral and chapter-house.

The Dean—*decanus*, was properly the head of the chapter, and chief person in the cathedral—the bishop not necessarily having the first seat and vote, but in some instances sitting in a lower stall in virtue of some benefice or canonry which he held. The dean had great power, and directed and controlled all the canons, chaplains, and other officers within the cathedral. Such power and duty often brought him in collision with the bishop, and very often the dean maintained the right of supremacy within the cathedral, but never asserting independence or equality with the bishop as to the rest of the diocese. The dean, presiding in the chapter, determined all questions touching the chapter and all appeals of the canons, corrected and punished all excesses of canons, vicars, and clerks of the cathedral. He had the induction and installation of new prebendaries, and the admission of all the clergy of the second form of the choir. In absence of the bishop he was bound to celebrate mass on the great festivals of the Church. It was the dean's office also to see and correct books, vestments, and other ornaments in the prebendal churches, which were exempt from the power and jurisdiction of the archdeacon and rural deans.

The reverence due to the dean is thus laid down for the guidance of the clergy of Moray:— All persons, members of the choir, great and small, shall bow to him in his stall on entering or leaving church. None of the choir, great or small, must be absent from the city for a single night without his leave. When he enters or passes through the choir or chapter-house, all members of the choir are bound to rise. Vespers and matins shall not commence before his coming, or message of his not coming. The sprinkling of holy water, and the procession and collect in Lent at compline, shall wait for his arrival or message to the contrary.

The Archdeacon was *archidiaconus* (διάκονος),

not *archidecanus*; and I must warn you against confounding him in any way or degree with the *dean*—which is not unlikely to happen, because, in Scotland, the vulgar generally called the archdeacon "ars-dene" or "ers-dene." The archdeacon administered the whole jurisdiction of the bishop, and was, by law as well as practice, the judge in the Episcopal Court. The diocese was sometimes divided into two archdeaconries, for example, St. Andrews, into the archdeaconries of St. Andrews beyond Forth and Lothian; Glasgow, into Glasgow proper and Teviotdale.

When court business became large and constant, the duty was discharged by a judge, apparently named by the archdeacon, styled the *Official*. The greater part of the law business of Scotland, both civil and ecclesiastical, before the Court of Session was established, was done in the Courts of the Officials of Edinburgh—St. Andrews principal and Glasgow wielding the authority of their respective archdeacons.

The Precentor or Cantor had charge of the music of the choir and the organs, where there were any. The careful provisions of boys for the choir, to be superseded when the voice broke at puberty, are very curious, and the more interesting to us as having been the foundation of those "sang schuils" which gave first a musical, and afterwards a general education in grammar. Many of these song-schools in cathedral towns, and, no doubt, in towns connected with great abbeys, like Jedburgh and Dunfermline, had taken the shape of burgh grammar schools before the Reformation.

The Chancellor of the diocese, along with other functions, had a general charge of theological and grammar education. He was very indignant at any extra-mural interloping or unauthorized teaching in his jurisdiction. Any free-trade in teaching was put down by him with proper spirit. It was his duty to superintend the service in church, and, amongst other parts of it, the preaching. He and the treasurer kept the chapter seal under double locks.

The general duties of the Treasurer are evident from the name of his office. One of our own chartularies says that he must, from his treasury, find lights and wine, the *host* — *hostias*, probably the expenses of the Communion elements—coals, incense, and necessary utensils in the church, keep the roof tight, supply straw for the chapter floor, or rushes at the great festivals. He had to pay the wages of the church servants—*et multa alia quæ vix possunt enumerari.*

Besides these chief dignitaries, there were a sub-dean, a sub-chanter, etc., and a crowd of acolytes and chaplains living on the foundation of their chaplainry or altarage, and assisting in the general service of the cathedral.

Another officer of the Church, whose name often leads to mistakes, was the Rural dean, quite distinct from the dean of the cathedral and chapter. The *decani rurales*, more often with us called *decani christianitatis*, had a jurisdiction over the clergy of a certain district quite well defined and known as a rural deanery. The Rural dean's jurisdiction was made up of a delegation of the general pastoral authority of the bishop and of the jurisdiction of the archdeacon, which that judge exercised in its highest form in the *curia christianitatis*. I do not find that the Rural dean acted as a judge, or had any court of his own.

In the chapters of seculars, each canon had a benefice or prebend as it was called, usually consisting of a parish in the diocese, of which he held the cure, with all its emoluments, and where he resided part of the year. The benefice is the prebend— *prebenda*, and the clergyman who holds it, the prebendary—*prebendarius*. But a prebend often consisted of land, or even of money-rent. One at Elgin was *prebenda centum solidorum*. For a certain part of the year each prebendary was bound to give *residence* and do duty at the cathedral.

The dignitaries and other canons of the cathedral bound to give residence at the cathedral for only part of the year had *vicars*, who took their place in the cathedral when they were out of residence. You must not confound these cathedral vicars—*vicarii stallarii*, vicars of the stalls, cathedral clergymen — with vicars of a parish—rural clergymen.

One other observation to remove a confusion in old church deeds. By a vulgar error which often passed into notaries' language, the dignitary who had his right designation from his cathedral office was often called after his country prebend. The dean of Moray had the parish of Auldearn for his prebend, and as he lived much at this pleasant rural parish, he was known as dean of Auldearn, as much as by his proper style of dean of Moray. In like manner the precentor of the cathedral and the chancellor were known or spoken of as chanter of Alves, and chancellor of Strathavon and Urquhart, from their rural prebends. But these were simply errors in colloquial language.

The fruits of certain churches and parishes were appropriated to the maintenance of the bishop —others to the support of the prebendaries in residence. The former were styled *mensal* churches, and the latter, *common* churches. Where a parish church was in its original independent condition, the minister was called *persona ecclesiæ* — parson or rector, and drew the whole tithes, great and small.

Where a church had been bestowed upon a monastery or a cathedral body, the cathedral or monastery was regarded as rector, called by English writers *parson imparsonee*, and was entitled to the rectorial or great tithes, leaving the small tithes for the vicar who served the cure of the parish church. This system — and it was thoroughly systematized, by which one set of men did the work, and another set drew the wages—gave rise in England to names which are not much used with us, but it is right that you should understand them. *Appropriation* is when a benefice was in the hands of a religious house—of monks for instance, or of a bishop and chapter, or of a college or university. *Impropriation* is where a benefice ecclesiastical is in the hands of a layman who is incapable of holding a cure of souls.

It happens that at the disruption of the Church in England many livings held by monasteries fell to the Crown, and were again often granted away by the Crown to laymen, so that the appropriated benefice became the impropriation correctly speaking, but somehow it often kept the name of appropriation which it had borne of old before the dissolution.

Our Lords of Erection were great impropriators of churches and church property, that had formerly been appropriated to monasteries or cathedrals.

It is difficult to say whether they were properly impropriators in virtue of their own position, or appropriators in respect of their title derived from the old monks or bishops, their authors.

The rectorial or great tithes were called *decimæ garbales* (from *garba* a sheaf), and consisted of the tenth sheaf taken from the harvest field; and woe to the tenant who pretended to remove his corn before the tithe was drawn! The vicarial tithes known as *decimæ vicariæ*, sometimes *decimæ fœni*—hay being the chief produce, came along with the tithes of the yearly produce of stock, lambs, calves, dairy, garden, to the vicar, where he had not covenanted away the *ipsa corpora* and accepted a stipend or pension instead. This was most frequently the case. The division of the fruits was not left to the common law, but the vicar, who resided and served the cure had a fixed pension — he was called *vicarius pensionarius*, vicar pensioner—leaving all the tithes to the great appropriator, unless otherwise covenanted.

You must not forget that a large part of the clerical emoluments of a parish consisted in oblations or offerings made at Easter and other feasts— nominally voluntary, but scarcely so in reality—dues of marriage, baptism, and the other numerous sacraments of the old church, and, heaviest of all, funeral dues. These were subject to the transaction between the vicar and the rectorial impropriator, but where a vicar compounded for a pension, I find they were paid over to the latter.

I need not tell you that the cathedral, as well as the monastery, was endowed largely with territories and landed estates, but I call your attention to this now to explain the form of ancient church rentals. These are generally divided into the *temporality*, that is the lands and tenements held in property, and the *spirituality*, meaning the income derived from the tithes and ecclesiastical dues of parish churches. The former were generally stated at a stated rental, more steadily fixed, perhaps, than the rentals of lay land-holders, of which last however we have few specimens extant earlier than the Reformation. It often happened that the church lord, whether regular or secular — I mean the bishop or abbot — held a whole district in property, including many parishes, and was at the same time entitled to the tithes and church dues as legally parson of the parish. The Bishop of Moray was lord of eight baronies, one of them Strathspey, apparently including the whole valley of the Spey from Laggan to Rothes, in which were many parishes. These old rentals are extremely useful for giving us sound ideas of the tenures and mode of cultivation in early times — a subject of which I shall have to speak in another lecture. The oldest rental is in the Chartulary of Kelso, dated 1290, and there are many later bringing us down to the Reformation.

If I have succeeded at all in my object, you now see what vast property and power were in the hands of churchmen, whether secular or regular; and you may judge how much a knowledge of the condition of churchmen, and the administration of their vast estates, would assist the student to know, not only the feeling of Parliament where churchmen held so important a place, but the state of the people and the manner of rural life in the early ages, and even in later times. We have abundant materials for the study; and, as I think that it has been very imperfectly pursued among us, I will detain you a few minutes while I describe some of these materials. And first of the Chartularies.

The chartularies, or registers of the charters of bishoprics and monasteries, afford the most ancient and authentic titles of lands in this country. These first tenures are, of course, of great consequence for the territorial history of a district. But hardly of less interest are the transactions, the sales, the exchanges, the dealings about lands and churches, and the judicial settlements about property of which the chartularies are so full. Few professional conveyancers will neglect such sources of information about the original and early tenures of the estates on which they have to make up titles, to settle boundaries, and to protect rights of all kinds.

So much for the local and territorial interest of these records. But there is another point of view in which the chartularies are of a higher interest. In this country, where we have as yet no *formulare* —no collection of ancient styles, these registers serve to supply what this Society (the Juridical) have given to modern times—the *Juridical styles* of an earlier day. We learn from them how all transactions were put in shape, whether in dealings about heritage or personality, and although we may not take them for our models now, be assured that a knowledge of ancient styles is important—I may say essential, for an accomplished lawyer. The chartularies afford us yet another class of valuable documents—I mean the valuations of church benefices, originally designed to regulate payments to Rome, but which were turned to many other uses.

One of these valuations, which our old lawyers knew as Bagimond's Roll, has become the laughing-stock of history from the incredible blunders that our professed antiquaries have committed about it. Sir John Skene says that "the Pope in the time of James III.,[1] sent in this realm an cardinal and legate, called Bagimont, quha did mak ane taxation

[1] A.D. 1460-1488.

of all the rentalles of the benefices." Bishop Lesly again places Bagimond still lower—in the reign of James IV.[1]

In truth, Master Benemund or Baiamundus de Vicci came from Rome to collect the tenth of ecclesiastical benefices in Scotland for the relief of the Holy Land in 1275—that is, two centuries before the date given by Skene. His valuation professed to be the *verus valor*, and as it was a good deal above the old assesment, the clergy for a time resisted and stood by their *antiqua taxatio*, from which it has happened that so many of the chartularies have recorded the ancient taxation of the district that concerned them. I need hardly point out to you how useful these valuations of benefices are, whether considered as the true value of livings, or as the comparative value by which taxes were imposed.

Of the Registers of bishoprics only four are extant, and they have been printed; those of Glasgow, Moray, Aberdeen, and Brechin. It is mortifying to think that the great Register of the bishopric of St. Andrews, so full of our early history, was known and has been lost almost within the memory of the last generation—only a few fragments of it having been preserved from copies.

The chartularies of monasteries, the religious houses of Regulars, that have been preserved, are

[1] A.D. 1488-1513.

much more numerous. First, let me enumerate those that are printed :—

    1. Arbroath.
    2. Balmerino.
    3. Cambuskenneth.
    4. Dryburgh.
    5. Dunfermline.
    6. Glasgow College Church.
    7. Glasgow Friars Preachers.
    8. Inchaffray.
    9. Holyrood.
    10. Kelso.
    11. Lindores.
    12. Melrose.
    13. Newbattle.
    14. North Berwick.
    15. Paisley.
    16. St. Andrews.
    17. St. Giles College Kirk.
    18. Scone.

The Registers of the universities of Aberdeen and Glasgow, which are not less useful, have also been printed, but not the Records of the mother University of St. Andrews.

In the second place, let me give you a list of the monastic Registers that are still in MS. and not printed :—

1. Charters of the Carmelite, Franciscan, and Dominican Friars at Aberdeen.

2. Register of the Nunnery of Coldstream.

3. Register of the Monastery of Coupar-Angus.

4. Register of the Collegiate Church of Crail.

5. Register of Holm Cultram in Cumberland —a house founded by Prince Henry of Scotland, to which many Scotch families granted charters.

6. Chartulary of the Abbey of Inchcolm.

7. Charters of the Priory of Restennet.

8. Register of the Collegiate Church of St. Nicholas, Aberdeen.

9. Register of the Chapel Royal of Stirling.

For reasons to be immediately explained, it is desirable to keep in mind that the Registers of the following religious houses, which cannot now be traced, were many of them quoted by writers of the last century :—

1. The Priory of Beauly.
2. The Abbey of Crossraguel.
3. The Abbey of Dundrennan.
4. The House of Fail.
5. The Abbey of Ferne, in Ross.
6. The Abbey of Glenluce.
7. The Abbey of Kilwinning.
8. The College of Lincluden.

9. The Monastery of Newabbey.
10. The Monastery of St. Mary's Isle.
11. The Abbey of Tungland.
12. The Priory of Whithorn.

The recovery of a single one of these missing volumes of Registers may be of inestimable value to the Scotch conveyancer for illustrating the tenures of the district in which the monastery had its possessions.

Observe that all those chartularies, of such interest for the topography and local history of their districts, are of bishoprics, or religious houses. Of lay chartularies—the Registers of property of laymen—we have but one of any note, or of any considerable antiquity. The Douglases of Lochleven and Morton have preserved a little chartulary of their early possessions, which goes back as far as the thirteenth century, but *that* also has now been printed.

I think there was no subject so fruitful of law disputes among churchmen as the distinction between tithes, rectorial and vicarial. The difficulty arose from the very nature of the case, but it was greatly increased by the innumerable transactions and covenants that took place regarding almost every benefice where there was a vicar.

Where the canon law had its course—I mean

where there was no special covenant—the tithes of the parish were simply divided into great and small; the great tithes—*decimæ bladi*, tithes of all corn, going to the rector or to the monastery or cathedral, which was in law the rector; the small tithes—*decimæ fœni*, that is, of hay, of garden produce, and of all other produce subject to tithe—and that was a matter depending too much upon use and wont—falling to the vicar, to whom also belonged the altar and personal offerings. It happened, I think, very often that the vicar's share at common law—I mean, of course, common church law—became the greater of the two, and I could give you many instances proving that it was so, and also showing the manner in which their respective incomes were arranged, when the abbey or cathedral grudged the whole legal vicarage to the vicar. But one shall suffice for the present, because I am not sure that I may not be encroaching upon the subject of Teinds, which our friend Mr. Kinnear has chosen for his course of Lectures.

Amongst the numerous benefices appropriated by the Abbey of Arbroath, one of the largest, perhaps, was the church of Inverness, with its chapels of Petty and others. I cannot tell you what the whole income was, but here is the arrangement between the Vicar of Inverness, and the Abbey of Arbroath, as rector, sanctioned by the Bishop of Moray, their diocesan, on the 2d of the nones of February, in the year of grace 1248. The vicar is to have the whole vicarage, that is proper vicarage tithes,—consisting, as I have told you, of tithes of hay, garden stuffs, young of animals, and many other products—with all its pertinents, reserving to the Abbot and Convent of Arbroath, as rector, the whole teind sheaves—*tota decima garbarum bladi*, that is, the proper rectorial tithes—the corn tithes or great tithes, also the tithes of the mill, and of herrings, and three marks from the tithes of the Lent confession—meaning the offerings of that season—also the whole lands belonging to the church of Inverness. He is also to have the vicarage house, and is taken bound to receive the Bishop and his train with becoming hospitality on their visitations, and see to the proper service of the church of Inverness—*in omnibus ad cultum dei spectantibus honeste faciet deserviri*—and its chapels; and he shall bear all episcopal dues.

A dispute between the same Abbey and the vicars of its churches within the bishopric of St. Andrews—the vicars complaining that an insufficient sustentation was given them by the monks, and the monks asserting the contrary—was settled in this manner by David Bishop of St. Andrews in 1249. The Vicar of Nigg, in name of vicarage, is to have *totum altaragium*, that is all dues and offerings levied and made at the altar; and on occasions of visitation the monks are to help the procuration with two marks. Let me explain that procuration means the expenses due on visitations of the Bishop, Official, Archdeacon, or Rural Dean, who were all entitled to be hospitably entertained. The vicar of the church of Inverkeithing is to have the whole altarage, excepting the land of the church (I don't think that this means that the land of the church formed part of the altarage), and bear the whole expense of procurations for himself and the Vicar of Inverlunan, besides paying to the monks five marks out of the altarage. The Vicar of Lunan, on the other hand, is to receive nothing but his altarage, and the bishops are to receive a procuration *in* the monastery for each of the churches of St. Vigeans, Barry, Arbirlot, and Ethy—showing, no doubt, that for those neighbouring churches the Bishop and his train could be most conveniently and hospitably entertained at the great Abbey. The Vicar of Arbroath has to provide a chaplain to serve in the church of St. Vigeans, and is to have fourteen marks of pension, which must content him, seeing that he has not to bear any of the bishop's visitation expenses. The Vicar of Barry is to have five marks and the whole church land of Barry in name of vicarage.

You will observe that the Vicar of Arbirlot is to have his altarage in name of vicarage, but he is to pay two marks to the monks, because he is relieved of the bishop's visitation. The Vicar of Ethy is to have the whole altarage in name of vicarage, and, in addition, to receive from the monks eighteen bolls of meal. I suppose the parish of Ethy was small or thinly peopled, so that the altar offerings and dues were not sufficient sustenance. There are other vicarages taxed in this decree—most having the altar and its dues, and some of them *land;* Glammis has *terra ecclesie*—the kirkland; and Newtyle has *una bovata terre*—an oxgate of land.

I give only one other settlement of this much-vexed question, for this special reason, that it affords us a valuation or estimated value of the vicarages—an estimate of what they would produce if left to law rights. It is a judgment in 1250, by Papal delegates, concerning the allowances that should be paid to the vicars of the diocese of Aberdeen.

The vicarage of the church of Banchory Ternan was valued at sixteen marks, and its vicar is ordained to have the whole altar dues, with one acre of land and the tithe of corn of the same town lands then cultivated, reserving to the fabric of the church of Arbroath—the appropriator of the parish—forty pence and the tithes of the corn of the lands to be hereafter cultivated, with the lands belonging to the church, and the other teind sheaves of the whole parish. The vicarage of the church of Banff is valued at thirty marks, and the vicar has for his share the altar dues with a manse, and also the altar dues of Inverbondy with one acre of land—the whole tithe of fish, white and red, and the lands belonging both to the mother church and chapel, and the teind sheaves of the whole parish remaining with the Abbot and Convent of Arbroath. The vicarage of Gamrie is valued at eighteen marks, and the vicar had the whole altar dues with two acres of land and the whole of the church land besides, the teind sheaves of the whole parish remaining with the Abbot and Convent. The Vicar of Fyvie, whose vicarage is valued at thirty-three marks, was adjudged to have his altar dues and the land of Ardincross, reserving to the monks five marks *in lana pacabili*, that is, in wool of a marketable quality, or lambs, and also the teind sheaves both of Ardincross, and of the said parish. The vicarage of Tarves was taxed at thirty-two marks, and the vicar had the altarage with one acre of land; while there were reserved to the monks eight marks, which were to be taken from the tithes of wool or lambs or both, and the corn tithes of the whole parish, with the kirkland.

There are other parishes where the distinction is drawn between the tithes of lands then cultivated, and of those that might hereafter be cultivated. So early was this distinction in favour of industry drawn, on which the very principle of our valuation of tithes depends, that the Judges-delegates append this general declaration : " The vicars of the foresaid churches shall sustain all the ordinary burdens (meaning chiefly the *procurations* I have mentioned above), and for the fabric of the chancels of their churches and extraordinary burdens, they shall bear their due proportion "—which is not explained.[1] The Pope, or rather the laws of the Church, in many cases, exempted from tithes, *novalia*—newly cultivated lands—lands which were cultivated by the hands of the monks themselves.[2]

It is remarkable how many of those settlements of vicarages took place about the same time. In the year 1251, Bishop David of St. Andrews fixed the portions to be paid to the vicars of the churches belonging to Holyrood in Lothian.[3] All the portions were payable out of the altar dues of the several parishes, ranging from the Vicar of Bolton, who was to have ten marks, to the Vicar of *Varia Capella*, or Falkirk, who had twenty, the same portion which the Vicar of St. Cuthberts had; and the Bishop declared that where the altar dues were not sufficient for the provision, the canons of the monastery must supply them from the other

---

[1] The parson was at common law answerable for maintaining and repairing the chancel, but he might cut timber for his remuneration.

[2] Bull of Lucius III. to Arbr. Moray, 152.

[3] *Portio vicarii*, the vicar's *portion* was now a word of style.

goods of the churches. The little churches of Mont-Lothian and Hamer are to be served by chaplains, being insufficient for the support of vicars—*cum sint insufficientes ad vicariorum sustentationem.*

Minute and complicated as most of these ancient settlements of vicarage and rectorial tithes originally had been, they were still further perplexed by a constant state of change and readjustment, as long as there was still a competent authority to adjudicate or sanction the transaction. But when the storm of the Reformation had swept away rector and vicar and all authorities cognisant of their rights, there remained the wonderful chaos of churches and church lands, tithes and dues, which nobody was willing to pay and everybody was eager to grasp; a state of matters which required much physical and moral courage for a court of justice to deal with.

It is worth noticing that church foundations mark the prosperity of the country. All our bishoprics were founded and endowed before the end of David the First's reign. Most, I may say all, of our great monasteries were erected before the end of the thirteenth century, or rather before the troubles which followed the death of Alexander III. in 1286.

The next revival of a church-founding spirit was in the fifteenth century, extending from James I.

to James IV. The taste however for monachism was somewhat abated during that time, and the religious efforts of the period took the shape of collections of secular clergy in what were called colleges or collegiate churches—sometimes named *prepositurœ* or *provostries* from the *prepositus* or chief of the college, though that officer was often styled *decanus* or dean.

Mr. Laing has given us a list of thirty-eight of these little cathedrals—for they imitated the service and constitution of cathedrals, only on a smaller scale—and has furnished a very instructive collection of the charters of eight of them within our own shire of Mid-Lothian, viz.—Soltra; Trinity College, Edinburgh; Kirk of Field; Restalrig; Corstorphine; Crichton; Dalkeith; Roslin.

Trinity College Church, so lately swept away, was endowed in 1462 by Queen Mary of Gueldres, widow of James II., for a provost, eight prebendaries, and two choristers.

Restalrig was erected into a collegiate church by James III. for a dean and certain prebendaries.

The collegiate church of Roslin was founded for a provost, six prebendaries, and two choristers by William Sinclair, Earl of Orkney, in 1446.

The members of the collegiate church were secular or parochial clergy, bound by their vows of ordination, but not subject to any *regula* or precise rule of discipline. None of them were very richly endowed. They furnished only maintenance for the prebendaries, and the expenses attending upon their handsome church and service suitable.

Let me explain a few words which, I think, have been mistaken in modern books. When a great church lord obtained additional benefices, when a bishop, finding his episcopal income too small, succeeded in getting an abbey or priory in addition, perhaps he could not become abbot or prior, as he may not have been of the right order, perhaps he was of no order of Regulars, and the matter was arranged by giving him the additional benefice *in commendam*, as it was called; thus, when the Prince, son of James the Fourth, Duke of Ross, Archbishop of St. Andrews, required still more revenue to afford him a princely living, he obtained three abbeys *in commendam*. He may never have visited them, never assisted in their chapters or convents, but he drew the revenues, and certainly without a thought of accounting for them to any one. He was *commendator* of those abbeys. But very frequently for some of the same reasons, a churchman who had no great benefice before, obtained an abbey where he could not preside as abbot, for some reason or other, and he also became *commendator* of that abbey; and latterly—say at the Reformation, and for a generation or two after—many laymen, with grants of monasteries and their lands, were styled *commendators*, like the Regent Commendator of St. Andrews and Earl of Moray. I prefer giving you an account of the thing as it was practised, instead of explaining the word by etymology; for I do not find a satisfactory etymology in the dictionaries of *commendam* and *commendatarius*.

When you meet with an abbot or prior, having a special grant of episcopal dress and ornaments, mitre, crosier, and the rest, which grants are very common, it is altogether a mistake to suppose that the abbot so honoured was thereby exempted from episcopal jurisdiction. The abbot of a mitred abbey had place and precedency in Parliament and Council in respect of his mitre, but no authority which freed him from the common jurisdiction of his diocesan bishop.

The word *curate*, at one time so well known in Scotland, was not known, or at least not much used, with us before the Reformation to express a class of men who did the work, while rectors and vicars drew the emoluments of the parish. Men were called *curatus* and *non curatus* as they had or wanted the cure of souls. But, to speak grammatically, I think the word with us was generally an adjective, and not a noun-substantive.

Forbes, the writer upon tithes, and who was, I think, professor of law at Glasgow, gives a learned expanation of the word *titular*. There is plenty of learning in the dictionaries about the word *titulus*, but it is somewhat thrown away here. In a question of teinds, and in any other question of Scotch law, the titular is simply the person who is *in titulo* of the teinds or benefice, having the title in him.

I hope it is hardly necessary to explain that a grant of an *ecclesia*—a church—carried more than the stone and lime ;· it carried with it all the parochial rights, all the tithes of the parish, the dues paid at the altar and at the cemetery, all manse glebe and land belonging to the church. If the grant was made to a Churchman, he might enjoy all these in person; if to a cathedral and chapter, or to an abbey and convent, they might, as patrons, present any qualified person, leaving the emoluments to be apportioned either by the common law, which was quite precise in the matter, or modified by special compact with their presentee or his predecessors.

You will sometimes find, especially in church grants, as pertinents, *can* and *conveth*. Tithes are granted by some of our ancient kings *de cano meo*, that is, from customs or rents paid *in kind*. We have the word still in *cain:* the cain fowls of a barony are quite well understood. Cain fowls are sometimes called reek hens — one payable from every house that reeked—every fire house. The old Lords of the Isles gave a grant to Paisley of a penny or some trifling sum *de unaquaque domo unde fumus exit.*

Conveth seems to have been a due collected by a lord from his vassals, perhaps on the occasion of journeys. Malcolm IV. granted to the canons of Scone, from every plough belonging to the church of Scone, which had been lately burnt, for their conveth at the Feast of All Saints, a cow and two swine, and four *clamni* of meal and ten thraves of oats, and ten hens and two hundred eggs, and ten bunches of candles, and four *nummatus* of soap, and twenty half *melæ* of cheese. The same charter granted the canons this privilege, that no one should take conveth from their men and lands except with their consent.[1]

In a dispute between the Bishop of St. Andrews and Duncan of Arbuthnot, tried in a Synod held at Perth 3d April 1206, witnesses swore that they had seen the preceding bishops in that land of Kirkton of Arbuthnot taking conveth as if the land and the native men upon it were their own, and that no one gainsaid them.[2] Not finding it easy to give any etymology of the word, I asked my ever-ready friend Mr. Skene's assistance. He pointed out to me the two occurrences which I have mentioned, and declined to suggest an explanation; and I follow his example.

[1] Liber de Scon, No. 5.   [2] Spalding Miscellany, vol. v.

Here are two or three morsels of Church History from the Register of the Priory of St. Andrews, which I am tempted to lay before you.

In the year of grace 1264, on Thursday next after the Feast of St. Scholastica the Virgin, the Lord J., Prior of St. Andrews, held his pleas—*placita*—at Dull in Atholl, near a great rock to the west of the house of Sir Thomas the Vicar, without any impediment, prohibition, or contradiction; on which day Kolin, son of Anegus the Souter, and Bridin, his son, and also Gylis, the brother of the said Kolin, did homage to the Lords Prior and Convent as their liegemen, in presence of all those present at the pleas, whose names are Sir Mauricius, called of Dull, Sir Richard, called of Pethkery, canons; Thomas, then Vicar of Dull, Rothryother, Duncan the clerk, called Makmulethir, Nicholas Makduncan, Makbeth Makgilmichel, Ewayn the doomster, Gilcolm Makgugir, MacBeth Makkyneth, Kennauch Makyny, John MacRothry, Makrath the priest, and many others whose names are unknown. The document is worth observing for the occasion of the meeting, but more for the remarkable attendance of Celtic suitors assembled at the standing-stone beside the vicar's house of Dull, where the country was gathered for the pleas and suits to be determined by the Lord Prior of St. Andrews, whose vassals they all were.

The next document records a similar event a few years later, when the Clerauch of Dul did homage to his Lord the Prior of St. Andrews, and points at a claim by some other party disputing the superiority.

On the day of St. Baldred, in the year of grace 1269, Andrew son of Gilmur, Clerauch of Dul, made homage to Sir J. of Haddington, Prior of St. Andrews, within the Priory of St. Andrews, on his bended knees, by putting his hands within the hands of the Prior, in the presence of Thomas Vicar of Dul, and William of Clatti, John of Norham younger, canons, and there swore on the holy Gospels to hold his homage to the said Prior and Convent, and that he had never done homage to any other, nor of right could do homage, than to the said Prior and Convent.

The following memoranda of the dates and dedications of certain churches consecrated by Bishop David de Bernham are not without interest.

In the year of the Incarnation 1242, 13th Kalends of June, was dedicated the church of St. Michael of Linlithcu, and also the following churches, by the Lord David Bishop of St. Andrews: the same year, on the 7th of the Ides of August, the church of St. Cyricus the martyr, of Eglisgrig; on the 2d Kalends of September, the church of St. Mernan the martyr, of Foules; in 1243, 4th Kalends of June, the church of St. Memma the Virgin, of Sconin; on the 15th Kalends of July, the church of the Holy Trinity of Kylrimund; on the 13th Kalends of August, the church of St. John the Baptist and St. Modrust the martyr, of Marchynche; on the 10th Kalends of August, the church of St. Stephen the Martyr and St. Moan the martyr of Portmuoch; on the 5th Kalends of August, the church of St. John the Evangelist and St. Athernisc the martyr, of Losceresch; on the Ides of August, the church of St. Lawrence the Martyr and St. Coman the martyr, of Rossinclerach.[1]

[1] Reg. Prior. S. Andree, p. 348. On the fly-leaf of my copy of the same Register, there is this note, dated at Paris, 30th May 1858:—

"M. Leopold Delisle writes to J. Y. Akerman of a MS. Bibl. Imper. fond Latin n. 128—a pontificale written in the beginning of the 13th century, which seems to have been à l'usage of David Bishop of St. Andrews. At the beginning is a long list of churches, titled, Hee sunt ecclesie quas dedicavit episcopus David : Ecclesia de Lessewade dedicata fuit anno gracie Millesimo ducentesimo quadragesimo 11 nonas Maii : Ecclesia fratrum predicatorum de Pert eodem anno iii idus Maii : Ecclesia Sancti Nicholai de Berewych eodem anno viij idus Julii : Ecclesia de Kirktun anno etc. quadragesimo uno xvij Kalendas Septembris.

"Le document finit ainsi : Ecclesia de Ketenes anno etc. quadragesimo nono xiiij Kalendas Maii : Ecclesia de Sancta hittenmantin (Stramartin) eodem anno xv. Kalendas Junii : Ecclesia de Clacmanan eodem anno nono Kalendas Septembris,

"Puis une main un peu plus récente a ajouté les articles qui suivent.

"Hee sunt ecclesie quas dedicavit episcopus Willelmus : Ecclesia de Dunothyr dedicata est anno gracie Millesimo ducentesimo septuagesimo vi. idus Maii : capella de Collyn eodem anno xi Kalendas Junii ita quod nullum prejudicium generetur matrici ecclesie de Fethyressach."

LECTURE V.

OLD FORMS OF LAW.

I MUST pass lightly over the institutions which we *certainly* had in common with the whole Anglo-Saxon peoples of Britain, but only because these have been well illustrated from Saxon or English sources and by English writers. Our laws are of the same family; our customs, judicial forms as well as others, even where identical with those of England, are not therefore to be held borrowed or imitated from England—for England was not even a name at the time when the institutions I am about to enumerate to you existed among us. For another reason I must not detain you on our earliest judicial forms—our aboriginal forms of process I may call them,—and that is because they have left little or no impression on our existing procedure.

It will startle only the youngest of my students to find that at a period within history the facts of a disputed case were not ascertained by documents or witnesses. Six or seven hundred years ago, when a man was accused, and denied the accusation—pleaded "not guilty" as we say now—his accusers did not call witnesses cognisant of the facts, but *he* was bound to find *compurgatores* to swear for him and with him, that they believed him guiltless—men of the vicinage, knowing the character of the parties accusing and accused. The number of compurgators necessary was defined very accurately, and varied with the nature of the accusation, from one to thirty.

You may suppose that reasoning beings were not quite satisfied with such witnessing to *character*, instead of witnessing to the *fact;* and we will believe, even without authority, that in that rude time the law prevailed, which we know well in after times, and which made speedy work with the homicide *red-handed*, or with the thief caught with the *fang*. There was little trial or form required to "justify" them. But failing such proof, and long before the machinery of evidence was adjusted, there came the *judicium Dei*—an appeal to Divine revelation of guilt or innocence. *That* was by the ordeal of hot iron, of water, or, finally, by the judicial combat—wager of battle. We have evidence of all these in fresh observance among us in Scotland, and chiefly in the hands of religious judges. A pretty island, which some of you may remember, opposite to Lord Mansfield's park above the bridge of Perth, was used by the monks of Scone as their place of judgment—*per ferrum et aquam:* and we had numerous other religious houses exercising the same jurisdiction.

A time came, however, when men no longer thought it convenient that he who was accused of the theft of a cow should go free, if twenty-four friends swore that they thought him incapable of stealing. The essoign by compurgators—*essonium compurgatorum*—went down. The trial by ordeal —walking over hot iron, floating in the river instead of sinking, and such like appeals to a present interposition of Providence—also fell into discredit. The trial of right by wager of battle—judicial combat—remained longer. In the time of David I. it was optional to the accused, or the defender, whether he would do battle or take purgation of leal men; and the laws of the judicial combat— *duellum*—were long carefully observed. It seems not to have revolted our forefathers to see the weak man obliged to fight the strong man, who wished to strip him of his inheritance. Yet this monstrous manner of settling a dispute about an estate in land or other weighty matter did at last offend common sense; and men looked round for other modes of civil and criminal judicature—other modes of getting at the truth.

In tracing our judicial forms to their sources, we meet first the broad partition between Church and Crown procedure, the former having, from the earliest period of history, all the apparatus of a well-studied and perhaps over-refined form of process; whereas the King's court, in its earliest stages, could have no written form of process, nor required any to obey the simple mandate contained in the King's brief. It was not merely that the churchmen were the educated class, accustomed to use their intellects, and trained in the schools of the most subtle philosophy: they had rules and precedents, and laws emanating from councils and Popes, of unchallenged authority. Before our poor country had emerged out of unlettered barbarism, Rome and the Roman Church had already a code of laws, not less coherent, not less carefully studied and followed, than the old code of Imperial Rome. Gratian had published his great collection of the decretals, or collected Canons of the Church, before the middle of the twelfth century; but long before that time the most important laws of that code were known and received over all Christendom with that unhesitating deference to authority which we find in the early stages of law everywhere.

I wish I had time to show you how Trial by Jury grew, and how it banished those old barbarisms. You may not be prepared to admit that the bulwark of our liberties originated in Church Courts, but the best English authorities are of that opinion; and a case that I will quote to you gives some additional support to that conjecture. Certainly if trial by Jury was introduced in the church courts, it was transplanted very early into the courts of civil jurisdiction. Without troubling you with an array of small facts from which I have made this deduction, I venture to assert that although the origin and rude outline of jury trial may be traced much higher, you will not find jury trial, according to modern use and phraseology, in England till long after the Conquest. The English lawyers think they can prove that criminal cases and civil suits were tried by jury in England in the reign of Henry III. We have evidence of trial by jury both in civil and criminal cases in Scotland about the same time, or a little earlier.

I have thought it desirable to show you jury trial in its infancy, and we have abundant materials for the inquiry. The most important are the Brieves upon which trials were directed to be taken. We have some of these of the time of the Alexanders still extant—the actual original brief or crown writ commanding a trial, with the verdict of the jury simply stitched or attached to it. Besides the few remains of the original brief and inquest of that early time, we have at least collections of styles of brieves for the different purposes required in two very venerable law manuscripts—the Ayr MS. and the Bute MS., both of the fourteenth century.

Amongst our materials for legal study I have not found a more simple and satisfactory form of trying a case than we meet in a dispute regarding the lands of Monachkeneran on the Clyde, claimed by the monks of Paisley as belonging to their church of Kilpatrick, but which were held by a contumacious layman, Gilbert the son of Samuel of Renfrew. We have the evidence of witnesses admitted very early; and in the manner in which the evidence is taken I find, as it were, the foreshadowing of the trial of an issue by a jury under a competent judge. Let me report the case which was tried in A.D. 1233.

The Abbot of Paisley obtained from the Pope a commission to three persons—the Deans of Carrick and Cuningham, and the Master of the schools of Ayr—for recovering the property of his abbey unjustly abstracted. In passing, it may be observed that this *magister scholarum* takes his place as coadjutor and equal with these deans—the *decani christianitatis* of the diocese. The trial took place in the year 1233, that is the twentieth year of King Alexander II. The Papal Commissioners sat at Irvine;

the monks of Paisley appeared for their interest, and proved the citation of the said Gilbert the son of Samuel, charging him for withholding the whole lands of Monachkeneran belonging to their church of Kilpatrick, which he illegally alienated. The monks gave in what I suppose would now be called a *Declaration*—commencing: The abbot and convent of Paisley intend to prove—*intentio abbatis et conventus de Passelet est probare:* in short, that the lands of Monachkeneran upon the Clyde were lawfully theirs, and that Gilbert the unlawful possessor should be ejected.

The first production of witnesses for the abbey in the parish church of Irvine is faithfully recorded. Alexander Fitz-Hugh swears that for sixty years and more he had seen Bede Ferdan dwelling in a big house made of wattles, on the east of the church of Kilpatrick, and had held that land of Monachkeneran which Gilbert the son of Samuel now holds. Interrogated: In whose name he possessed the land? Answers: That he held it in the name of the church, doing no service therefor except only receiving and entertaining strangers coming there— *recipiendo et pascendo hospites illuc venientes.* He says also that when he was a boy he and his father were sometimes received there as guests.

Thomas Gaskel swears that he also had seen Bede Ferdan dwelling in the said house in the land of the church of St. Patrick, and adds that he saw afterwards Christinus, son of the said Bede, possessing the said lands on the same tenure as his father had held them; and that the whole church lands were divided into four parts: one of which the said Bede Ferdan possessed, the three other parts being held by three other persons, each of whom in the name of the church entertained strangers. Interrogated: as to the time? He says that it is more than forty years since; for he was brought up there from his infancy. Interrogated—a strange interrogation we should think — What are the lands belonging to the church? He answers: Cochmanach, Fimbelach, Edinbernan, and Cragventalach, and certain other lands which Dugald son of the Earl now holds.

Of this Dugald, son of the great Earl, we know something; but I must not go into that piece of church scandal—only thus far: he was a priest, and had been presented to the church of Kilpatrick by his father, and having obtained colourable but illegal titles of the lands of the church, pretended to hold the same in heritage, until through conscience or fear he yielded them up to the abbot in open court. It seems strange to us that the charters were not produced nor called for; but perhaps that is an omission in the record. Dugald son of the Earl being then sworn, concurred in everything with

Thomas Gaskel, and adds that the said lands of Monachkeneran and many other lands, through his fault and carelessness, have been alienated from the said church, because he would not offend his father or his brother, or his relations. The second production of witnesses for the monks was in the parish church at Ayr, on the Saturday after Martinmas of the same year. You observe that the places of proof were made to suit the Commissioners, who were all of Carrick and Cuningham.

Malcolm Beg, the first witness, swears that he saw Bede Ferdan keeping his house beside the cemetery of the church of Kilpatrick, and that he held the land of Monachkeneran in name of the church; and for that land and others which he held of the church he received strangers coming to the church, and did no other service therefor. Interrogated: In the time of what Earl he had seen this? He says: It was in the time of Earl Alwin—no doubt the Alwin Fitz-Arkil whom heralds give as the first of the great Earls of Lennox —and that that Earl gave to St. Patrick and the church that land of Kathconnen which he, the witness, afterwards held and sold for fear — *pro timore*. He further says that all these lands of the church which Bede held, and Dugald and others now hold, were free and quit from all temporal service, and that the men dwelling in them were always defended by the church and in the church court against all men.

Anekol agrees in all things with Malcolm Beg, and adds that Earl David, the brother of King William — that was David Earl of Huntingdon and of many Scotch lordships—at the time when he held the earldom of Lennox, wished to have an aid— *auxilium*—out of those church lands of Kilpatrick, as he had from the other lands of his earldom, and could not, because they were defended by the church. Gilon concurs in everything with Malcolm Beg. Gilbethoc concurs in everything with Malcolm and Anekol, and adds that Bede was slain in defence of the right and liberty of the church. Fergus son of Cuningham concurs with Gilbethoc in everything. Hilarius concurs in everything with Fergus and Gilbethoc. Nemias swears to all that Anekol had witnessed, and adds, with regard to the time, that he had seen this fifty years ago, and is sure of what he says, because he was born in that parish. Ressin agrees in everything with Nemias; Gillmor with Ressin and Nemias. Rotheric Beg of Carric concurs with Malcolm Beg his brother: being interrogated how he knew this, answered that he had seen it from his youth, as he was born and brought up in the parish of Kilpatrick; Rathel agrees in everything with Rotheric; and Gillekonel Manthac, brother of the Earl of Carrick, in everything with Malcolm Beg. We have no proof for the layman: he was cited often and failed to appear, being contumacious; at least so says the writer of the record, who, I fear, had a leaning to the monks.

Then the two deans, Lawrence of Carrick and Richard of Cuningham, and the Master of the schools of Ayr, as delegates of our Lord the Pope, certify to the Bishop of Glasgow, their Ordinary, that the suit was rightly contested before them; and after having heard the witnesses and examined the whole cause, it appeared to them that the Abbot and Convent of Paisley had sufficiently proved their Declaration—*intentionem suam sufficienter probasse*—and therefore, by the advice of men prudent and skilled in the law, they had adjudged to them the possession of the disputed land, and had condemned Gilbert in the lawful expenses, to wit, in £30, which they had taxed and modified—*a nobis taxatis et moderatis*. You see how far back that little style of process goes for its origin. Wherefore they enjoin the Bishop, for the reverence and obedience due to the Pope, to put their sentence to execution against the said Gilbert, compelling obedience by Church censure.

The Bishop appears to have done what he was required, but the Lennox was far away and in a wild country, and perhaps not very careful of Church censures; and so Gilbert remained a long time under sentence of excommunication, despising to obey the judgment. Then the Pope's delegates supplicated the King, Alexander II., to extend the secular arm against him—*brachium seculare extendere* —for the honour of God and Holy Church; and in observance of the approved process, the King had complied with their request—for which the delegates render thanks, and intimate to his royal majesty that, in other cases, when any one is excommunicated for contempt—*pro contumacia*—if he find caution to obey the law, he is absolved; but when he is excommunicated for disobeying a definitive sentence he is not absolved, even upon finding caution for obedience, unless he shall first satisfy or perform what is adjudged—*satisfaciat judicatis:* and so they supplicate the King not to withdraw his secular arm, which he had extended against the said Gilbert, until he shall obey the sentence and perform what is adjudged. That is all we have of the case, and we do not know whether the extending of the secular arm ultimately prevailed over the contumacious Gilbert, who had shown himself so regardless of Church censures and even of excommunication.

I have occupied perhaps too much of your time with the details of this case; but I think it is a very important one. It is the earliest I know which consists of a definite and carefully recorded declaration, and of evidence given by a large number of witnesses strictly confined to its proof, with a relevancy worthy of a more advanced age ; and I don't think that the judge could have much difficulty in finding that the Abbot and Convent *intentionem suam sufficienter probasse.*

We have no specimens, I think, of lay procedure —procedure in lay courts—so early as that church case from the chartulary of Paisley. The contemporary biographer of King David I. tells us of the King hearing cases in person : that of a morning when he was going out hunting—when his foot was actually in the stirrup—the good King would stop and sit down patiently to hear the complaint of some poor petitioner ; and we have evidence scattered through all the chartularies of that great Prince's attention both to the making of laws, and giving the sanction of his great name and authority to statutes and codes of customs, and to adjudicating in lawsuits. He settled marches, forest rights, and rights of pasture ; but he recorded his decisions simply by a cross on the oak-tree, which was shown for generations after—by cutting ditches on the hillside—by setting up tall stones—done by the King, certainly by the King in person. His grandson, William the Lion, more clerkly, directed written instruments concerning the marches and other conditions which *he* adjudged to be executed for preservation. But of the machinery of proof—the machinery for ascertaining the facts in lay courts—during those reigns, we know nothing.

But even so early as King David, the King had, as I have already mentioned, his great law-officers, his Justiciar, his Chamberlain, his Chancellor, his Constable, each with his own jurisdiction; and then, or very soon after, Scotland was divided into Sheriffdoms, where the law was administered in the name and by the authority of the King, and where the sheriff was, both in theory and practice, the minister of the Crown, for executing the King's writs as well as judging and trying cases civil and criminal, with the full authority of the Crown. Let me describe some of those brieves, the writs which our old Kings—Alexander II. and Alexander III.—addressed to their sheriffs, and some of the process which followed upon them. We have some of the little writs themselves—the brief of vellum—just as it issued from the King's Chancery—and attached to it, or bearing marks of having been once sewed to it, there is the verdict of the assize returned by the officer to whom the brief was addressed.

Speaking of that period, then, which we may call the period of the Alexanders, those royal writs are sometimes addressed to the king's justiciars, or the justiciar of Lothian, that is, the justiciar be-south Forth, but much more commonly to the sheriff of the county, and direct trial to be taken about such a variety of matters, civil and criminal, of rights heritable as well as possessory questions, of questions of status and legitimacy, that I cannot find any class of litigation that can be supposed to have been excluded.

I thought it right to print a few specimens of these old writs amongst the *prolegomena* of the first volume of the Acts of the Parliament of Scotland —*Formulæ Agendi*.[1] You will find there an inquest taken at the Castle of Dumfries, before the bailies of our Lord the King, upon the death of Adam the miller, who was killed in a quarrel by Richard, son of Robert, son of Elias. The bailies tried the case *per sacramentum*, that is, by sworn jurymen; and their names are given—not twelve, but thirteen in number, with a tail *et aliorum*, which shows, I think, how little attention was paid to any exact number of jurymen. Observe, too, that the jurymen were probably, according to the ancient practice, witnesses in the cause—men of the vicinage, best knowing the truth. You see how the words run from *vicinage*—*visnetum*, to the English *renew*.

Whether jurymen or witnesses, or both, they

[1] P. 87.

swear to all the details of the squabble, although using only a dozen lines for the purpose. They also tell what is worth your attention, that the barons on that jury agreed with the burgess jurors in all things; and the said burgesses and barons say upon their oath that Richard, the survivor of the fray, was a true man—*fidelem in omnibus;* but the other, Adam, was a thief—*et defamatum*, a phrase which, I suppose, we may translate *habit and repute*. This was only, you see, the report of a proof upon oath. There may have been a verdict and judgment separate, but if the jury were required to give a precise verdict, it would seem to be one of "not guilty."[1]

Next, the King issued his mandate to his sheriffs and bailies of Lanark, to ascertain the tenure of Adam of Liverance—I suppose it is here a surname, but derived from the duties of his office, which consisted in delivering food, drink, etc., in the King's household, and specially clothes, hence called *liveries*—in the land of Paduinam, which he holds of the King in chief, and what service he ought to pay to the King therefor, together with the extent—*extenta*, which Thomas de Normanvil holds from him. Charters were ordered to be produced, and the trial took place at Lanark, by men of the baronies and burgesses: and the jury find that Adam was bound to pay to the

[1] Acts of Parliament, i. p. 88.

King the service of two archers and of one sufficient servant on horseback for making all manner of liverance, which ought to be made in the King's Court to the grooms and the dogs—in which service *did* serve six persons named, who received nothing from the King except their food. Further, when ward, relief, or marriage fell, it belonged to the King; and further, the extent of the whole land is 13 merks—meaning, I think, of the land held by Thomas de Normanvil.[1]

The next is a remarkable inquest. It is called a *new* inquest—*nova inquisitio*, and was taken evidently on the allegation that the previous inquest was fraudulent. Here are the words of the twelve jurymen—who being all sworn, said in their verdict that the inquest taken formerly about the said lands of Hopkelchoc by Sir Gilbert Fraser, Sheriff of Peebles, was faithfully and reasonably made, and by reasonable persons, and not suspected in any way in that matter; and that they all swore faithfully, but they certified that two of the jury said that a person open to suspicion—*una persona suspecta*, was upon that first inquest, namely, one of the tenants of the party.

The next writ is by Alexander III., addressed to Alexander de Montfort, Sheriff of Elgin, commanding him to make diligent and faithful inquest, by good, true, and free men of the country, that is of

[1] Acts of Parliament, A.D. 1259, i. p. 88.

his rural sheriffdom, and by the best and most faithful of the burgesses of Elgin, concerning a right which Robert Spink, the crossbowman—*Spinc, balistarius*—claims to have, by reason of Margaret, his wife, to the King's garden of Elgin, and to the lands belonging to the same garden. It is dated 13th August, the thirteenth year of the King's reign, that is 1261.

The inquest takes place on Saturday next before the decollation of St. John the Baptist—the decollation, you know, is the 29th August—in the year 1261, in the full court of the Sheriff, Alexander de Montfort. The jury consists of twelve men, half barons, half burgesses, but intermixed apparently without design of giving precedence to the barons. Two of the jury are thanes, and I observe that they are placed first, before the Provost of Elgin. The assize find that the ancestors of the said Margaret, during all their lives, possessed the said garden and land in peace, and died vest and seized, as of fee and heritage—*ut de feodo et hereditate*—and their service therefor was to find cabbages and garlic—*olera et allia*, for the King's kitchen, when the King stayed in the castle of Elgin; and if it happened that the King brought any falcon or goss-hawk there, the ancestors of the said Margaret were to receive one penny a day for the food of the goss-hawk, and twopence for the food of each gerfalcon, and should have a chalder of oatmeal annually for taking care of the birds—for which cause, say the jury, the said garden and the said land ought to descend to the said Margaret and her heirs, as of fee and heritage, according to the law of the land —*secundum assisam terre*, according to what the witnesses had sworn. You will observe in this case that the verdict is against the King, or against some of his officers, who wanted to oust Margaret and her husband.[1]

Here is another brief of the same reign, nearly of the same date: Alexander King of Scots, to Eimer de Maxwell, Sheriff, and his bailies of Peebles. We command you to make inquiry by good and faithful, free and lawful men of the country—*per probos, fideles, liberos et legales homines patrie*, whether Robert Cruik keeps by force our petary of Waltamshope from the burgesses of Peebles, which they allege was given to them by our father and ourselves, and whether the said Robert has ploughed, or in any other manner occupied our land, and the common pasture of our said burgesses. It is a good issue, and the jurymen confine themselves nearly to it, returning this verdict. They say upon their oath that the burgesses cut their peats in the petary of Waltamshope, and that the said Robert violently cut and broke the said peats, and impeded

---

[1] Acts of Parliament, A.D. 1262, vol. i. p. 90.

them from carrying them away; and that he took one horse with heather, and still detains the price of the horse, which is four shillings, and the price of the heather, which is one penny, as his escheat, saying that it is his escheat, because they had pulled the said heather in his common. And the said burgesses took the price of the said horse and heather to borch and pledge—*ad vadium et ad plegium*, that they could not have them, because he said it was his escheat. Further, the jury said that the same Robert Cruik had built his hall where the men of our lord the King used to common, and also ploughed upon the common of Peebles. As Clerk of Court, I should have no difficulty in writing out the verdict "for the pursuers."

Another interesting document of the same kind, is the brief and retour of the inquest concerning the succession of Dugald of Lennox, which carries back to the reign of Alexander III., a very simple and accurate form of jury trial.[1]

Even from the Justiciar, as well as from all inferior courts, lay an appeal or falsing of dome to the Supreme Court or King's Council, which gradually grew, you know, into a yet greater jurisdiction, as the Court of Parliament. It has been asserted by a high authority that Parliament, as a court of justice, had only an appellate, and no

[1] Chartulary of Paisley, p. 191.

original jurisdiction. In later times, when we have a full record of the proceedings of Parliament, the judicial work was performed entirely by a committee elected for the purpose—*electi ad causas et querelas—auditores causarum et querelarum*,[1] and a considerable body of the causes tried in that committee during the reigns of James III. and James IV., is preserved and published in the same shape with the Acts of the Parliaments of Scotland. It happened with us as in England, that although Parliament was looked to as the great judicial body of the kingdom, yet a Court of high authority continued to sit and act under the name of the King's Council, and for a considerable time appeals were heard and lawsuits determined by both these Courts—the judicial Committee of Parliament and the King's Council sitting at the same time—apparently often in the same chamber, and with the same clerks and officers of court. The actual judges were no doubt often the same, and I have seen traces of processes taken from the King's Council to the Parliament.

A separate volume is printed of the proceedings of the Council and their judgments in civil cases during the reigns of James III. and IV.,[2] under the title of *Acta Dominorum Concilii domini regis*.

[1] A.D. 1466-94.   [2] A.D. 1478-1495.

These concurrent jurisdictions and the want of trained lawyers in either Court, with the uncertain times of the sittings of both, led to the establishment of the Court of Session in 1532, which, beginning with great unpopularity, and deserving the condemnation that it met with at the time, has lived down that censure, and has become the worthy rival of the learned judicatures of England in their purest time.

It is well known, says Daines Barrington,[1] that there is no legal argument which has such force in our courts of law as those which are drawn from the words of ancient writs, and that the *Registrum brevium* is therefore looked upon to be the very foundation of the common-law; and he quotes for his authority Sir Edward Coke, who supposes that the Register of Writs is the most ancient book in the English law.

Even without that, we cannot but look with interest upon these writs, which show us the earliest subjects of controversy, and the original manner of obtaining redress in the King's Courts. Seen by the light of these original brieves, with their verdicts attached to them, we can better appreciate the value of those collections found in our old MS. law books, headed "Brevia," written as styles for use—styles, that is, for the royal precepts to form the foun-

[1] Barrington, p. 126.

dation of civil suits, and bring them into court. Our collections of styles of *Brevia* have not been printed. Mr. Dickson has been good enough to make fine copies for me of the two most important ancient collections from the Ayr and the Bute MSS.

You will not expect me, in a lecture like the present, to give you a detailed account of these writs, the foundation of all civil process of old; but let me try to convey to you some idea of the subjects about which men went to law in the old time; and then see with what precision and in what nice terms the various proceedings are set forth.

I pass by the common actions for compelling payment of debts, for compelling implement of contracts—the brieves of mortancestry, of novel diseisin, of recognition, of perambulation, brieves of partition, of ward; and I come to one that was in constant demand, the brief *de nativis et fugitivis*, and you have the whole law to be drawn from the words of this brief. It runs in the name of the King, addressed to justiciars, sheriffs, provosts, and their bailies, commanding them that wherever the bailies or attorneys of I. de B., the bearer of the present writ, shall find his native and fugitive men —*nativos et fugitivos homines*—outwith the king's lordship, burghs and wards, who ought to be his, of law and reason—*qui sui esse debent de jure et ratione*—of his lands, or of the land of R., that they shall have the said natives for inhabiting the said lands, and no one is to withhold them upon the King's full forfeiture. Observe, first, that the natives were to be *nativi sui*, or *nativi de terra sua*, as the English lawyers have it, *neyfs in gross*, or *neyfs regardant*, slaves to their master, or serfs bound to the soil. Secondly, the King's writ does not infringe the protection given by his own domains, his own royal burghs, or wardlands within which no man might seize fugitives on a general warrant.

The next brief is not a commencement of law pleadings; it is rather a stop to all such. It is a style of a royal writ, however, in common use. The King in the simplest terms declares that he has made R., who was his slave and native man—*servus et nativus homo noster*—a *free* man, a "Frank," as the emancipated villein in England loved to call himself.

In the time of these venerable styles churchmen still looked to the State and to the King's courts for recovering their rights, and even for enforcing the jurisdiction of the Church. In one of them the King commands his justiciars, sheriffs, and other officers to compel payment to churchmen of the rents, duties, etc.—*de redditibus canis, etc.*

In another the King commands his officers to imprison those in their bailiaries and burghs who have been for forty days or more under the greater excommunication by sentence of the bishop or official, despising the keys of Holy Mother Church, and to compel them to satisfy God and the Church. Another brief of the King commanded his civil officers to seize and to deliver over to their ecclesiastical superiors apostatizing members of religious fraternities.

But while thus stretching out the civil arm to enforce the jurisdiction of the Church, our sovereigns drew the line and boundary of that jurisdiction. One brief, addressed to archdeacon or dean, prohibits them from entertaining in their courts a plea respecting a lay fee held of the King *in capite*, seeing that that belongs to the King's Court; and a similar writ is directed to an abbot. The next writ is addressed to a bishop or his commissary; and the King writes thus: " A. has complained to us that B. prosecutes him in the Consistorial Court before you, concerning a lay tenement—*super laico tenemento*—for which he does *forinsec* service—the cognition of which ought to pertain to our royal Court—wherefore we command, etc. Next, in a similar cause, a writ is addressed to the lieges to compel the contumacious prosecutor in the court of Christianity to desist from his prosecution by distraining of goods, etc.

We find all the initiatives of giving and taking and recovering seisin, of fixing the amount of dowry, terce and tutory, and we have others not now so well known. The King addresses his writ to the relatives and friends of B., commanding them to relieve him in the poverty into which he has fallen, and to free him from the fine which he incurred for the death of a certain person imputed to him; "each of you according to that belongs to you—*quantum ad eadem pertinet*, as was the custom in the time of King David."

Again the King commands his sheriff to make inquiry whether A., the bearer of the present writ, from the inconsiderate heat of anger, and not by *murthir* nor *forethoct felony*, killed B., and whether B. gave occasion to his death, and how far, and what were the circumstances. That and most of the brieves addressed to the sheriff were for making inquisition *per bonos et fideles patrie non suspectos*, and the first duty of the sheriff was to proclaim the writ in his court, and then to empannel an assize for trying it, and for making answers to the points of the brief.

I shall now lay before you the steps of procedure, which are minutely described in the brief of right

—perhaps at one time the most common of all the brieves. First, within burgh, the brief is presented to the bailies in full court, which is opened in such manner that a small piece of the seal shall stick at the tag of the brief, so as to mark its authenticity. When the brief is formally read, the bailies shall order their serjeant and a witness to go to the dwelling-house of the wrong-doer, and summon him to appear before the bailies on a day named, and to answer to the charge contained in the brieve. No other excuse for the defender's absence from Court on the day specified will be accepted, than that he is bedridden, or engaged in the King's service, or going to a fair; and if absent from any other cause, the pursuer will ask the Court to give judgment in his favour. If the defender appears in Court on the day specified, the pursuer's counsel will challenge him thus: Thou defender who stands there, the pursuer who stands here says to thee, and I for his part, that thou unjustly deforces one rood of land [it is most minutely described], as the said brief of the King more fully bears.

The defender shall answer: My Lord Bailie, the defender who stands here denies every word of the charge, and all the right of the said pursuer in the said subjects. The defender shall then ask sight of the brief, to be advised in the premises, and on receiving it, he shall leave the Court and seek counsel. When he appears again in Court, he should as before deny the right of the pursuer, state his exceptions either to the brief or to the right of the pursuer, or he may demand to see the ground in dispute, or he may put off till a day and term to call his warrant.

One brief *in re mercatoria* is remarkable, and it would be very important, historically, if we could fix more precisely its date. The King, addressing the great customers of a burgh, commands that any merchant arriving at their ports who can prove by letters of cocquet that they have paid the due custom in England, shall not be obliged to pay a second custom, and *that* so long as Scotch merchants have similar privilege in English ports.

Take next two brieves in rural matters. By the first, which is entitled against " scabbed sheep," the King directs the sheriff to inquire as to the existence of the disease called " pilsoucht " among sheep, and to slay forthwith those infected—to stamp out the pestilence, as we should say, and to allow none to be moved beyond their own pasture without special license. Another writ is a style of a royal precept for speedy justice against unfair fishing of salmon. It is general and summary enough. The King sets forth the destruction of fish by cruives throughout the kingdom, and commands the sheriff to destroy forthwith all cruives upon waters within his sheriffdom, and to permit none of them to be repaired.

Everything was in favour of the band of lawyers —experienced, learned, zealous, not only for their own court, but to maintain the superiority of the spiritual power in everything. Everything was in their favour but one. Our Scotch kings, from William the Lion to Alexander III., maintained vigorously the jurisdiction of the civil magistrate, and even when that great race had gone, and when public feeling, as well as the prosperity of Scotland, had been much lowered by continual war, some of our Stewart kings still acted upon the old tradition. I take an instance from a private charter-chest in the reign of James IV. A dispute had arisen between the Bishop of Moray and the Roses of Kilravock about certain marches, which was submitted to arbitration; and it would appear that the Bishop was proceeding to enforce the decreet-arbitral in the ecclesiastical Court, when the King interfered in this manner: He sends a mandate to his sheriffs of the county, setting forth that the King was informed that the reverend father in God, Andrew, Bishop of Moray, tends by censure of Holy Kirk, and by force, to compel the opposite party to consent to the perambulating of the lands by certain pretended commissioners, without any brieves cognisable of the King's chapel, notwithstanding that the lands of the lay party were held of the Crown, and the sheriffs are ordered to cause the Bishop to desist and cease from such ecclesiastical procedure, and from any attempt to perambulate the lands except by brieves of perambulation of the King's chapel, under all the highest pains and charge that may follow.

Nevertheless the Bishop, at his own hand, and in contraire to the command of the King's letters, persisted in acting in his own Court; whereupon the King sends more peremptory order to the Bishop himself to cease from all troubling of the Roses, and from impediment making to them in brooking of their old heritage of Kilravock.

Consider the amount of business arising from the proper jurisdiction of the ecclesiastical Court. The Bishop's official was the only judge in matters of *status*—legitimacy, bastardy, divorce. He was kind enough to take charge of the affairs of widows, orphans, and all *personæ miserabiles*—all questions of slander, all disputes between churchmen, the whole management of Notaries Public, questions arising upon covenant where the covenant was sanctioned by an oath (and what covenant of old wanted that sanction?), the large class of business connected wills, testaments, probates, executry—in a word, of all moveable succession, and perhaps of succession in heritage, for there was a time when Scotch heritage could be left by will. In addition to all these you must take into account the business brought into their Courts by consent of parties, and add to that all the influence of all the notaries, the largest class of "men of business," as we call them, and who were all churchmen or dependents of churchmen, and so preferring the ecclesiastical courts. I say, when you consider all this, you need not be surprised that the business in the Officials' Courts of Glasgow, St Andrews, Edinburgh, was larger and of more importance than the business transacted in all the Sheriff Courts, where there were, you know, no lawyers, and greater also than the King's Council or the Judicial Committee of Parliament, with its occasional sittings, could ever have transacted.

I told you that the Consistorial Court took care of the cases not only of the widow and the orphan, but of all the *miserabiles personæ*—all the poor who could not buy the help of lawyers. That is the foundation of jurisdiction in a fable of Henryson's, which, with your leave, I mean to tell you, as the best account we have of the jurisdiction and form of process in the Consistorial Court. You know Robert Henryson held office as teacher of the Abbey School in the great Monastery of Dunfermline. He was not a churchman, or at least not in orders; but when you have listened to my fable, you will not doubt that he had had some experience in the Consistorial Court.

My fable is called "The Tale of the Dog, the Sheep, and the Wolf."[1]

[1] See Appendix.

LECTURE VI.

RURAL OCCUPATION.

THE earliest information we have of rural matters is from the Registers of the great religious houses; for the monastery was the great cultivator of lands as well as improver of the arts; and the very oldest connected description of rural tenancy, rents and culture, is from a rental of Kelso, of 1290. The date is worth noting, because it shows us that the state of things described in the rental must have been put in shape and methodized before the end of that prosperous time, the reigns of the Alexanders. The monks had immense territories, which they still for the most part held in their own hands, *in dominico*, and cultivated from their several granges. Their lands were measured in plough-gates, husband-lands, and oxgates, where the land was arable, and by the number of sheep maintained, where pasture. The oxgate, or what effeired to the cultivation of one ox, "where pleuch and scythe may gang," was thirteen acres, in the Merse and Teviotdale. The *husbandus* or cultivator who kept two oxen for the common plough and possessed two oxgates, had of course twenty-six acres, and that amount was called a *husband-land*. Four *husbandi*—neighbours—I think generally joint tenants—working their common plough, their whole possession was a ploughgate; that is, the quantity of land tilled by eight oxen, or 104 acres. These joint tenants were bound to keep good neighbourhood, and the rules were strictly enforced.

On their land in the valley the monks reared oats, barley, and wheat, as their successors do. They got hay from their pasture-lands by *haining* (as we say) a portion of natural grass on marsh or meadow. You will observe that made a late hay harvest compared with our sown grass—for the ballad of "Chevy Chase" tells us the famous battle

"Fell upon the Lammas tide
When marchmen win their hay."

They had waggons for their harvest, and wains of some sort for bringing peats from the moss and over-sea commodities from Berwick, which implies that there were roads passable for such carriages; but indeed we have evidence of the existence of such roads in that country a good deal earlier, as early as the time of William the Lion; and it is worth noting the mention of king's high roads in the time of the Alexanders, through all Scotland, from Berwick to Inverness, although it may be doubted whether these were in all cases roads for wheel-carriages, or not rather in many cases only for horses, whether for saddle or pack-horses. At the date of the rental the monks had large flocks of sheep, as much as a thousand ewes upon one farm; and there are careful provisions for shifting their pasture ground in summer and winter. Wool was the great produce of their estates, convertible into money. It does not seem that they sold either corn, sheep and cattle, or the remaining produce, the fish of their river.

These particulars are gathered of a state of occupancy previously. But to come to the period of the "Rotulus reddituum"[1] itself, we find the "grange," or farm-stead of the abbey, the chief house in each barony or estate. In it were gathered the cattle, implements, stores needed for the cultivation of their domain lands or mains, the *nativi*, serfs or carles who cultivated it, and their women and families. Some monk of the abbey occasionally looked after the grange, but the proper steward was a lay brother, or *conversus*, who dwelt there, and rendered his accounts to the cellarer of the monastery.

Of the inhabitants of the grange the lowest in the scale was the *nativus*, neyf or villein of the English law, who was transferred like the land which

[1] A.D. 1290.

he laboured, and might be caught and brought back if he attempted to escape, like a runaway ox or sheep. Outside the grange, but near it, dwelt the cottars, *cottarii*, a class a good deal above that which we call *cottars*, for each occupant had from one to nine acres of land along with his cottage, for which they paid rent, although perhaps that word was unknown; but they paid, nevertheless, some money and services in seed-time and harvest. Beyond the mains and the hamlet, or cottar town, lived each in his separate farm-stead—the *husbandi*, or husbandmen, holding each a definite quantity of land called a *husband-land*, and, as I have already said, *four* of these united their oxen to work the common plough of the ploughgate. As a fair specimen of the footing on which the husbandmen held their land, I will tell you the rent and services due on the barony of Bolden.

The monks had there twenty-eight husband-lands, that is, seven ploughgates, each paying 6s. 8d., or half a mark of money rent: four days' reaping in harvest—the husband with his wife and all their family; one day carrying peats: the service of a man and horse to and from Berwick once a year. A horse-load was three bolls of corn, or two bolls of salt, or one and a half bolls of coals, or somewhat less in winter when the ways were bad. The husbandman was further bound to plough an acre and a half, and to give a day's harrowing with one horse; to find a man at sheep-washing and one for sheep-shearing; to serve with a waggon one day for carrying home the harvest. All were bound, as primary duty, to carry the abbot's wool to the abbey, and to find carriages across the moor to Lesmahago. The service, and I daresay the rent also, were heavy enough; but then, as in England still, the Church was a fair and merciful landlord. It is worthy of remark that no farm service is imposed on women except harvest work, and also that all services at the period of the rental were in process of being commuted for money-rent —a remarkable step of progress. The writer of the Rental speaks of the vestiges of an ancient practice which he calls *stuht*, plainly equivalent to our ancient practice of *steel-bow*.[1]

The rental which I have been using was the title by which the abbey levied its rents, and by which its husbandmen or tenants held their lands. They were the kindly tenants of the Church lords, and had many privileges, as well as a certain fixity of tenure.

---

[1] A custom described by Lord Stair as "goods set with lands upon these terms, that the like number of goods shall be restored at the issue of the tack." I think the practice can be traced back to Anglo-Saxon times, and even its name is not peculiar to Scotland, but is found in the *eisern vieh* of Germany, and the *beste de fer—bestia ferri* — in French and old Latin.

A tenant of a superior class held his land by charter and seisin; he held it in perpetuity, and could not be ejected. His tenement was small, and he gave services and a rent by no means elusory —sometimes paying for half a plough eight shillings of money-rent. Above these, again, the great Church vassals held a place only second to the barons and freeholders of the Crown. Their tenure was in a manner baronial, though holding of the abbey. They held their lands free of all predial service, and had the abbot's license to hold courts of *bloodwit* and *byrthensak*—assault with bloodshed, and theft which the thief could carry off on his shoulder, and petty causes. They had "merchet" for the marriage of their vassals' daughters, and paid to the abbot merchet for the marriage of their own. In the very earliest of the charters of the abbey, long before the Rental that I have been quoting to you, we find grants concerning mills, minute regulations for order and precedency at the mill, and a strict thirlage established. At the period of the Rental the mill of Bolden, with its thirlage, was rented at eight merks yearly. Four brewing-houses were let for ten shillings each, and were bound to supply ale to the abbey at the rate of a gallon and a half for a penny. Each fire-house of the barony paid a hen at Christmas, which was worth a halfpenny. Although a money rent is more apt to mislead us than payments in produce and services, yet it is worth noting that the lands of Abbots-Selkirk, a plough and a half of land, had given ten merks of silver rent.

Alexander II. granted to the monks the land held by Richard, son of Edwin, on both banks of the Ettrick, for the maintenance of the bridge, which may have been of timber;[1] and such a grant serves to mark the civilisation and progress of the period. There are other bridges noticed over smaller streams, some of them in the middle of the thirteenth century, stated to be of stone, and all of them calculated for the passage of heavy waggons and carts.

An inquisition held at Bolden in 1327, for determining the boundaries of the ploughgate of land in Priestfield, found that it was part of the territory of Bolden, and was given to be held by four husbandmen, and that it was wont to find one man at arms, who ought to be the captain of thirty bowmen —*architenentium*—found from the barony of Bolden, for the king's army.[2] As with Priestfield and its barony of Bolden, the other tenants and vassals of the abbey were no doubt bound to relieve the monks of the military and other public services.

The wealthy abbey and its monks, themselves employed in agriculture, and enlightened land-

---

[1] Kelso, No. 395.   [2] Kelso, No. 471.

holders, have probably left us the best specimen of the tenures, rents, services, and general condition of the agricultural classes of the best period of our national prosperity—for Scotland had never been so prosperous as under William the Lion and the two Alexanders; but we find marks of some methodical arrangement of estates and rules of cultivation soon after the date of the Kelso Rental.

The earliest lease of lands approaching to what we call an agricultural lease that I know, is a contract between the Abbot of Scone and the Hays of Leys—neighbouring lairds, not properly of the class of cultivators or agricultural tenants. The lease is more remarkable as containing perhaps our oldest specimen of *Scots* in interlined glossings or translations of its terms; but it is also of some importance for our present purpose. The date is 1312—two years, you see, before Bannockburn. The abbot sets the lands of Balgarvie with all their pertinents, and by the same boundaries by which husbandmen—*husbandi*—used to hold them *in ferme*. The lease is for thirty years, the rent at first two marks, rising a mark *per annum* for six years, six marks from the sixth to the twelfth year, eight marks from the twelfth to the twentieth year, and ten marks from the twentieth to the thirtieth year. The Hays themselves are to give suit—*facere sectam*

—in the three head Courts of the abbot yearly; and their *husbandi*, the real cultivators of the soil, to give suit at *all* the abbot's Courts in the barony of Scone. The Hays are bound to the mill of the abbot, and to pay the twenty-fourth measure for multure, besides knaveship. The husbandmen and their cottars are to pay the sixteenth measure of all kinds of corn for multure like the other husbandmen and natives—*husbandi et nativi*—of the abbey, and to take their share in the making and upholding of the mill. The Hays are to do the king's military service, and to bear all the other burdens of the land during their term. They and their men dwelling on the land are to have fuel from the common for their own use only, and which they may neither give away nor sell. Small quarrels emerging between the Hays and their men are to be decided among themselves; but greater disputes, such as belong to the lord, are to be reserved for the abbot's Court. The covenant concludes with two remarkable provisions:—(1.) That if it should happen that the King revoke his gift of the land from the abbey, the Hays and their husbandmen shall quit without payment of their rent of the year of their quitting; (2.) The Hays are to make suitable buildings for themselves and their husbandmen, which are to be so left at the end of their term. There is here no prohibition of sub-letting, as we find in similar covenants, which prohibit sub-tenancy—*exceptis cottariis.*

The next Rental I have noted is that of the Bishopric of Aberdeen, dated 1511—perhaps the most intelligible and consistent of these old rentals, but I have no time to describe it. A large part of the Bishopric's revenue seems to have been derived from the parish of Clatt, situated in the western extremity of the Garioch. The conditions on which Robert Blak held the haugh of Bolgie are very instructive, and might furnish a lesson to many a landlord in our own time. He pays only twenty shillings for a ploughgate of land, and it is declared that he obtains it at such a low rate because the lands have but lately been reduced to culture. He is bound, however, to build three outsets, which must be inhabited by himself or his dependants within a time specified, and, failing in that condition, he loses his tenure. The lands of Clatt were divided into ten tenements, each consisting of little less than three ploughgates of land. The number of tenants was about forty, so that each tenant held on an average about five oxgates of land. Most farms were held by several tenants in joint tenancy. The average rent of a ploughgate may be thus stated:—£3, 7s. 9d. in silver maill, the grassum generally one year's rent; 1s. 8d. for bondage (*pro bondagio*, meaning commuted services), one firlot of oats, one firlot of malt, one firlot of meal, a quarter of a mart, one mutton, a quarter of a kid, five capons, seven domestic fowls, four muir fowls, along with a pig from the mill, and two stones of cheese from one pastoral holding.

Fethirnyr, another division of the lands of this Bishopric, shows the conditions under which sub-letting was permitted on this great estate. A crofter was bound to build one rood of the fold for every cow which he had in the town of his master. The tenants were answerable for the conduct of their crofters in the grazing of their cows, and in other things that belonged to good neighbourhood. There were fourteen crofters or sub-tenants on this holding, besides the tenants proper. The average rent payable by each crofter is 9s. 9d. in silver maill, one firlot of barley, ten fowls. No grassum appears to have been exacted from these small holders, and so we may safely infer that they were tenants at will. A profitable source of revenue in this barony were the mills, which paid a rent often as high as £4 each.

As an example of the tastes of the clergy, overlords, we find that the forest of Glenrinnes was not let out like Keithbeg, of which it was a part, but was reserved, along with its foggage, " to my lord " — no doubt for my lord's rural enjoyment or sport. The tenants were bound to build houses on their farms; and in two cases they were allowed to *retain* and apply part of the rent for that object. A very common service which was performed by the tenants in the district of Birss was the carriage of wood, indicating the abundance of wood in that quarter. *Good neighbourhood* is stipulated on the part of the tenant, under forfeiture of his right. This was rendered more necessary by the system of common and joint holdings—running, we may believe, often into "runrig," that fertile source of quarrels among cultivators of the soil. The foggage of the Bishop's forest of Birss, that is, I suppose, both its pasture and game, is let along with a good many farms adjoining to a neighbouring gentleman, at a rent which was probably below the value. We should judge so, if from nothing else, from the circumstance of the tack being set with the solemn consent of the chapter; but this might apply to other questionable terms of the lease, which was granted for nineteen years—apparently much longer than the country practice, and which included sub-tenants and assignees.[1] A curious item in these payments in kind is the return made from the farm of Dulsak. Finlay Reauch, the tenant, pays evidently at his entry a grassum of 26s. 8d., and a rent in silver maill of

---

[1] The tenant was a kinsman of the Bishop—Elphinston of Selmys.

26s. 8d.; besides, he is bound to furnish four dozen plates, four dozen dishes, four dozen salvers, eight *lie* chargers, and four great basins. These utensils he is bound to manufacture of dry wood, and not of green wood, under pain of the forfeiture of his right. Mr. Reauch evidently exercised the trade of a *mugger*. His wares were turned, but not the " beechen bowl "—they were probably of birch or plane. I fear the old manufacture is extinct.

On the lands of Fetternear (on Don side) the meadow and hay—*pratum et fenum*—are reserved to the bishop, and the tenants of the lordship are bound to guard them from all animals, whether their own or others, from Easter to Michaelmas; and when the hay was cut, they were to win it and cock it, and my lord was to pay only for the cutting of it. The forest and fishing of Fetternear were reserved for the bishop in like manner. The fishing reserved would go to show that the cruives on Don were not an absolute impediment to the salmon in those days.

The bishop was lord of the forestry of Birss, from which he drew some money rents and a little corn; but some part of the parish was then, as now, covered with growth of natural wood; and the bishop has from many of the farms six loads of wood, *sex onera lignorum*,[1] which, I think, means logs

[1] Horace used the same word (1 Ep. xiv. 42).

or billets for the fire. The tenant of the foggage of the forest pays four bolls of nuts, small hazel nuts, which are still produced in those glens, and are much in request at all the village fairs.

The next definite description that I have met with of rural tenures is after no long interval. There is preserved in Lord Forbes's charter-room a rental of the old Forbes property made up in the year 1532.[1] The land here also is divided into ploughs, each of eight oxen. The ploughgate of land is sometimes let to four tenants, each of whom contributed the work of his pair of oxen to the common plough. These joint tenants were bound to keep *good neighbourhood*, that is, to perform their respective shares of the farm labour at the sight of umpires called "birleymen," chosen by themselves.

Let me say something of this rural officer chosen by the people. I think he is not yet extinct in some Northern districts—not forgotten anywhere in Scotland. The birleymen were the arbiters— the referees in rural differences—between tenants of the same estate. The settlement of the rights of outgoing and incoming tenants, of the value of meliorations, and all such matters, was in their hands for the most part; and in the old time, to dispute the award of the birleyman left a stain on a man's character. The rent is sometimes in money,

---

[1] Forbes Rental, 1532.

but more frequently in victual. The Castle-hill of Druminnor — a plough of land — a situation not favoured by climate, if I remember—is let to four tenants for forty bolls victual. The farm of Buthny, in the parish of Forbes—one plough—is let for thirty-eight bolls victual. One plough of Kirktown of Forbes—you will find the *terra ecclesiastica* often the best land—was let to two tenants at a rent of twenty-seven bolls one firlot common victual, and four bolls wheat. Sillavathie, containing two ploughs, and let to three tenants, is rented at fifty bolls of victual. Four ploughs at Carndard are let for a money-rent of £8, 18s. 8d. One plough of Cushny is let for a money-rent of £2, 4s. 8d. In the parish of Forbes, the farm of Logie, containing two ploughs, and divided among four tenants, is rented £6, 13s. 4d. Stralouing, two ploughs, is rented at £8, with a grassum of £8. In addition to these rents, whether payable in kind or in money, there were somewhat heavy custom dues, a wedder or two, many capons and poultry, leits of peats, and for the mill, swine, swine and geese, and certain services, such as three days' ploughing of all the strength. You will find over the whole rental that the average rent in victual is 32 bolls for every ploughgate, and the average rent where in money varies from £2 to £3.

Let me observe that in this rental there is no

appearance of a servile class. The *nativi* had before this time, all through Scotland, been enfranchised or absorbed into the free population. Like other ancient possessions, they were still found in the lord's charters, but the last process which I have met with for claiming a neyf, was in the Court of the Sheriff of Banffshire in 1364, when Alexander, Bishop of Moray, having sued out a brief from the King's chapel, obtained the verdict of an assize, finding that Robert, Nevyn, and Donald were the natives and liege men of the said Lord Bishop and the Church of Moray, and his property.[1]

After another considerable interval, we have a very minute account of the management, tenures, and rents and customs of the great estates of the noble family of Gordon in the northern counties.[2] Beginning at the Enzie on the Banff coast, the Gordon territory at that time, went in a broad stripe through Strathbolgy, Strathspey, Badenoch, and Lochaber to the west sea. This rental shows us the agricultural holdings—very often about two ploughgates each—set to eight tenants in joint occupancy, each holding two oxgangs, and contributing two oxen to the common plough.

The payments, like the labour, were in common.

---

[1] Registrum Moraviense, p. 161. In England the lord could not prosecute for more than two villains in one *Nativo Habendo.*

[2] Gordon Rental, A.D. 1600, Spalding Club.

A very small sum was paid in money, distinguished as *maill* or *silver-maill*. Next come certain bolls of oatmeal and bear, which is always distinguished as *ferme*—that is, the real and solid part of the rent, producing on a barony of moderate extent such a quantity of oatmeal and bear fit for malting as to require distinct barns for holding the lord's share.

Under the head of "customs" are included several commodities in small quantities. These are generally a *mart* or ox to be killed at Martinmas, two or three wedders or muttons, as many lambs, grice or young pigs, geese, capons and poultry, chickens, eggs, and almost universally the ancient tax of a *reek hen*, or a hen for every fire-house. A very little tallow is paid from the alehouse of the barony, and there are customs of butter and cheese in very small quantities. Besides these commodities for the kitchen, the low-country farms often pay a few ells of cloth, not of *wool*, but linen cloth of three-quarters broad for my lady's napery. I observe it might be commuted at ten shillings an ell.

Let me give you a few specimens of the rental. The farm of Wttingstone in the parish of Dunbenane in Strathbogy was set for five years from 1600. It consisted of two ploughs, and was held by three tenants, one of whom held eight oxgangs, and the other two each four oxgangs. They paid a ferme victual of 4 chalders, 8 bolls, and 12 bolls custom meal, 4 wedders, 2 dozen chickens, a reek hen for every fire-house, and a leit of peats.

Take another farm. Kirktown of Cabrach, measuring one plough of land, was set for a money-rent of 40 pounds maill and 2 stone of butter; no *ferme* is payable from this tenancy, and the Cabrach is still better adapted for dairy than corn cultivation.

Now to notice a much wilder country. In Lochaber the tenancy is measured in marklands. Mamoir in Lochaber measures 40 marklands, and every markland pays to my lord "tua markis." The land is possessed by Allan Macolduy. I suppose he is the head of the clan Cameron—the Locheil of his day. Gargavach consists of 40 marklands, but it pays only 40 marks. Glenavis is a ten markland, and pays only ten marks; but I think these rents cannot be taken as the value of the holdings, but probably as some remainder of an old compact between the Gordons and Camerons.

In Badenoch we have again the measurement by ploughs. Kingussie Beig was four ploughs, and paid yearly £5, 6s. 8d. of money maill; and of custom two marts, two wedders, eight poultry, each tenant (the number not given) paying a kid or a lamb, with "areadge and careadge" and due service.

I observe through all the lordship of Badenoch

a small money-rent, which I told you was not the case so commonly in the low country. Even now the harvest is very uncertain in Badenoch, and the landlord chose to have the cattle produce in money, except such marts as he could consume himself.

The most prominent items in the rental of the lordships of Huntlie and Enzie are the *silver maill* and *ferm victual*,—Huntly paying yearly in silver maill a sum of £1777, 3s. and of ferme victual 2385 bolls. Enzie, making a return yearly of £462, 16s. 8d. in silver maill, and of ferme victual 968 bolls, 2 firlots, $2\frac{1}{2}$ pecks. From the lordship of Badenoch, a rent of £261, 2s. 10d. was obtained, while only 173 bolls of ferme victual seems to have been paid, and *that* from one parish only, Skearalvey. A large quantity of bear was paid in multure in the lordship of Badenoch, and stands a fair comparison with that derived from the lordship of Huntly—the former returning 185 bolls $2\frac{1}{2}$ pecks ; the latter 218 bolls, 3 firlots. Wheat is to be found only once in this rental. It formed a small item in the return made as ferme victual by the lordship of Enzie. Badenoch being a pastoral country, makes a great return in marts, the number being $92\frac{5}{8}$. Huntly comes next, its number being being $42\frac{3}{4}$, and Enzie last, the number being $21\frac{1}{8}$. Huntly again makes a return of $167\frac{3}{4}$ gryse—the other lordships making no return in this species of revenue. Capons, geese, poultry, chickens, and eggs also form a considerable item in the revenue, more especially in the lordship of Huntly. In the lordship of Enzie a quantity of *brew* tallow was paid. This duty seems to have been specially exigible from alehouses, one of which appears to have been attached to every farm in this lordship.

But to enable you to judge more definitely of the difference in rents between a Highland and a Lowland country, I shall take as good specimens the parishes of Kingussie and Bellie.

In the parish of Kingussie there are altogether 23 holdings, each generally held by several joint-tenants. There are 73 ploughgates, 4 mills, with their crofts, and the return is as follows:—

Maills in money,	£110.
Multer,	73 bolls 2 firlots.
Ferme,	173 bolls.
Teynd,	8 bolls.
Marts,	$33\frac{1}{2}$
Mutton,	$33\frac{1}{2}$ wedders.
Lambs or kids,	22.
Capons,	12.
Poultry,	146.
Butter,	1 stone.
Cheese,	2 stones.

You may take a rough average of the rent of

this parish per ploughgate—the ploughgate being the work of 8 oxen, that is equal to eight times 13 acres Scotch, or 104 acres.

Taking the average, then, in the parish of Kingussie, every ploughgate paid as follows :—£1, 1s. 1d. of silver maill ; one boll of multure ; two bolls, one firlot of ferme ; two pecks of teind ;[1] half a mart ; a third of a lamb ; one-sixth of a capon ; two poultry fowls ; also a small portion of butter and cheese, and everywhere "areadge and careadge and due service," which I can only explain as the carriage required for my lord's house, and the agricultural service at seed-time and harvest.

Turning now to the parish of Bellie, which is in the lowest part of the lordship of Enzie, I have summed the whole of the farms, and the different items exigible from the tenants in the name of rent, and I find there are about thirty ploughgates in this parish, and the aggregate rent may thus be stated :—

Silver Maill,	£72.
Ferme victual,	590 bolls, 2 fir., 3 pecks.
Multer bear,	39 bolls, 2 firlots.
Marts,	$8\frac{5}{8}$.

[1] Here you will observe a small payment under the name of teinds. I do not know the state of the Gordon investitures at that time, but I suppose the Earl of Huntly had a tack of teinds, conveying to him the whole parsonage and vicarage teinds of his estate at a fixed rent, and he levied the amount, no doubt, somewhat increased from the tenants, but commuted or fixed.

Muttons,	54½.
Lambs,	39½.
Swine,	4.
Capons,	259.
Geese,	44½.
Poultry,	283.
Chickens,	136.
Eggs,	1044.
Tallow,	17 stones.
Custom linen,	141 ells, 5 nails.
Salmon,	40 barrels.

You will keep in view that in this parish the rent is not derived from land alone—by far the largest item of silver maill being that derived from the fishing, and that the mills, of which there are six, with their respective crofts, and the alehouses, ten in number, contribute a proportion of the custom exactions.

By taking, again, the average rent of a ploughgate, including the rent paid for mills and alehouses, the result may approximately be thus stated:—£2, 8s. of silver maill; twenty bolls of fermo victual; one boll and a half of multer bear; one-third of a mart; two wedders; one swine; eight capons; one goose; nine poultry fowls; four chickens; thirty eggs; half a stone of butter; three ells of custom linen; one barrel of salmon.

You will remember that we calculated £1, 1s. 1d. to be the average rent of a ploughgate of land in Kingussie, whereas in the parish of Bellie the same measure of land paid £2, 8s. This difference in rents between the two parishes can only be accounted for by supposing that the patriarchal relation between the chief and his clansmen counted more in Kingussie than in Bellie, or that the two districts were in different states of agricultural improvement and occupation; or, again, that the lands of Bellie were *twice* as productive as those of Kingussie—which is the most probable reason for the difference of rents. The fishings of Bellie pay a rent of £323 in silver maill. One does not expect to find the fishings of a small north country parish yield four and a half times more in silver maill than the revenue derivable from the land. But the cruives of Spey are in Bellie.

In all that vast estate reaching from sea to sea, and across ranges of mountains—now everywhere pastured by sheep and cattle—there is no payment of wool or woollen cloth, nor of hides or skins, nor any amount of sheep and cattle, beyond the occasional mart or wedder for the lord's table.

In fact there were at that time no cattle or sheep reared in large flocks and herds in our Highlands. The space and pasture were the same as we know them now, but the thousands and millions of sheep which graze them now had not yet taken possession. The first introduction of large flocks of sheep into the Highlands was in the last quarter of last century. Gough the antiquary, writing in 1780, says that Mr. Loch's plans for introducing sheep had been "attended with some success," and that the sheep promised to thrive very well in the Highlands.

But at this time—1600—there was nothing but the petty flock of sheep or herd of a few milk-cows grazed close round the farm-house, and folded nightly for fear of the wolf or more cunning depredators.

You will observe in this rental, over a wide district of the north, and sufficiently low in the scale of cultivation, we find no difference of degree or rank except indeed what arises from the size of the farm, and except where we run into the country held in the old patriarchal manner by the chiefs of clans. I have told you elsewhere of the injustice wrought by turning these chiefs into feudal barons. Here I think they seem to have consented to hold their own possessions under the new lords for a rent. The lordship of Lochaber, as I have already told you, is thus rentalled: every markland pays to my lord two merks, and the forty markland of Maormor is noted as possessed by Allan Cameron, *Macconel dhui.*

The length of lease is generally five or six years. In cases where the old wadset was redeemed, a lease was granted of the lands for nineteen years. I need not tell you that the nineteen years' tack, now so common, was intended to define a twenty years' possession, and to avoid questions about the moving of the tenant, and the right to the way-going crop.

With these short leases of five or six years was joined a system of grassum, or what the English would call a *fine for renewal.*

The rental of the Gordon estates indicates rather than expresses that the land was mostly cultivated by recognised sub-tenants. But it tells us nothing of the different ranks and classes of these.

We learn something of this at a later period from another source. After the storm of last century had banished some of the great proprietors of Highland districts, and their estates had come to the Crown, it became necessary to inquire into the state of the population. It happened that, in 1762, the factor upon the Drummond estates in Perthshire had made some extensive clearances, removing and ejecting the inhabitants of the glens. This produced a remonstrance from the poor people, who had influence enough to have their case considered, and the factor was required to make a report upon the condition of the agricultural people and their tenures. It gives additional interest to the correspondence between Mr. Campbell and the commissioners on the annexed estates that Lord Kames, himself no mean agriculturist, took an active part in it. I have not time for the details of that correspondence, but the factor's report gives us definite information of the following classes of inhabitants. After the tenants holding by lease, and the common class of sub-tenants, he enumerates:—

1. A *Bowman*, whom he calls a hired servant of the tacksman. But we know better from other parts of the country that the bowman was, or I may say still is, a person who farms for a season the tenant's milk-cows, and the pasture to maintain them.

2. The Perth factor next mentions *Steel-bowman*, a class of tenants who received stock and cattle along with their farm. The practice is still well known in other districts, and I do not think it necessary to dwell upon it. The system of steel-bow could only come into use when the agricultural tenant, as a rule, had no capital.

3. A *Pendicler*, according to the factor, is one who has a certain small quantity of grass and corn land. The tenure is sometimes from the proprietor, sometimes from the tenant, and accordingly he pays his rent to *his* landlord.

4. The *Cottar* paid for his cottage and bit of land in services and a little money. He had no work cattle. The tacksman under whom he sat ploughed and harrowed his ground, and carted his dung to the field, and for the most part carried home his peats.

5. The *Crofter* nearly resembles the cottar, but his arable land does not change like the cottar's, who was moved about at the pleasure of the tacksman. So too the crofter differs from the pendicler, for the crofter's cattle are herded and pastured along with those of the tacksman, at least in summer and harvest.

A *dry-house Cottar* is one that has neither corn, land, nor pasture—nothing but his cottage and kail-yard.

Let us add to the statement of the Perth factor some information derived from a report on another Highland estate similarly situated. The estate of Robertson of Struan, forfeited after the '45, lies, you know, all around Loch Rannoch, a district separate and then almost inaccessible for all but a Highlander. A rental of that estate was made up in 1755, from which we have some important results. There were on the estate 138 tenants in all. The aggregate rent payable in money was £448, giving an average you see of about £2 (but you will observe that now the factor counts in *sterling* money).

The other payments in name of rent were:—
39 wedders; 87 pecks of corn; 46 thraves of straw;[1] 12 stones of cheese; 6 stones of butter; 12 veals; 80 long carriages; 288 loads of peats; 9 days of casting and leading peats. All which customs and carriages are stated by the factor to be convertible into money at £26, 7s. He values the wedder at 3s. 4d.; the veal at 3s. 4d.; a thrave of straw at 1s. 10d.; a load of peats at three half-pennies, each long carriage at 1s. 10d.; each hen and cock at $3\frac{1}{3}$d.

From the factor's report we gather that most of the inhabitants had a right of common pasture, and that there were constant quarrels about the number kept by each, which the baron-bailie referred to the adjudication of the birleymen of the district—you see how far the Saxon institution had penetrated into the Highlands—who fixed the number of cattle and sheep in proportion to the soumes (soum—a cow's grass, or equivalent): thus, a cow is one soume; a horse or mare is two soumes; six (big) sheep counting one soume; a three-year-old cow at May-day to be regarded as a big cow at the Martinmas following; a three-year-old horse or filly at May-day to enter to be one soume, and if kept after the Michaelmas following to be two soumes. Every two-year-old wedder to be looked

[1] Thrave = 24 sheaves.

upon as a big sheep at the Martinmas following.[1]

I think it appears plainly that a large part of the population of the Highlands had no written tenures, and it suited the factors of those days—the Bailie Macwheebles of the time—to represent and to treat those immemorial occupants and dwellers on the land as holding at the absolute will of the first chief who was knowing enough to obtain a Crown-charter.

I am afraid it results also that the population, at least of the Struan glens, far exceeded what the country could support with its own produce, or honestly.

The power of the chief or *laird* was measured by the number of men he could turn out under arms, and he had every inducement to maintain the full number of dwellings and inhabitants. In summer the people of the glen might exist upon the produce of their pasture lands, and there was a little corn for the beginning of winter, but for the rest of the year they must necessarily have sought

---

[1] I copy from the old Statistical Account of Bedrule a good explanation of *souming* and *rouming* :—

"It seems probable that the land *outfield* in many places was occupied in common by the proprietors or tenants in a certain district, parish, or estate, having been thereby entitled to *soum* or pasture on the outfield in summer, in proportion to the number and kinds of cattle he was thus able to *roum* or fodder in winter by means of his share of *infield* land."

sustenance elsewhere. They could not dig—to beg they were ashamed. There was a third alternative, they left their glens and *lifted*.

We find in these rentals indications of the Old Extent and its relation to the actual rent and value of the land. A plough of land consisted of 8 oxgates or 104 acres. This we found to be the measure in the Merse and Teviotdale, and it applies very well to the shires of Aberdeen, Banff, and Moray.

Now a ploughgate of land is found to have been rentalled in the old extent (which is nothing else but a rental of the times of the Alexanders) at three marks or forty shillings, and in this I think we have the foundation of the old county qualification throughout Scotland. A proprietor of a ploughgate held of the Crown had a vote for a member of Parliament, and that is expressed in parliamentary language to be a forty-shilling land of old extent.

Observe the forty-shilling land is the same as a three markland; but knowing that a forty-shilling or three markland is a ploughgate averaging 104 acres, we find that a markland ought to be on an average $34\frac{2}{3}$ acres.

The money measure of land established by the old extent of the Alexanders over all Scotland, *or else* some other money valuation and measure of land, was for some reason more used and longer preserved on the Western coast than in the more agricultural part of Scotland. I have shown you how, at the very turning of the declivity from east to west, in the great Gordon territory, and just where wind and water shears, you come from land designated by ploughgates and oxgangs to lands designated in merklands. Various reasons will suggest themselves for the difference. Among others it may seem that some agricultural enterprise was already at work by which arable land was increasing in great arable districts, and when such improvements had rendered the old rental of Scotland no longer available, the landlords and tenants were driven to a measurement available in all situations, and suiting itself to the amount of cultivation.

A *Davach* is somewhat more difficult of explanation. It was a measure of land known chiefly over the north-eastern counties. In the earliest charters of the bishopric of Moray, a very great number of the parishes of the diocese are described as having a *terra ecclesiastica* or kirkland of half a *davach* in extent. I have tried to ascertain the extent and average value of these church lands, but without success. In a cultivated country, long subsequent rents or valuations helped but little to ascertain a term of ancient measurement. I wish I could submit an etymology for the word satisfactory to you or to myself. But it has happened here as in other cases, my Gaelic oracles give no certain sound in the matter. My friend the Rev. Dr. Reeves has spared no trouble, and has brought into the field two great Celtic scholars, Mr. Stokes and Mr. Hennessy. I myself naturally lean much on Mr. Skene, but whether the word 'davach' has reference to some certain number of oxen for pasturing the land or for tilling it, or finally to be paid as rent for it—or whether it means a vat or certain liquid measure by which the produce of the field or the lord's proportion of the produce is to be measured —I am not yet in a position to assert with any confidence. So situated, I beg to leave here the etymology, and to give you in a few words instances that seem to me to settle the meaning and extent of the word ' davach.'

On the 4th October 1381, in a court of Adam Bishop of Aberdeen, held at the Chapel Mount of St. Thomas the Martyr, beside the canonry of Aberdeen, for the production of charters of tenants claiming to hold from the Lord Bishop and the church of Aberdeen[1]—one of the tenants, Bernard de Cargill, undertook to produce his charter showing how he held the lands of Cloveth from the Bishop and the church of Aberdeen.

[1] Aberd. Reg., vol. i. p. 135.

The Bishop's lands of Cloveth, which had been given by Malcolm Canmore in dower to the church, according to the evidences and registers of the church, are entered in these registers as *half a Davach*.

In the Bishop of Aberdeen's rental, dated 1511, the same lands of Cloveth are entered as *two ploughs*. It seems to follow that the lands of Cloveth, of the extent of half a Davach, consisted of two ploughs, and that a whole Davach would be equal to *four ploughs*.

Such is the guidance of record. That the understanding of the country was the same, appears from a MS. account of the Scottish bishops, preserved in the library at Slaines, and which, though without date, can be ascribed without much doubt to the year 1726. That MS., evidently the work of an intelligent churchman of the district,[1] contains this account of the valley of Huntly: "Strathbogie[2] was of old divided into forty-eight Davachs, each containing as much as *four ploughs* could till in a year."

The "Aucht-and-forty Dauch of Huntly" is still spoken of in the north, and by the natives of the district with affectionate remembrance.[3]

[1] Antiquities, Shires, vol. iv. 460. We are indebted for its publication to the late Joseph Robertson.

[2] Antiquities, Shires, vol. ii. 164.

[3] At farmers' meetings in our own time a favourite toast was "The auld aucht-and-forty!"

We have now little of the old interest in Old Extent, but it may be well to remember that a century ago, and down to the year 1832, territorial taxation was the basis of our elective franchise, and that claims and objections to that qualification called forth the greatest exertions in our courts, and also helped to raise among us a race of men of business thoroughly learned in election law, and in feudalism and all the legal antiquities which enter into it.

In seeking for evidence of an ancient taxation of Scotland, Mr. Thomson thought that the earliest marks of it were to be found in the terms *carrucata terræ, bovata terræ,* which are met with in writs of the twelfth century (Mr. Thomson says, the eleventh century), but I am unable to follow my master in that supposition. These measures—ploughland, oxgate, seem to me to be the natural divisions which would be adopted as soon as agriculture was introduced or any transactions took place regarding occupation of land. I cannot connect them—the ploughgate, the oxgate of land—by any necessary link—with taxation.

It may be somewhat different with the money designations *librata, marcata, denariata terræ*—these seem to explain at any rate a fixing of money value and perhaps of money payments, to definite portions of lands, but were these payments of the nature of a tax, or were they of a methodized rental? We have them back so old that they can scarcely have been prepared for the allocation of any general national tax known in our history. But whether these money measures, which have stuck so fast in the memory of the people, were *extent* or valuation with the view to tax—or valuation or appraising for the purpose of claiming a rent, is a difficult question, and now only of historical importance.

As a problem of history—perhaps the oldest problem of our history—it would be of great interest to ascertain when and by what authority, by what masters — political masters, or territorial — the western half of Scotland, the wildest shores of our Highlands, and the wildest islands, were measured and valued in marklands, shillinglands, pennylands, farthinglands, long before money—coined silver—was generally used or known as an element of rent, on the other side—the agricultural side of Scotland.

The popular belief (opposed to Mr. Thomson's theory) is, that these are marks of an ancient territorial rental, not connected with national taxation. The people attribute them to the mysterious great lords, whom they know only by name—the Somerleds and Torquils, whom, so far as I know, they believe also to have been their own leaders and patriarchs. I do not like to build upon tradition, but this popular belief may be in part correct, if we examine it by the light of history. The northern chiefs, the pirate

Jarls and Kings, who swarmed down our west coast in the eleventh and twelfth centuries, and who were absolute masters of the Western Isles—choosing Isla, the most fertile, for their dwelling-place—while cousins or brothers of theirs, or at any rate men of the same lineage and customs, grasped the northern islands of Orkney and Shetland—those Norse chiefs were indeed the territorial lords of those wild and wide possessions, and as such had an interest, if they had intelligence and knowledge of affairs enough, to lead them to establish fixed rentals of their lands. But then those great landlords were also independent princes, hardly acknowledging any sovereignty in their own Norse Kings, and certainly none in the King who ruled Lothian, Fife, and Forfar, and claimed some shadowy authority over the mountains and islands of the west.

Now while these lords necessarily levied rents on which to live, they required also payments in respect of their position as princes. Every warlike expedition, every piratical cruise—and both enterprises came as often as summer came—required a fleet of galleys or birlins to be manned and provisioned, and some valuation or arithmetical arrangements for apportioning these burdens with some degree of fairness. In this way, the rental of the territorial lord might serve the purpose of a stent-roll for political assessment, and indeed it could hardly fail, that the divisions, marked deliberately and probably fairly, to pay so much rent, should be used when it was necessary for the same territory to levy taxes, or payments equivalent to taxation.

Let us not dispute, then, whether that old valuation of western Scotland was for rent or for taxes. So far as taxes are known in a very primitive state of society the valuation probably served both purposes.

Why the rents in those old Norse possessions, both on the West Coast and Islands, and in the northern islands of Orkney and Shetland, should have been fixed in money instead of produce, opens a wide inquiry, which I will not even enter upon here; but from the earliest period in which we have any light concerning their customs, it was the practice amongst all those lands of the Norsemen; we find it even existing to this day in a land now so agricultural as Caithness, formerly, you know, a great possession of the northern Jarls.

I wish you to remember that the great high road of northern commerce—of trade, of pilgrimage and crusade, of piratical adventure, of war—flowed down the Baltic, and poured in full stream upon our shores and islands, bringing with it a knowledge of money—a received coinage and currency which is necessary for war and plunder, no less than for peaceful commerce.

The earliest of those island rentals preserved, is one of 26th August 1507, which is among the Rolls of the Great Chamberlain of Scotland.[1] The different subjects are merely mentioned by name (distinguished, however, by the islands in which they lie), and the valuation is expressed in marks, or pounds, shillings, and pence. In one part of this great rental which I analysed more particularly, I was struck with the very great number of farms or possessions set down as of thirty-three shillings and four pence value, while some are entered at 16s. 8d. and others at 8s. 4d. I at one time thought that these multiples which do not correspond either with our pound or with our mark coinage, pointed to some money standard of the North, which might yet be found by the diligent student. But I have learned better from an Islay friend, who has the advantage of studying these curiosities of tenure on his own ground. He pointed out to me that the merk and its aliquot parts were the real foundations of all that money measurement, and in this manner :—There are still some tenements designated ten merklands, and there probably were many of old. These, divided into two, gave five merklands—again divided, gave two and a half merklands. But two and a half merks are *the* 33*s.* 4*d.*, *de quo queritur*—the commonest designation in the great rental.

[1] Roll 339.

That halved gives the 16s. 8d. land—divided again, the 8s. 4d. land, both of which are found in the rental of 1507.

In those western regions there are also found 50s. lands and 25s. lands, but my teacher points out that these also are probably founded upon the mark, as the unit of the arithmetic—thus, $2\frac{1}{2}$ marks are equal to 33s. 4d., and if a farm of this rent were divided into two, each half is 16s. 8d. — again halved 8s. 4d. Now, if to a $2\frac{1}{2}$ merkland there were joined one-half of another land of that rent, the lands so joined would bear a rent of $3\frac{3}{4}$ marks, or more simply, a 50s. land—this halved, a 25s. land, and so on.

The rental of the Bishopric of the Isles prepared about the time of the Reformation is comparatively insignificant. Very few subjects are valued, and all that I have observed worth your notice is, that the lands named from money measures are always rentalled at that amount; as, for instance, the twenty-pound land of Icolmkill, £20—the twenty-four penny land in Uist called Ungenab, 24d. This rental does not contain any statement of customs, or any payment in kind.

You must not suppose that in this inquiry I have passed over the curious rentals of the northern islands; but I am sorry to say that they add to the difficulties rather than remove them. There are rentals preserved, and even published, of the northern islands of Orkney and Shetland, most careful and minute, and going as far back as 1497. Many of them show the valuation in actual progress and the fixing of rents going on, with generally from four to five years' tenure. But it is extremely difficult to get at the principles of taxation. It seems plain that the same collector levied *pro rege* and *pro episcopo*. There are no agricultural measures of ploughgate and oxgate, nor of soums' grazing. The measures are *merkland, pennyland, farthingland,* and *urisland*. The ure or ore, you remember, is a coin not unknown in our own old laws; but who can explain the different payments of *stent,* and *scat,* and *mail,* and *cost,* and *flesh,* and *wattel,* and *forcops!* This last I have fancied to mean *grassum.* Fortunately there are some zealous Orcadians working on the antiquities of their country, and we must look to them for the explanation of these various payments as well as of the measures by *bismar* and *leispund*,[1] and *fathoms of peats,* and *spans* and *barrels of butter.* I only mention them now to show you the family resemblance between the manner of designating tenements by money valuations in the two great districts where the Norsemen have left traces of their administration—the Hebrides and the Orkneys; and also to show you the early pro-

[1] These are *manvers* or *implements* of weighing rather than weights.

pensity to break down the payments of the tenant, as if to cheat him into the idea of paying less, because the payments were levied under the names of money-rent, ferm, multure, teinds, customs, cain —which I take to be something equivalent to the multitude of payments exacted from the poor tenants of Orkney and Zetland.

Having a whole country occupied by an agricultural population who defined their tenements in oxgangs, husbandlands, ploughgates, with only the memory of an ancient measure and valuation in money values—poundlands, shillinglands, etc., down to penny and farthinglands—used for a long period for apportioning the public burdens—taxes and others—but in our time, only for fixing a parliamentary franchise—*a forty-shillingland of old extent*—and finding the other side of Scotland with its lands measured and still named from denominations of money—merklands, half and quarter merklands,—I thought it very interesting to try to ascertain the equivalents in the two kinds of valuation; and I am happy to say I find that fixed authoritatively—I mean by the proper tribunal— 300 years ago, though I think it has not been noticed by any of our constitutional writers. It had escaped the notice of Mr. Thomas Thomson.

In 1580-1 a tax was imposed for the expenses of putting down what was called the rebellion of the Maxwells and the troubles of the Borders. The Acts[1] imposing the tax are conditional, confused, and altogether a very discreditable piece of legislation; but one part is clear enough, that the temporal lands of all Scotland were assessed at the rate of 6s. 8d. on the poundland of Old Extent; and that Lords of Erection of the temporality of the Church, though first liable, were to have relief against their feuars and vassals, the real proprietors of the lands of which *they* were superiors.

Now at that time, Adam Bothwell, a very well known man (the Bishop of Orkney, who married Mary to Bothwell in the hall of the abbey 15th May 1567), was Commendator of Holyrood Abbey, with an erection of its temporalities into a lordship. When my lord Commendator was called on by the tax-gatherer for the sum of tax effeiring to his barony of Broughton—a very extensive barony in this neighbourhood, including not only Broughton, Warriston, Pilrig, on one side, but Liberton, St. Leonards, Pittendreich, Saughton, and Saughton-hall, and lands all the way to Linlithgow, on the other —the soil as various as you can imagine—my lord claimed relief from his feuars at the rate which he himself was bound to pay, namely, a half merk for every poundland of old extent. But the memory of Old Extent was then vague and indistinct, and a

[1] Acts of Parliament, vol. iii. pp. 192, 189.

dispute arose between the Lord of Erection and the feuars about the meaning and value of a poundland of Old Extent. The case came to be argued in the Court of Exchequer on 11th May 1585, and a full account of the proceedings is preserved, and of an elaborate judgment pronounced by the Lords Auditors of Exchequer, who, regarding this as a leading case, with all solemnity "Find, decern and declare that 13 acres of the complainer's lands, lying within the barony of Broughtoun, extendis and sall extend to ane oxgait of land, and that four oxgait of the saids lands extendis and sall extend to ane pund land of auld extent in all tyme to cum" —thus ruling that a forty-shillingland of Old Extent is equal to eight oxgaits, or in other words, one plough-land, and that indiscriminately over the best land of Lothian and some of the poorest.

I told you before that, notwithstanding local variations and accidental exceptions, an oxgait in the south of Scotland—at any rate all through the Merse and Lothian—measured thirteen acres, and if there were any doubt it should be removed by this authoritative decision; and so much for oxgaits and ploughgates. But here we have, *for the first time*, the old agricultural measurement of oxgates and plough-gates brought face to face, and weighed in the balance —with the technical money measurement then and now known as £ s. d. of Old Extent. It seems from the peculiar phraseology of the judgment, it was meant to settle from thenceforth that the forty shilling land of old extent was to be held neither less nor more than a ploughgate of land, or 104 acres. Consequently one merkland should contain $34\tfrac{2}{3}$ acres of arable land.

Another point or set of points connected with old measures and valuations of lands on both sides of Scotland was, I hope, cleared to your satisfaction, and it rewards you for some laborious investigation and attention to dry figures, if we have really settled beyond reasonable doubt what is an oxgait, a husbandland, a ploughgate, and—more mysterious than these—what is the davach of the north!

When I say these hitherto disputed measures are now ascertained, I must not be held to the letter. From the principle and very names of these measures—perhaps connected with the *labour* of *oxen*, perhaps with their *pasture*—the amount may vary in lands more than commonly difficult to labour—or more than commonly unproductive of food; but these are exceptions which do not touch the general rule.

Perhaps these are the most practically useful of the matters which our little course of study has enabled us to make clear; but a few years ago, quite within my own memory, it would have been considered a still greater triumph—a greater rescuing out of the obscurity of ages—to have fixed, as I hope we have done, what was the real meaning and intention of a 40s. land of old extent—the primitive foundation of our electoral franchise.[1] I think we have ascertained, with no great research, that a 40s. land of Old Extent was neither more nor less than a ploughgate of 104 acres.

But it was not for working out and settling points like these—it was not even for satisfying a rational curiosity about the antiquities of our country, that I proposed this short course of lectures to men of your profession and standing. I thought it a worthy object of your study if I could guide you to know the original shape and first meaning of our laws and forms of process. I have endeavoured to show you these in their very earliest state, to lay bare the roots of our national institutions, and I trust you have received some pleasure in the search. It is one that might be carried on with still increasing pleasure, and for those of you who think of prosecuting it I have suggested a few books that may facilitate your studies.

---

[1] It may be necessary to remind some of my readers that the Act 1681, cap. 21, provides that none shall vote at elections but those who stand publicly infeft of a 40s. land of old extent, holden of the King or Prince, or in £400 of valued rent.

LECTURE VII.

BOOKS.

If you have observed, or if you look back on our little course, you will see that hardly any of my Lectures are founded on printed books. I do not say that I have shut out from myself, or from your knowledge, the speculation of greater masters. I hope it is far otherwise; but those things which were in print I held to be already your property, at any rate *vestri juris*. Men living in a legal atmosphere, and domiciled in our noble Library, must soon become aware of what scholars, in all ages, have done for our science. But scholars and authors in this country have, in my opinion, somewhat erred in neglecting the sources and very foundations of our law and constitution. I thought some light might be derived from sources which they had overlooked, and you will judge whether our study of charters—whether those brieves which we disinterred, after their sleep of many ages—have not given you some new and striking lights upon the foundation of legal process in our country, and upon the foundation of property itself.

I told you honestly that my account of the ancient Church among us, its officers, its property, its jurisdiction, was not to be found, so far as I knew, in printed books. Other legal antiquities, such as the process about the lands of Monachkeneran, may be in print indeed, but where it lies as little known as in the most difficult MS. I think no books could tell us those things which we made out from our own calculations of the measures of land and the meaning of the terms expressing its measurements.

Having spent my own life among records, I have ventured to introduce you to that novel study, and my success must be judged from the interest which you feel in it. I hope you will not allow the petty difficulty of reading old hand to deter you from continuing our course and diving even into the *penetralia* of charter and record.

Even independent of those deeper studies which are necessary for mastering any worthy object, a Scotch lawyer ought not to be ignorant of the shape and form of all our records. Mr. Dickson will lay before you the very Ordinance, signed with the royal hand, under which the Court of Session now sits. He will exhibit to you tall presses crowded with the Register of the Great Seal—that foundation of land rights of which we are proud, not without some cause. Gentlemen, these objects of intelligent curiosity are now as open as can be desired to the whole world. For purposes of study, not only are fees abolished, but you have a staff of learned record scholars ready to help your intelligent inquiries. I tell you there is more of history, more of the history of the Scotch people, their institutions, their laws and customs, to be found in that room—that noble room where Mr. Dickson spends his days in the footsteps of Thomas Thomson, than in all libraries besides. And yet how few of you have visited and studied in that room! It is in this sense that I just now quoted to you the lines of Lucretius—" Juvat integros accedere fontes atque haurire, juvatque novos decerpere flores." But that you may follow out those studies with greater profit and pleasure, I will point out a few books to help and direct— mostly the works of men who have travelled the same road before you, and perhaps without your advantages—books that may be like the grammars and dictionaries of your new language.

A fitting commencement of your charter studies will be the great work of James Anderson, the "Diplomata et Numismata Scotiæ." I think you are all aware of the purpose for which that great collection was made — for proving and setting forth with due parade the proofs of the antiquity and independent royalty of Scotland, at a time when that was still necessary; for the Union was approaching, and there were some men found in England unworthy enough to propose dealing with Scotland as an old feudal dependant, instead of an ancient and always independent neighbour.

The country took up Anderson's work, and Parliament voted it such supplies as the Scotch Parliament could then give. Anderson was fortunate in the assistance he received from Thomas Ruddiman. The apparatus for this great collection of coins and charters—I mean the preliminary dissertations—are very valuable; and the lists of persons and places, composed when all our chartularies were still in manuscript, are wonderful proofs of industry, and, in general, very accurate.

A similar collection of Anglo-Saxon Charters by John M. Kemble, published in six or eight volumes octavo, will be found a very useful help in charter study. I have borrowed more from Kemble's Introduction than from any one printed book. With all his ready and confident assertion, you will find him generally very trustworthy. I have traced him through some of the greatest collections of Anglo-Saxon charters in England, and have admired his laborious accuracy.

Benjamin Thorpe's collection of the Ancient

Laws of England is an indispensable book for any man who sets himself to study the ancient laws of Scotland. Thorpe is now *facile princeps* of Anglo-Saxon scholars, and his only defect as an editor is, that he is somewhat grudging of expressing his own opinions, especially when he has only a conjecture to offer. His book, in two volumes octavo, with its glossary, is a ready repertory of English legal antiquities. Mr. Thorpe has also edited a volume of Anglo-Saxon charters.

For helps in general, let me mention the most wonderful book in our department of study—L'Art de vérifier les Dates, the greatest work of the Benedictines of St. Maur—a book supplying all helps for chronology so fully as to amount almost to history.

A little book by Sir Harris Nicolas, which he calls the Chronology of History, taken entirely from the great French work, except as regards the personal chronology of our own sovereigns, should be on your table. At the end of my copy I have filled in a few pages with the regnal years of our Scotch kings.

I need hardly tell you of the mass of topographical and family history contained in the huge volumes of George Chalmers. Disfigured as it is with almost every fault in plan, manner, and execution, the work is yet the great repertory of all that kind of learning for Scotland.

The Origines Parochiales Scotiæ puts forward something of the same design not quite so ambitiously. You will find in it a great deal of parochial, local, and also some pedigree information for the dioceses of Glasgow, Argyle, the Isles, Ross, Caithness, and Orkney. I did not intend that it should come below the Reformation, but it was difficult to draw a line when interesting materials turned up. You will find, I think, some useful short *notes* of ancient topography prefixed to a book called Scotland in the Middle Ages.

Mr. E. W. Robertson, in a book named Scotland under her Early Kings, has some very valuable dissertations upon points of prehistoric antiquity. I think my friend Mr. Robertson is not so studious of *our* national antiquities as of Teutonic antiquities generally. His history is to Scotch history somewhat like what Sir Thomas Craig's book is to Scotch law.

Lord Hailes's Annals must be open before you in all study of ancient law or history of Scotland.

The only book which Thomas Innes left in print was the Critical Essay on the Ancient Inhabitants of the Northern parts of Britain. He was, as Mr. Joseph Robertson says, the first labourer in that field, and the "Essay" has great merit in careful research and honesty. The works which he left in MS. are to my mind more valuable, but none of them were in a state which he thought fit to meet the public eye. Some little volumes of his MS. Notes, now in the hands of Mr. Laing, will one day be turned to account, and may supersede Keith's Catalogue of the Scottish Bishops, which is chiefly drawn from T. Innes's MS. notes, still extant. Though sadly imperfect, Keith is a necessary tool for the charter student. So is, in a less degree, Crawford's Lives of the Great Officers of State.

Of mere chronicles we have the Chronicle of Melrose, the Chronicle of Holyrood, Fordun's Scotichronicon, which Mr. Skene is now editing in a worthy manner, specially distinguishing the work of Fordun from that of his Continuators.

Barbour is something better than a chronicler, but he has some of the merits of one. I tried an experiment in editing his Bruce for the Spalding Club, in establishing a uniform spelling, such as I thought the Archdeacon of Aberdeen himself would have used if he had felt the propriety of spelling uniformly.

Wyntoun's Chronicle had been edited on a different principle, but carefully and scholarly, by David MacPherson. His index is curious and valuable. He has also done something for old Scotch geography in a little quarto volume with a map. It might serve as a foundation for a good Scotch geography.

The Scotichronicon and the Chronicle of Lanercost contain some new facts.

Our oldest written history, Adomnan's Life of St. Columba, has been edited with all learning and affectionate zeal for the memory of the old Saint, by Dr. Reeves, the greatest historical scholar of the Celts—himself a Saxon.

Dr. Reeves has also given us a summary—a very conclusive summary—of the history of the Culdees.

A great many chartularies have been printed for the different literary clubs of Scotland. The registers of three bishoprics, Glasgow, Moray, Aberdeen, and books of register of nearly all the great monasteries of Scotland, carefully printed, are now accessible in all our libraries, and contain in themselves—it is not too much to say—they contain a fuller history of ancient Scotland than ever has been written. No doubt the registrar of the bishopric was chiefly taken up with the property, the benefices, the honour and glory of his own cathedral; no doubt the monk who wrote the chartulary of his abbey was most careful to engross the charters of kings and magnates which were the titles of their broad lands; but they did more, they recorded their transactions with their neighbours, peaceful or contentious, the dealings with their tenants and vassals, the mighty industries which they conducted, the churches they built—all the incidents that interested the most intelligent class of society are to be found in them. Any one of our poorest chartularies would furnish texts for lectures for several sessions in the lower Advocates' Library.

I mentioned to you before some of the works of Mr. Joseph Robertson. I think I told you of his five or six volumes of County Collections for the Spalding Club. The index to these is now printed, and completes the great repertory for northern county history. I am sure I have spoken to you already of Mr. Robertson's two great works, his edition of the Inventories of Queen Mary's Jewels, and his Statutes and Councils of the Scotch Church—two works unmatched for fulness and richness of learning and illustration.

I thought of giving you a list of the works of my great master, Thomas Thomson; but I find a full and accurate account, furnished by Mr. Laing, at the end of a memoir of his life,[1] and I will not repeat what I have there said. There are none of his works which will not well repay your study.

For all that concerns heraldry, you will find two volumes of Ancient Scottish Seals, by Mr. Henry Laing, very useful.

Mr. David Laing, whom I quote so often, is, I am sure, known to most of you as the learned Librarian. But he has filled some shelves with his own

[1] Memoir of Thomas Thomson, p. 244.

books—all useful, all most accurate. There are two departments in which he stands above competition. He is a zealous Presbyterian, and not less a hearty Scot. His edition of Knox—no easy work—is excellent; but if the reader of Knox wants to supplement his reading with a knowledge of the later Scotch Reformed Church, where is he to find the history of all the "godly bands," and covenants, and the counter-covenants, but in the works of Mr. Laing! His editions of our old Scots poets—his Dunbar, Lindsay, Henryson—contrast advantageously with those of the scholars of the last generation, who really knew little of the old Scots language.

For the mere language of charters we have no guide so good and so full as Du Cange. I use a little edition by Adelung, which embodies Carpentier's Supplement,—there is also a convenient abridgment in one volume, published by the Abbé Migne; but the book in its glory is to be seen in the last quarto Paris edition which stands over the fireplace in our catalogue-room. Big and exhaustive as it seems to be, I need not tell you that a Frenchman can never be a satisfactory guide to Scotch charters, but the Supplementum Scoticum to Du Cange's Dictionary is yet to be written. All that Sir John Skene did in his little book De Verborum Significatione, was known and used by Du Cange, and it is mortifying to say that some of the worst errors in that grand Dictionary of Middle-age Europe are those copied from our countryman's hasty, ill-considered work.

I have told you already of the great national work, the Acts of the Parliaments of Scotland, the foundation, of course, of all history and law of the country; but I wish to direct your attention to some circumstances which make the first volume of that collection more than a mere gathering of old laws and Acts of Parliament. The apparatus placed at the beginning of that volume contains a selection of what we thought most curious and valuable of ancient charters, of old forms of process, of vestiges of prehistoric legislation—of great inventories of the muniments and records of the kingdom before they were lost or destroyed. That edition, which is only now finished, embraces, at the end of Vol. VI. Part II., the documents of the Government of Scotland during the time of Cromwell and the Commonwealth. There will also be soon published a General Index of the Acts of the Parliaments of Scotland, full of our law and history from David I. to the Union, A.D. 1124 to 1707.

Amongst English books one of the most pleasing to read, and, I believe, a book of great accuracy, is the Honourable Daines Barrington's Observations on the Statutes, a goodly quarto.

Thomas Blount's Ancient Tenures and Jocular Customs of Manors, you will find a very entertaining and instructive book.

Oughton upon Consistorial Form of Process is full of the curiosity of the old subject, and with great precision and legal learning.

On a subject which we Scotsmen must take help from England to study, you will find valuable assistance in the works of White Kennet, who studied the law of parishes, of tithes, of rectorial and vicarial rights, of impropriations and appropriations, and has left us the results in a great many volumes of very pleasant and popular reading. He wrote about the beginning of last century.

The works of Madox—his *Firma Burgi*, his *Formulare Anglicanum*, his History of the Exchequer, are very useful upon subjects where the law and custom of England are almost identical with our own.

Sir Henry Spelman, Hickes, Skinner, Lye, Fleetwood's *Cronicon Pretiosum*—an attempt to fix the value of money at different periods—Sir Henry Ellis (especially his Dissertation upon Domesday Book), Dugdale's *Origines Judiciales*, Cowell's Dictionary, not for its politics, the *Registrum omnium Brevium*, London 1595, Stubbs's Documents of English Constitutional History, should at least be known and accessible to the student of Scots law and history.

I need only mention the Record publications of our own country since the time when Mr. Thomson introduced the study of records. Besides the Acts of Parliament, he published two volumes of Judicial Proceedings—the oldest reports of law cases we have, for they are of the middle of the 15th century. These are not so well known as they should be. The *Registrum Magni Sigilli* is a careful print of the Great Seal Register, from the reign of Robert I. to that of Robert III. The *Retours* condensed in three volumes, down to the year 1700, are already very well known to the profession of the Law, and extremely useful. It may not be so well known that Mr. Lindsay has made some progress in continuing the series upon a still more condensed plan. The Chamberlain Rolls, that is, the Public Accounts of Scotland from 1326 to 1453, a mine of vast richness, has hardly been worked at all by our historians. It is a poor apology that it is difficult reading, and that the difficulty does not disappear when the original MS. rolls are turned into print.

A great series of the most authentic materials of the law and history of England has been produced in our own time with admirable care and correctness under the direction of the Master of the Rolls. To Sir Thomas Duffus Hardy and his assistants in Chancery Lane it is owing that the historical student of England can never again be left to the guidance of rash speculation or reckless mis-statements. So much done for a neighbouring country is not without its effect upon ours.

APPENDIX.

The fable to which I allude at page 240, and which I read to my class in illustration of the forms of the old Consistorial Court, is one of Henryson's, which has had the good fortune to be commented on by Lord Hailes, edited by Mr. D. Laing, and illustrated by Lord Neaves. Henryson calls it the Tale of the Dog, the Sheep, and the Wolf.

A false Dog schemed to defraud a simple Sheep, who, he alleged, owed him a loaf worth five shillings. The innocent Sheep was the common victim. Pleading poverty, the pursuer prosecuted in the Consistorial Court, where a fraudful Wolf was judge, that time, and bore authority and jurisdiction, who sent out a summons in common style.

"I, Maister Wolf, partless of fraud and gyle,
Under the pains of high suspension,
Of great cursing and interdiction,
Sir Sheep I charge thee straitlie to compear
And answer to a Dog before me here."

The Sheep appears, but without advocate, and answers, "declining" the judge and all the members of the Court as his known enemies, and with reason, for, said he,—You

"Sir Wolf—with tuskis ravenous—
Has slain full many kinismen of mine;
Therefore as judge suspect I you decline."

And the corbie whom they had made apparitor, pykit had full mony sheep's eyn.

> " The fox was Clerk and notar in the cause,
> The Gled—the Graep (hawk and vulture) at the bar could stand
> As Advocates expert into the laws
> The Dogis plea together took on hand,
> Who were confederate straitly in a band
> Against the sheep to procure the sentence,
> Though it was false—they had no conscience.
>
> And shortly of this Court the members all,
> Both Assessories, Clerk and Advocate,
> To me and mine are enemies mortal,
> And aye have been, as many shepherds wot."

The Sheep's exception is regularly submitted to arbiters—the Bear and the Badger—who hold a long disputation, seeking decrees and glosses of the law, and revolving many volumes, the Codex and Digests new and old :

> "As trew judges, I beshrew them that lie."

The arbiters, swearing full plain, the sentence gave, and process fulminate against the Sheep, who had no appeal from that sentence.

The Sheep, again brought before the Wolf, without advocate, humbly takes his trial, and Tod Lourie (the Fox) writes the proceedings as clerk.

> " And thus the plea unto the end they speed,
> This cursed Court corrupted all for meed,
> Against good faith, law, and eke conscience,
> For this false dog pronounced the sentence."

The Sheep—dreading their execution, sold the wool from his back, then bought the loaf, and to the Dog made payment, as it commanded was—naked and bare then to the field could pass.

The *moral* likens the Sheep to poor commons that daily are oppressed by tyrannous false men—

> " In hope this present life shall ever last."

> " The wolf is like a sheriff stout
> Who buys a forfeit at the kingis hand,

> And has with him a cursed Assize about,
> And dytes all the poor men up on land."

The Raven is like a false crowner, who has a porteous of the indictment, and, when he comes in Court, scrapes out John and writes in Will or Wat, and takes bribes on both hands.

The "Tod" and the Gled need no commentary. But for the Sheep, the poet overheard his moan and repeats it. It is all against the common sin of covetousness, which has exiled from the world love, loyalty, and law.

> "The poor is peeled, the lord may do no miss;
> Now is he blyth with usury most may win;
> Gentrice is slain, and piety is ago,
> Alas, good Lord! why suffers thou it so!
>
> Thou suffers this even for our great offence.
>
> We poor people as now may do no more
> But pray to Thee, since that we are oppressed,
> Into this earth, grant us in heaven rest!"

Although the example of legal oppression is taken from the Church Court (perhaps levelled at some notorious Archdeacon of the time), the moralist gives no preference to the lay process—to the "Sheriff stout," even with his Assize or jury. Henryson had no reason for painting the Consistorial Court but that he was best acquainted with consistorial process. He took no thought of the feud that had raged so long in England between the Church Courts and the common lawyers. The moralist aimed wider,—at the oppression of the poor by the rich and powerful, at the baseness and venality of lawyers; he cared not to distinguish—all lawyers alike. Lawyers were not in good odour in his country then!

INDEX.

ABBOT: head of the monastery, 170; specially summoned to Parliament, 123; mitred, his privileges, 203.
Abbots-Selkirk; rent in silver of, 247.
Abercromby, Francis, created Lord Glassford *for life*, 146.
Aberdalgy, reddendo for, 67.
Aberdeen; Bishop of: Robert III.'s grant to, 39; bishopric of; foundation charter, spurious, 87; rural deaneries, 174; rental, 250-4; confederacy of free burghs from, northward, 114; charters of the friars still in MS., 192; register of the Collegiate Church of St. Nicholas in MS., 192; University of, register printed, 191.
Aberdeenshire, extent of a ploughgate, 270; Robertson's *Antiquities*, 293.
Aberlot, vicar of, his income, 196.
Absolute; our Kings ruled at no time absolutely, 98.
Acts of Parliament, 294-5; *The General Index*, 295.
Adomnan's Life of St. Columba, Rev. Dr. Reeves's, 292.
Advocate, King's, 77.
Advocates' Library: Lectures read in, 1; founded by Sir George Mackenzie, 4; MSS. of John Riddell presented to, 18.
"Aforethocht" felony: brief distinguishing it from *chaudee melee*, 234.
Agricultural measures of land; where found, 271; balanced with money measures, 281-4.
Agriculture: outline of the Lecture, 24-5; Act in favour of the labourers of the ground, 125; best information from the Kelso rental, 247-8.
Aid (*Auxilium*), 111; lands held of the Church free of, 218.
Alehouse; superseded the brewhouse, 48; originally the hostelry, *ib.*; reddendo for, *ib.*
Almonds, Bruce's dish to the monks of Melrose, 38.
Almoner, The, his office, 78.
Anandale, Bruce's first charter, 33.
Anandale; rural deanery, 176.
Ancient Laws of England, Thorpe's collection, 289, 290.
Ancient Tenures, Blount's, 295.
Anderson, James, W.S.; his patriotic works, 15; *Diplomata et Numismata Scociæ*, 288-9.
Anekol, witness in an ancient jury trial, 218.
Anglo-Saxon charters; Scotch charters founded on, 31; Kemble's collection, 289.
Angus, ruled by a Maormor, 97; four bailliaries of, each ruled by a Maor, 78.
Angus, rural deanery of, 174.
Annexation, Statute of, 148.
Antiquaries, Legal; small number, 2; list of, 2-18.
Antiquities, Legal, materials for the study of, 6, 9.

Antiquities of the Shires of Aberdeen and Banff, Joseph Robertson's, 293.
Annals of Scotland, Hailes's, 291.
Apostates, brief against, 233.
Appeals; Committee of Parliament for, 119-122; made to the Supreme Courts, 228, 229.
Appropriation, meaning of, 185.
Aquis, in, rights to waters in a grant of barony, 44—*Aqua* meaning running water, *ib.*
Aragon, Constitution of the Cortes of, 106.
Arbroath, Abbey of; the Barons' Letter to the Pope dated, 104; a house of the Benedictines of Tyrone, 165; account of the house, 166; disputes with its churches, 194-5; chartulary printed, 191; vicar, his income, 196.
Archdeacon, 181-2.
Archdeaconries, 174-6.
Argyll, bishopric of, 176; bishops sometimes called of Lismore, *ib.;* deaneries of, 177.
Arrow, price of, 65-6; head of, valued, *ib.*
Articles, Lords of; their origin, 119-122; election, 146-7; usurp the power of Parliament, *ib.*
Athole, Earl of, earldom of Stratherne granted to him *for life,* 145.
Athole, deanery of, 174.
Auxilium, translated aid, 111.
Ayr MS. the most Scotch of the ancient styles, 42; brieves from, 214.
Ayr, Master of the Schools of, 214; National Assembly in the parish church of, 104.

BADENOCH, rental of, 258-9.
Bagimond's Roll, historical mistakes about, 189.
Bailie, his office, 84.
Balgarvie, lands of, lease of, 248-9.
Balgony, reddendo for, 67.

Ballia or *Ballivatus,* meaning of, 84.
Balmaschennan, reddendo for, 67.
Balmerino, chartulary printed, 191.
Banchory-Ternan, vicarage of, valuation of, 197.
Banff, vicarage of the church valued, 197-8.
Banffshire, *nativi* claimed last in the Sheriff-Court of, 256; plough of land, 270; Robertson's *Antiquities of the Shire,* 293.
Banrents, specially summoned to Parliament, 123; who they were, *ib.*
Baptism, dues on, 186.
Barbour's Chronicle, 292.
Barons; their Letter to the Pope, 104; regard seat in Parliament as a burden, 115; relieved of attendance in Parliament, 122.
Baron-bailié, refers tenant-quarrels to the birleyman, 268.
Barons' Courts, process used in, 59.
Barony, no grant of, in Bruce's charters, 33; grant *in liberam baroniam,* 42; head court of, the oldest in Scotland, 98.
Barrington's *Observations on the Statutes,* 295.
Barr, vicar of, his income, 196.
Beauly, register of, lost, 192.
Bellie, rental of, 261-2; rent of a ploughgate in the parish, 262.
Benedictines: of St. Bernard, 164; their religious house, *ib.;* of St. Maur, authors of *L'Art de vérifier les Dates,* 290; of Tyrone, 165— their houses, 165-6.
Benefice; what it implied, 183; valuations of, 189.
Bernham, De, Bishop David, churches dedicated by, 207-8.
Berwick, one of the "Four Burghs," 114; high-roads from, to Inverness, 242.
Birleyman, office of, 254; baron-

bailie refers disputes to him, 268.
Birss, forest of, rent of the foggage, 252.
Bishops; specially summoned to Parliament, 123; their disappearance from Parliament, 141; how appointed, 177; Keith's *Catalogue*, 291.
Bishoprics, list of, 173-7; usurpation of the patronage, 178; chartularies, 188-90; foundation, 200; registers, 292-3.
Black Friars, the Dominicans, 171.
Blantyre, reddendo for lands in, 67.
Blench duties, 64-8.
"Blood, corruption of," 150.
Blount's *Ancient Tenures and Jocular Customs of Manors*, 295.
Bludwites, jurisdiction in, 60.
Boar, value of, 66.
Bolden, barony of, rents and services on, 244, 246.
Bolingbroke, Lord, on the historical study of law, 26-7.
Bolton, vicar of, his portion, 199.
Bondman, grant of a barony *cum bondis et bondagiis*, 50. *V.* Native.
Books recommended for the study of Records, 288-296.
Bow, value of, 66.
Bowman, a sub-tenant, 266.
Boyne, rural deanery of, 174.
Brechbennach, custody of, 166.
Brechin, bishopric of, 175; an abbey of Culdees originally, *ib.*
Brew-houses; pertinents of landed estates, 48; superseded by the alehouse, *ib.;* rents paid for, 246.
Bridges, land granted for the support of, 247.
Brieves; oldest traces of civil process, 22; extant at the time of the Alexanders, 213; collection, in the Ayr and Bute MSS., 214; to whom addressed, 222-3; matters of which they treat, 223; royal, 222-237.
Brigham, Treaty of, term *Parliament* first used in, 102, 118-19.
Broom, grant of lands *cum genestis*, 45.
Brude, King, noticed in the chartulary of St. Andrews, 29.
Brushwood (*cum brucis*) pertinent of a landed estate, 44.
Buchan, ruled by a "Maormor," 97; rural deanery of, 174.
Burgesses, names of those bound for the ransom of David II., 107-8.
Burghs; royal burghs granted to Thomas Randolph *in capite*, 40; President of the Court of the Four Burghs, 76; grant an obligation for the ransom of David II., 107-8; their constitution, 113; Parliament of the Four Burghs, 114; form Third Estate, 115-6; were they the Third Estate in the early Parliaments of Bruce? 116; regard representation as a burden, 115; royal, holding of vassals, 116-7; such tenure declared illegal, 117; Acts in their favour by James IV. and Queen Mary, 129; grouped by Cromwell, 139; ten commissioners for them in the British Parliament, *ib.;* to send two commissioners, 141; afterwards only one, 142; commissioners sitting on "furmes," 142; commissioners paid for attendance in Parliament, 151-3.
Burton, Mr., noticed, 13.
Bute MS., brieves from, 214.
Butter, stone of, value of, 66.
Byrthensak, court of, 246.

CAITHNESS, bishopric of, 175; Caithness-shire, uncertain tenure of, 93; money measures of land, 277.
Caledonia, George Chalmers's, 290.

Cambuskenneth, Abbey of; famous Parliament held at, 103 — the burghs represented in that Parliament, 116—its constitutionalism, 117-8; a house of the Canons of St. Austin, 163; chartulary printed, 191.
Campbells, frequently Chancellors, 76.
Can, meaning of the word, 204.
Canmore, Malcolm, *V.* King Malcolm Canmore.
Canons of the cathedral, 179; two classes, *ib.*
Canons Regular of St. Augustine, 163; their houses, *ib.*
Cantor, his office, 181.
Cantyre, deanery of, 177.
Capon, value of, 66.
Capons of Ross, Buchan and Moray valued, 66.
Carnwath, reddendo for, 68.
Carriage, long and short, valued, 66.
Carric, Earl of, grant of chiefship by, 74; his brother witness in a jury trial, 219.
Carric, dean of, a judge in an early trial by jury, 214; rural deanery of, 176.
Carmelites, an order of friars, 172.
Castille, constitution of the Cortes, 106.
Catalonia, constitution of the Cortes of, 106.
Cathedral; constitution of, 178—sometimes borrowed from England, 179; dignitaries, 179—minor dignitaries, 182—often styled after their country prebend, 184; vicars, distinguished from those of the parish, 184.
Cattle, herds of, belonging to the monks of Kelso, 243; few, in the Highlands, 263-4.
Causes and Complaints, Auditors of, a Committee of Parliament, 229.

Cawdor, thanedom of, reddendo for, 82.
Cellarer, his duties, 170.
Celtic law, early disappearance of, 96.
Celtic officers in the time of Canmore, 97.
Celtic suitors, 206.
Chalmers, George; his contribution to topography, 17; to family history *ib.*; his *Caledonia*, 290.
Chamberlain, an early officer in Scotland, 96; President of the burghal Parliament, 114; his office, 76; Rolls, edited by Thomas Thomson, 13.
Chancellor, an office in Scotland in the time of David I., 96; his office, 76; Chancellor of the diocese; his office, 182.
Chaplains, churches served by, 200.
Chapter, constitution of the, 178.
Chapter-house, dignitaries of, 179.
Charter, oldest Scotch, 29, 35; bad Latin of French charters, 33; Lecture on, 29-91; old charters brief, 33; styles of the granters, 34; persons addressed, 35; causes of grant, 36-37; subjects granted, 37-39; *Quæquidem* clause, 39; *Modus tenendi*, 40; Faciendo clause, 61-8; how authenticated, 68; spurious charters, 87; extending the meaning of their words, 155; royal, preserved by the monks of Melrose, 168; no written tenures in the Highlands, 269.
Chartularies; their importance, 188; described, 188-192; printed, 191; still in MS., 192; lost, 192-3; lay, 193.
Cheese, stone of, value of, 66.
Chief; injury to the clansman by his lands being feudalized, 156-7; how his power was measured, 269; advantage to him by the change of patriarchal to feudal holding, *ib.*

INDEX. 307

Chiefship, grant of, 74.
Chronicles, list of, 291-2.
Chronology: Records of David II. misdated, 32.
Chronology of History, Sir Harris Nicholas's, 290; *L'Art de vérifier les Dates*, 290.
Church; history of, neglected by historians, 9, 13; defect supplied by Joseph Robertson, 13; outline of the Lecture, 22-3; Druids' circles filling the original idea of a church, 98; brief limiting its jurisdiction, 233; excommunication by it, 149; Lecture on the Old Church, 161-208; government, 173; property, 184-8; chartularies described, 188-193; valuations of benefices, 189; foundation of churches, 200, 201; grant of an *ecclesia*, 204; dedication of churches by Bishop David de Bernham, 207-8; brief, compelling payment of church rents, 232; Church, vassals of, 246.
Church Courts; procedures different from those of Civil Courts, 212; extensive jurisdiction, 238; juries originated, 283.
Churchman, the Chancellor generally, 76.
Cistercians; of the order of St. Benedict, 162; their houses, 167; exempted from taxes, 168-9.
Civil and Church Courts; procedures in, 237-240.
Clackmannanshire, to be represented by one Commissioner only, 122.
Clansmen; their holdings feudalized, 156-7; injury to them by change of tenure.
Claremathen, law of, for recovering stolen goods, 56.
Clatt, rent of a ploughgate in, 250-1.
Clergy, the first of the Three Estates, 141; sat on the "Benches" in Parliament, 142; Seculars and Regulars distinguished, 161.
Cloth, ells of, paid as customs in the Highlands, 257.
Clerk of Register, his office, 77.
Cluniacs; of the order of St. Benedict, 162; their religious house, 167.
Coal; early dispute, 165; first workers, 168.
Coalpits, grant of lands *cum carbonariis*, 45.
Coke, Sir Edward, quoted, 5, 43.
Coldstream, nunnery, 172; register still in MS., 192.
Collegiate churches; when founded, 201-2; members secular, 201.
Colliers, till recently "astricted," 50.
Commendators; who they were, 202.
Commissioners to Shires and Burghs, 151-3.
Committees of Parliament, 22, 119-122; whole power of Parliament intrusted to a Committee, 127.
Common churches, 184.
Commons, unjust divisions of, 154-5.
Complaints and Causes, Auditors of, 22.
Comptroller, his office, 76.
Compurgation: witnessing to character, 210.
Compurgators in a disputed case; their number, 210.
Concilia et Statuta Scotiæ, Joseph Robertson's, 13.
Conies, pair of, valued, 66.
Consistorial Court; its extensive jurisdiction, 238-9; Henryson's Fable illustrating old forms, 239-240, 297-300.
Consistorial Form of Process, Oughton's, 295.
Constable, his office, 38, 75; an early officer in Scotland, 96.
Constabulary, grants of, 38, 84.
Constitution of Scotland compared

with England's, 94; defects in the former, 148.
Constitutional Government in the reign of Robert I., 117-8; on the Continent in the 14th century: causes of its failure there, 106.
Contracts, brief, concerning, 231.
Contumacy, how punished, 220.
Conveth, meaning of, 205.
Conveyancers, learned, list of, 14-16.
Cornage, lands held for blowing a horn, 63.
"Corruption of the blood," imported by the Act of Union, 150.
Corstorphine, collegiate church of, 201.
"Costages;" Commissioners of Shires and "Speakers" to be paid, 123.
Cottar; a subtenant, 267; dryhouse cottar, *ib.*; deprived of his right in Commons, 155, 244; extent of his holding, *ib.*
Councils of the Church, list to be found in the *Statuta Ecclesiæ*, 173.
Coupar-Angus, register still in MS., 192.
Court, earliest, in Scotland, 98.
Courts; appeal, 228; civil and ecclesiastical Courts—their jurisdiction, 237-240.
Court of the "Four Burghs," 114.
Court of Session: its origin and institution, 119-122, 132, 230.
Cow, estimated at, 66.
"Cowdeche," price of, 65.
Craig, Sir Thomas, as a feudalist, 2.
Craignish papers, example of Maorship from, 78.
Crail, register of, still in MS., 192.
Crawford, Earl of; grant to him of the Dukedom of Montrose for life, 145.
Crawford's *Lives of the Great Officers of State*, 292.
Crichton, collegiate church of, 201.
Croft, rent of 251.
Crofter, a sub-tenant, 267.

Cromarty, sheriffdom and burgh of, holding of a subject, 116.
Cromwell; his government of Scotland, 139; unites England and Scotland, *ib.;* Scotland represented in the British Parliament, *ib.*
Crops in Teviotdale, 242.
Cross-bow, value of, 66.
Crossraguel, register of, lost, 192.
Crown, "the Four Points," 60; deeds regulating succession to the Crown, 108-9; procedure in Church and Crown Courts different, 212.
Crowner; his office, 84.
Culdees, monks of Irish origin; rise and progress of the order, 162-3; Reeves's History of them, 292; their religious houses, 163; Brechin, a Culdee abbey, originally, 175.
Cumbria, uncertain tenure of, 93.
Cumin seed, pound of, value of, 65-6.
Cuningham, Dean, judge in an early jury trial, 214; rural deanery of, 176.
Curate, meaning of the word, 203.
Customs; on the Forbes estates, 255; on the Gordon estates, 257; on the Struan estate, 268; their money value, *ib.*

DALKEITH, collegiate church of, 201.
Dallas's *Styles*, 14.
Dalrymple, Sir James, on the "Scottish British Church," 8.
Dating, early charters without dates, 30-1; how the date may be ascertained, 31; the *annus domini* introduced, *ib.;* *annus domini* and *annus regni* differ in charters of David II., 32; *L'Art de vérifier les Dates*, 290; Nicholas's *Chronology of History*, 290.
Davach of land; division found chiefly in the north-eastern shires, 271; etymology of the word, 271-

INDEX. 309

272; extent of, 272-3; "Aucht-and-forty danch of Huntly," 273.
David, Earl, notice of his holding the earldom of Lennox, 218.
Davidson, John, W.S., learned Conveyancer, 11, 16.
Dean, chief dignitary in the cathedral, 179-180.
Deaneries, rural, 174-6.
Debates in Parliament, 143-4.
Debts, brief for compelling payment of, 231.
Decisions, collections of, 5; Kames's *Remarkable Decisions*, 10.
"Declaration," contained in early jury trial, 214-220.
Deer, Book of, oldest writing connected with Scotland, 29.
Desnes, deanery of, 176.
Dewar lands, in Glendochart, reddendo for, 67.
Diplomata et Numismata Scociæ, 15, 288-9.
Dirleton's *Doubts and Questions*, 4.
Dog collars, pair of, valued, 65.
Dominicans, account of, 171.
Doomster (latinized *Judex*), his office, 97.
Doorward or usher, his office, 77.
Dornoch, see of the bishopric of Caithness, 175.
Doubts and Questions in Law, Dirleton's, 4.
Douglas, William Lord, created Duke of Hamilton for life, 145-6.
Douglas, Sir Archibald of; sale of the earldom of Wigton to him, 73.
Douglases of Lochleven; their chartulary, 193.
Doves, pair of, valued, 66.
Dovecots, grant of land *cum columbariis*, 45,
Dowry, brief of, 234.
Drengs, who they were, 36.
Drontheim, bishopric of the Isles, its suffragan, 177.

Druid's Circles, filling the original idea of a church? 98.
Drumalbane, rural deanery of, 174.
Drummond Estates, Factor's Report, 265-7; different classes of subtenants mentioned, 266-7.
Dryburgh, chartulary printed, 191.
Du Cange's *Dictionary of Mediæval Latin*, 294.
Duck, wild, valued, 65-6.
Dugald, son of Earl of Alwin, witness in the case of Monachkeneran, 216.
Dukes, specially summoned to Parliament, 123.
Dull, pleas at, 206-7.
Dulsak, rent of, 252.
Dumfries, Castle of, inquest at, 223.
Dunblane, bishopric of, 175.
Dundrennan, register of, lost, 192.
Dunfermline, Abbey of; Walter Fitzalan's grant to, 37; foundation charter, spurious, 87; a house of the Benedictines of St. Bernard, 164; account of it, *ib.*; chartulary printed, 191; Grammar School of the burgh originally a "sang-schule," 182.
Dunkeld, originally a monastery of the Culdees, 163; bishopric of, 174; rural deaneries, *ib.*
Duplin, reddendo for, 67.

EARL, specially summoned to Parliament, 123.
Earldom, grant of, 38, 40; sale of, 73.
Easterlings, "sterling" their coinage, 64.
Edinburgh, Parliament of the Four Burghs to meet at, 114; one of the Burghs composing the burghal Parliament, 114.
Education Acts, 129-30.
Edward III.; Parliamentary reign of, 106; letter from Torwood to him, *ib.*

INDEX.

Eggs; estimated per dozen, 66.
Eglisgrig, dedication of the Church St. Cyricus's, 207.
Elcho, nunnery of, 172.
Elections, Law of, Wight's, 11.
Election; Acts for sending Commissioners to Parliament, 122, 136-7.
Elgin, burgh of; holding of a subject superior, 117; inquest concerning the King's garden at, 225, 226; rural deanery of, 175.
Emancipation, grant of, 38; brief of, 232.
Emerald Charter, 88.
Encroachments on the rights of the people, 154-8.
England, liberty of the subject in, 149; neyfship in, 160.
English Acts of Parliament, language of, 153-4.
Enzie, rental of, 259.
Episcopacy; government of the old Church episcopal, 173.
Erskine, David, learned Conveyancer, 14-5.
Erskine, John, author of the *Institute*, 6.
Ethy, vicar of, his income, 197.
Ewirland, Cramond Regis, reddendo for, 67.
Excommunicates, brief against, 233.
Excommunication, 149.

FABLE, Henryson's, illustrating the forms of process in the Consistorial Court, 239-240, 297-300.
Fachalos (? Frithalos), meaning of, 70-1.
Faciendo clause, 61-8.
Fail, register of, lost, 192.
Fairs, grants of, 38.
Falaise, treaty of, the independence of Scotland surrendered by the, 112.
Falkirk, vicar of, his portion, 199.
Family history, Chalmers's service to, 17.

Fang, thief caught with, 210.
Farnes, deanery of, 176.
Fatal Chair of Scone, Mr. Skene's history of, 164.
Fawfield, reddendo for, 67.
Feather, white plumash, value of, 66.
Fergus, son of Cuningham, witness in a disputed case, 218.
Ferm: rent in oatmeal and bear, 257.
Ferue, register of, lost, 192.
Fetternear, forest and fishing of, 253; hay and meadow of, *ib.*
Feudal; injury to the cottar by the feudalizing of lands, 155.
Fife, rural deanery of, 174.
Findhorn, James II. hunting on the banks of, 124.
Fishers; recent attempt to "astrict" them, 50; the law against seeking for bait, 155.
Fishings, grants of, 38; grant of land *cum piscationibus*, 45; clause *cum piscariis* unjustly extended, 155; brief for putting down cruives, 236-7; large rent paid for the fishing of Bellie, 263.
Fish-stanks, rights *in vivariis* in a grant *in liberam baroniam*, 44.
Fitz Alan, Walter, his grant to Dunfermline, 37.
Fitz Alans; Stewarts descended from, 75, 167.
Fitz Hugh, Alexander, witness in an early jury trial, 215.
Flocks possessed by the monks of Kelso, 243.
Florin of gold, value of, 65.
Foggage of Birss, rent of, 252-3.
Forbes, rental, 254-6.
Fordun's *Scotichronicon*, by Mr. Skene, 292.
Forest; the most extensive right in the time of Bruce, 33; right of property precedes that of forest, 41; grants in free forest, 41; the forest laws of the Normans not known in Scotland, 41; rent of

the foggage of the forest of Birss, 252-3; the foggage of the forest of Glenrinnes, reserved "to my lord" the bishop, 251.

Forfeiture, Bruce's charters proceed on, 39.

Forms of Parliament, 142-3.

Forres, burgh; holding of a subject, 117.

Forth, David I. King benorth, 30; justiciar for Scotland proper benorth, 75.

Fothrif, rural deanery of, 174.

Foules, dedication of St. Mernan's, 207.

France; constitution similar to Scotland in the 14th century, 106; serfdom till the great Revolution, 160; States-general, their constitution, 106.

Franciscan friars, 171.

Fraser, Sir Gilbert, Sheriff of Peebles, inquest by, 225.

Friars; account of, 170-1; their chief orders, 171-2; Franciscans, known as Minors, 171; Dominicans, as Preachers, 171; chartulary of the friars at Glasgow printed, 191.

Frostleys, reddendo for, 67.

Fugitivis et nativis, de, brief, 231.

Funeral dues, a source of church revenue, 186.

Furniture, household, exempted from taxation, 108.

Fyvie, vicarage of, valuation of, 198.

GAELIC, spoken by Malcolm Canmore, 94.

Galloway; bishopric of, 176; its deaneries, *ib.;* David I. King in Galloway, 30; grant to the Galwegians of their peculiar laws and liberties, 38; uncertain tenure of Galloway, by the kings, 93.

Gallows, grant of a barony *cum furca*, 58.

Game, provisions regarding, in the charters of Melrose, 45-6.

Gamrie, valuation of, vicarage of, 198.

Garden, King's; inquest concerning, 226.

Garlic head, a blench duty valued, 66.

Garviauch, rural deanery of, 174.

Gask, reddendo for, 67.

Gaskel, Thomas, a witness in an early jury trial, 215.

Germany, serfdom in, till recently, 160.

Gibson-Craig, Sir James, as a Conveyancer, 16.

Gilbert, son of Samuel, defendant in the case of Monachkeneran, 214-220.

Gilbethoc, witness in an early jury trial, 218.

Gilon, witness in a disputed case, 218.

Ginger, pound of, valued at, 66.

Glamis, thanedom of, reddendo for, 65.

Glasgow; archbishopric, 176; archdeaconries, *ib.;* rural deaneries; suffragans, *ib.;* constitution of the cathedral borrowed from Sarum, 179; College Church, chartulary printed, 191; University, register of, printed, 191; Assembly of 1638, 141.

Glassary, deanery of, 177.

Glassford, Lord, Francis Abercromby created *for life*, 146.

Glenelg, reddendo for eight davochs and five pennylands of, 67.

Glenluce, register of, lost, 192.

Glenrinnes, forest of, reserved to my lord the bishop, 251.

Glensaucht, reddendo for, 67.

Glentilt; thane of, progress of titles showing how he became Toschach of Monivaird, 80-1; thanedom of, reddendo for, 82.

Gloves, pair of, valued, 65-6.
"Goodman," holding of a, 36.
Gordon, Charles, W.S., a learned Conveyancer, 14.
Gordon, frequently a Chancellor, 76.
Gordon rental, 256-265; holdings, in joint occupancy, 256.
Goose, valued, 66.
Government, change of, how effected, 144.
Gowrie, rural deanery of, 174.
Grammar Schools, origin of, 181-2.
Grange of the abbey, 243; inhabitants of, ib.
Grant, Isaac, a learned Writer to the Signet, 14.
Great Officers of State, Crawford's, 291. V. Officers of State.
Great Seal, affixing of, implied the presence of the sovereign, 68; Keeper of, usually the Chancellor, 76.
Grey Friars, Franciscans known as, 171.
Greyhound, valued, 66.
Grouping of shires and burghs by Cromwell, 139.
Gum, pound of, valued, 66.

HABEAS CORPUS, not known in Scotland before the Union, 149.
Haddington, nunnery of, 172; rural deanery of, 174.
Hailes, Lord, as a historical inquirer, 8; *Annals of Scotland*, 9, 291; neglected Church history, ib.
Hay, "fudder" and load of, valued, 66.
Hayning—hay cut from pasture land, 242.
Hamer, church of, to be served by a chaplain, 200.
Hamilton, Duke of, Lord Douglas created, for life, 145-6.
Hanse, a confederacy of free burghs beyond the *Munth*, 114.
Hawk, value of, 65-6.

Hawk-glove, value of, 65.
Hawk-hood, value of, 66.
Hawkings, grant of land *cum aucupationibus*, 45.
Hays of Leys, early contract of lease between them and Abbot of Scone, 248.
Heaths (*cum brueriis*) a pertinent of an estate, 44.
Hen, valued, 66.
Henryson's Fable, illustrating procedure in the Consistorial Courts, 239-240, 297-300.
Heraldry, 294.
Herds, owned by the monks of Kelso, 243.
Hereditary right, asserted in the earliest Scotch charter extant, 34-5.
Heriot (herizeld), grant of a barony *cum herezeldis*, 53.
Heritable jurisdictions fatal to political liberty, 148; Act abolishing them, 149.
Hides, no payment of, in the Gordon rental, 263.
Highland parish, rent of, 260.
Highlands, excessive population in the, 269-270.
Highlanders; how they lost their holdings, 156-7; tenants at will, 269.
Hilarius, a witness in an early jury trial, 218.
History of law, Bolingbroke on the importance of, 26-8.
Holm Cultram, register of, still in MS., 192.
Holyrood, Abbey of; a house of the Canons St. Austin, 163; beautiful charter, 32; chartulary, printed, 191; portions of vicars of their churches, 199; chronicle, 292.
Homage, grant of a barony *cum homagiis*, 50.
Home of Wedderburn, George, a learned Conveyancer, 15.

INDEX. 313

Hope, Sir Thomas, described as *juris nostri peritissimus*, 4.
Hopkelchoc, lands of, *a new* inquest concerning, 225.
Horses, exempted from taxation, 108.
Horse-load, description of, 244.
Horse-shoe, valued, 66.
Hospitals, their intention, 172-3.
Hot iron, ordeal of, 210.
House, made of wattles, notice of, 215.
Household, Master of the, 77.
Hunting, grant of land *cum venationibus*, 45.
Huntly, rental of, 259; the "aucht-and-forty dauch," 273.
Husbandland, extent of, 241-2.
Husbandmen, their holdings, 244.

IMMIGRATION from England, 94-5.
Impropriation explained, 185.
Impropriators, the Lords of Erection, 185.
Incense, pound of, value of, 66.
Inchaffray, chartulary of, printed, 191.
Inchcolm; bishopric of Dunkeld followed Columba to, 174; chartulary still in MS., 192.
Index to the Acts of Parliament, 295.
Infangthef, jurisdiction in, 57-8.
Inglis, Sir William; grant to him of the barony of Manor, 37.
Innes, Thomas, his Critical Essay, 291-2.
Inquests; for assessing all property, 108; taken by order of Alexander II. and Alexander III., 222-8; a *new* inquest, 225; inquest regarding the death of Adam the miller, 223-4; inquest by Alexander de Montfort, Sheriff of Elgin, 225-6—the jury half barons, half burgesses, 226; concerning the petary of Waltamshope, 227-8.
Inventories of Queen Mary's Jewels, 293-4.

Inverkething, vicar of, his income, 196.
Inverness, rural deanery of, 175; vicar of, his income, 194-5; high-roads to, 242.
Investiture, 19, 20, 85-91.
Iona, Island of, seisin taken of, by Columba, 20; the see of the bishopric of the Isles, 177.
Isles; bishopric of 177; changes it underwent, *ib.*; suffragan of the see of Drontheim, *ib.*; rental of the bishopric, 279; oldest rental of the, 278-9; measures of land, in, *ib.*; merk, the foundation of valuations, *ib.*

JEDBURGH; Abbey of, a house of the canons of St. Austin, 163; Grammar School of, the burgh originally a "sang-schuil," 182.
Judicial combat, 210; in use in the time of David I., *ib.*
Judicium Dei—appeal to Divine revelation, 210.
Jungle (*cum bruscis*) a pertinent of an estate, 44.
Juridical Society, Lectures read before, 1; *Styles* by the Society, 17.
Jurisdiction of the civil magistrate upheld by the Scotch King, 237-8.
Jury, trial by, in its infancy, 213; in England in the reign of Henry III., *ib.*; in Scotland about the same time, *ib.*; originated in church courts, 213; an early case foreshadowing a jury trial, 214- 220; number of jurors, 223; jurors probably witnesses too in the cause, 223; early trials, 223-8; in an early case the barons said to agree with the burgesses, 224; jurymen on an inquest, half-barons, half-burgesses, 226.
Justice-Clerk, his office, 77.
Justice-Deputes, in Parliament, 142.
Justiciar; his office, 75; two justi-

ciars in Scotland, *ib.;* an early officer in Scotland, 96; appeal from, 228.

KAIN-LIME, boll of, valued, 65.
Kames, Lord, his contributions to Scotch law, 10.
Keith's *Catalogue of Scottish Bishops*, 292.
Kelso, Abbey of; charter still preserved, 32, 166; house of the Benedictines of Tyrone, 165; account of the Abbey, 165-6; chartulary printed, 191—supplying the best information on rural matters, 241; monks great cultivators of land, *ib.;* held their lands *in dominico*, *ib.;* kindly tenants of, 245-6; rental, 243-248.
Kemble's collection of *Anglo-Saxon charters*, 289.
Kennet's *Law of Parishes*, 295-6.
Kid, valued, 66.
Kilrimund, Holy Trinity at; dedication of, 208.
Kilwinning, register of, lost, 192.
Kindly tenants of the Abbey of Kelso, 245.
King Malcolm Canmore, no charters of his reign extant, 29; King of united Scotland, 93; spoke Gaelic, 94.
King Duncan, oldest writ a charter of, 29.
King Alexander I. (the Fierce), his investment to the cathedral of St. Andrews, 19-20; National Assembly in his time, 99.
King David I., charters begin in his reign, 29; his title, 30; King benorth Forth, and in Lothian and Galloway, 30; claimed allegiance of Scots, English, French, and Galwegians, *ib.;* his beautiful charters to monasteries, 32; persons to whom his charters are addressed, 35; the National Assembly in his reign, 99; free burghs in Scotland from his days, 114; all bishoprics founded before his death, 200; wager of battle or compurgation optional in his time, 211; how his decisions were recorded, 221.
King Malcolm IV., National Council under him, 99; taxation in his reign, 111; his great charter to Kelso still preserved, 166.
King William the Lyon, National Council in his reign, 100; taxation imposed for his ransom, 112-113; how proof was ascertained in his reign, 122.
King Alexander II.; National Council under him, 101; inquests made by his order, 222-5; grants of land for support of bridges, 247.
King Alexander III.; National Assembly, 101-2; monasteries founded before his death, 200; inquests taken by his order, 225-8; high roads in his time, 242.
King John Balliol, Parliament in his time, 102; Parliament first called itself by that name, 119.
King Robert I.; his first charter of Anandale, 33; grants the "King's" dish to the monks of Melrose, 38; his charters proceeding on forfeiture, 39; grants the earldom of Moray in regality, 40; Parliament under him, 103; Scotch version of his Statutes, 104; his unconstitutional Acts, 116-7; the burghs not represented in his earliest Parliaments, 116; but formed the Third Estate in 1326, *ib.;* his death-bed letter preserved by the monks of Melrose, 168.
King David II., his records misdated, 32; money subscribed by the Estates for his ransom, 107; declared illegal for a royal burgh to hold of a subject, 117; importance of his Parliaments, 119-122.

INDEX.

King Robert II.; records of Parliament in Scotch, 110.

King Robert III., grants the barony of Manor to Sir Wm. Inglis, 37; his grant to the Bishop of Aberdeen, 38; his coronation, 108; the first Act of Parliament in Scots, 110.

King James I.; his constitutional ideas, 122; collegiate churches founded between his reign and that of James IV., 201-2.

King James II.: his parliamentary history, 123; hunting on the banks of the Findhorn, 124; his Act in favour of the labourers of the ground, 125.

King James III., power of Parliament intrusted to a committee, 127.

King James IV., Education Act, 129; Acts in favour of burghs, 129.

King James V., Parliaments of, 130-5; Act establishing the Court of Session, 132.

King James VI., representation established in his reign, 123-137; his parliamentary history, 138.

King Charles L.; commissions for surrender of teinds, 23; Act establishing parish schools, 130; parliamentary feeling spread in his reign, 138.

Kings; styles of English and Scotch, 341.

Kings, Early, Scotland under her, 291.

King's agent, in Parliament, 142.

King's Council, notice of, 22; *acta dominorum concilii*, 229.

King's Court, partition between it and Church Courts, 212.

"King's Dish;" grant to the monks of Melrose, 38.

Kingussie, rent of, 260; rent of a ploughgate, 4, 261.

Kinross-shire, to send one commissioner to Parliament, 122.

Kirk of Field Collegiate Church, 201.

Kirkland (*terra ecclesiastica*), half a davach, 271.

Kirktown of Cabrach, rent of, 258.

Kirkwall, St. Magnus's, the cathedral of the bishopric of Orkney, 176.

Knights Templars: their origin, 169; their chief house, *ib.*

Kyle, rural deanery of, 176.

LABOURERS of the ground, Act in favour of, 125.

Laird; his tenure, 36; how his power was measured, 269.

Laing, Mr. David, on the Reformed Church, and the Scots poets, 294-5.

Lanark, rural deanery of, 176.

Land; measures of land, in Merse and Teviotdale, 241; earliest information touching rural matters derived from religious houses, 241; lecture on early occupation of land, 241-285; measures of land, on the Forbes property, 254; on the Gordon estates, 256, 258; pasture on the *infield* and *outfield*, 269.

Lanercost, Chronicle of, 292.

Language of the English and Scotch Acts of Parliament, 153-4.

Latin of Scotch and French charters, 33.

Law, old forms of, 209-240.

Laws, Ancient, collection of, by Benjamin Thorpe, 289-290.

Laws, unjust, 154-8.

Lawyers, attempting to defeat the Act in favour of the labourers of the ground, 125; straining clauses in charters, 155.

Lay Courts, procedure in, 221-2.

Lease, contract of, 248; language and conditions, 248-9.

Leases on the Gordon estates, 265.

Leni charter, spurious, 87.

Lennox, Dugald of, inquest concerning his succession, 228.

Lennox, earldom of, held by Earl David, 218.
Lennox, rural deanery of, 176.
Lesmahago, a cell of Kelso, 166.
Liberty, less protected in Scotland than England, 149.
Limestone; grant of lands *cum lapide et calce*, 45.
Lincluden, register of, lost, 192.
Lincoln, constitution of the Cathedral of Moray formed after, 179.
Lindores, chartulary of, printed, 191.
Lindsay, Lord, presented MSS. of John Riddell to the Advocates' Library, 18.
Linlithgow; rural deanery, 174; St. Michael's Church, dedication of, 207.
Lismore, Bishop of, Bishop of Argyle sometimes styled, 176.
Liverance, Adam of, a royal mandate to ascertain his tenure, 224.
Liveries, origin of the word, 224.
Lochaber; Thane of, progress of titles showing how he assumed the surname of *MacTosche*, 81-2; thanedom of, reddendo for, 82-3; rent of farms in, 258; measures of land in, *ib*.
Lochaw, reddendo for, 66-7.
Lochindorb, reddendo for, 64.
Lords of Erection: appropriators or impropriators? 185-6.
Lords of Parliament, specially summoned to Parliament, 123.
Lorne, deanery of, 177.
Losceresch, dedication of the church of, 208.
Lothian; David I. King in Lothian, 30; a Justiciar for, 75; archdeaconry of, 174; rural deanries, *ib*.
Lowland parish, rent of, 261.
Lunan, vicar of, his income, 196.
Lyon's Usher, in Parliament, 142.

MACBETH, noticed with Lady Macbeth in the register of Priory of St. Andrews, 29.
MacIntosh, *V.* Toschach, 81-2.
Mackenneth, Malcolm, laws ascribed to, 3.
Mackenzie, Sir George, not a historical nor constitutional lawyer, 4.
Mackenzie, Colin, a learned Writer to the Signet, 16.
Maill, rent in money, 257.
Mair of fee, several in Scotland, 78.
Mairdoms, numerous, 78.
Malcolm Beg, witness in the case of Monachkeneran, 217.
Manor, barony of, granted for the slaughter of an Englishman, 37.
Mantle, red, value, 66.
Manuel, nunnery of, 172.
Maor, his office, 78; one in each of the four bailiaries of Angus, 78.
Maormor, his office, 79; superseded by *comes* or count, 79, 97; in Moray, Buchan, Mar, Mearns and perhaps Angus, in the time of Canmore, 97.
Maorship, example of, from the Craignish papers, 78.
Mar; rural deanery of, 174; earldom of, ruled by a "Maormor" in the reign of Canmore, 97.
Marchynche, St. John and St. Modrust's Church, dedication of, 208.
Margaret, Queen, her influence on Scotch customs, 94.
Marischal, his office, 75; in Parliament, 142.
Mark, foundation of money valuations in the Isles, 278-9.
Markland, equal to $34\frac{2}{3}$ acres, 270, 284; was the measure connected with national taxation, 275-6.
Marriage; dues on, 186; Tax on, 52-3.
Marshes, rights *in maresiis* conveyed in a grant *in liberam baroniam*, 43.
Mart, valued, 66; killed at Martinmas, 257.

INDEX. 317

Mary, Queen; Act in favour of Burghs in her reign, 129; histories of, 138; *Inventories of her Jewels*, 13, 293-4.
Maxwell, Eimer de, Sheriff of Peebles; inquest before him concerning the petary of Waltamshope, 227-8.
Meadows, conveyed in a grant *in liberam baroniam*, 43.
Meal, stone of, valued, 66.
Mearns, The; ruled in the time of Canmore by a Maormor, 97; rural deanery of, 174.
Mediæval Latin, Dictionary of, 294.
Melrose, Abbey of; provisions regarding game in the charters, 45-6; a house of the Cistercians, 167; account of the Abbey, 167-8; chartulary printed, 191; chronicle, 292.
Mensal churches, 184.
Merchandise: brief *in re mercatoria*, 236.
Mercheta mulierum, a marriage-tax, 52-3.
Merse, The; rural deanery, 174; measures of land, 241; extent of a plough of land, 270.
Meute, a cry of hounds, 46.
Middle Ages, Scotland in the, 291.
Midlothian, collegiate churches in, 201.
Milk, Bruce's grant of a dish of rice and milk to the monks of Melrose, 38.
Mills; frequently granted, 38; grant of lands *cum molendinis*, 47; right, a grievous oppression, *ib.*; no monopolies in England, 48; reddendos for mills, 49, 246, 251; bringing home the mill-stone, 47-8.
Mirror, valued, 65.
Mitchelson, Samuel, a learned Conveyancer, 14.
Mitred abbot, his privileges, 203.
Modus tenendi clause, 40.

Monachkeneran, dispute regarding the lands of, foreshadowing trial by jury, 214-220.
Monastery; officers of, 170; heads in Parliament, *ib.*; chartularies, 188-193; chartularies preserved, 191; printed, *ib.*; still in ms., 192; foundation, 200; monks great cultivators of lands, 241; improvers of the arts, *ib.*; registers recommended for the study of Records, 292-3.
Money extent of a ploughgate, 270.
Money measures of land; where most used, 270; marks of national taxation, 275-6; balanced with agricultural measures, 281-4.
Monivaird, Toschach of, formerly known as Thane of Glentilt, 80-1.
Monks; different houses of, 162; their chief orders, 162-170.
Mont-Lothian, church, to be served by a chaplain, 200.
Montfort, Alexander de, Sheriff of Elgin, takes inquest, 225-6.
Montrose; dukedom of, granted to the Earl of Craufurd for life, 145; charter of the burgh spurious, 87.
Monymusk, a house of the Culdees, 163.
Moors, rights *in moris* conveyed in a grant *in liberam baroniam*, 44.
Moray; Bishop of, lord of eight baronies, 187; dispute between him and Rose of Kilravock, 237-8; last process for claiming a neyf by Alexander, Bishop, 256; bishopric, account of, 174-5; rural deaneries, 175; cathedral, its constitution, 179; earldom, granted in regality to Thomas Randolph, 40; uncertain tenure of, by the kings, 93; ruled in Canmore's time by a Maormor, 97; ploughgate in, 270.
Mortancestry, brief of, 231.
Morton chartulary, 193.
Morven, deanery of, 177.

Mugger, trade of, 253.
Muirhouse, barony, reddendo for, 67.
Multure dues, grant of lands *cum multuris*, 47.
Munth, confederacy of free burghs beyond, 114.
Muttons of Ross, Buchan, and Moray valued, 66.

NAIRN, royal burgh, holding of a subject, 117.
National Assembly or Council; under Alexander I., 99; under Malcolm IV., 99; under William the Lyon, 100; under Alexander II. and Alexander III., 101-2. *V.* Parliament.
Native, neyf or villein; grant of a barony *cum nativis*, 50; neyf in gross, 51, 232; deed of sale of neyf in gross, 52, 232; neyf regardant, *ib.*; brief touching natives and fugitives, 231-2; neyf or villein, the lowest of the inhabitants of the Grange, 243; disappearance of neyfs before 1532, 256; last process for claiming a neyf, 159, 256.
Neighbourhood, rules for keeping good, 242, 251-2, 254.
Nemias, witness in the case of Monachkeneran, 218.
Newabbey, register of, lost, 193.
Newbattle Abbey; a Cistercian house, 167; account of, 168; chartulary printed, 191.
New Park (Stirling), reddendo for, 65.
Neyf, *V.* Native.
Nicolas, Sir Harris; his *Chronology of History*, 290.
Nigg, vicar of, his income, 195-6.
Nithsdale, rural deanery of, 176.
Nobility in Parliament, 142; eldest sons of Peers in Parliament, *ib.*
Norsemen; money measures of land in their Scotch possessions, 277.

North Berwick, nunnery of, 172; chartulary printed, 191.
Novel Diseisin, brief of, 231.
Numismata Scotiæ, 288-9.
Nunneries, 172.

OBLATIONS, source of Church revenue, 186.
Observations on the Statutes, Daines Barrington's, 295.
Offerings, a source of Church revenue, 186.
Officers of State, list of, 74-8; not different from those of England, 96; in Parliament, 142, 146; in Scotland in the reign of David I., 222. *V.* Great Officers of State.
Offices mentioned in charters, 85.
Official, The, 181; his jurisdiction, 238-9.
Old Extent; Thomas Thomson on, 12; 40s. land = 104 acres or one ploughgate, 270, 284.
Old forms of Law, Lecture on, 209-240.
Onions, per barrel, valued, 66.
Orcadian customs, 280-1.
Ordeal, jurisdiction of, 61, 210.
Origines Parochiales Scotiæ, 291.
Orkney, bishopric of, 175; cathedral, 176; money measures of land, 277-280; rentals, 279-280.
Oughton's *Consistorial Form of Process*, 295.
Outfangthef, jurisdiction in, 58.
Ox, valued, 66.
Oxgate = 13 acres, 241, 284; four oxgates = one pound of Old Extent, 284.

PADUINAM, tenure of, 224-5.
Paisley Abbey; house of Cluniac Benedictines, 167; account of the abbey, *ib.*; chartulary very interesting, 167; printed, 191; monks, the pursuers in an early jury trial, 214-220.

Pannage, right of, 41.
Parish; vicars, distinguished from those of the cathedral, 184; Parish schools, Act establishing, 130.
Parishes, White Kennet's Law of, 295-6; *Origines Parochiales*, 291.
Parliament, Wight's History of, 11; Outline of Lecture on, 21; Lecture, 92-160; the word first formally used in England in 1272, 101; Parliament of Brigham, the first national assembly called by that name, 102, 118-9; under John Balliol, 102; under Robert I., 103—name common in his reign, 103; complete, 105; held at Cambuskenneth,—its constitution, 105; similar constitutions abroad, 106; constituent parts of Parliament, 99-111; Records in Scots, 110; imposing taxes, 111; Parliament of the Four Burghs to meet at Edinburgh, 114; burghs, the Third Estate, 115; burghs, not an Estate in the early Parliaments of Bruce, 116; importance of the Parliaments of David II., 119-122; small barons relieved from attendance, 122; persons specially summoned, 123; clergy as the First Estate, 141; persons admitted, but not allowed to vote, 142; forms of Parliament, 142-3; the places where the members sat, 142-3; rules for debate, 143; sitting of Parliament, 143; riding of Parliament, *ib.*; summons, 150; proxies, 151; heads of monasteries in Parliament, 170; appeals, 228-9; Auditors of Causes and Complaints, committee of Parliament, 229. *V.* National Assembly.
Parson or rector, 184.
Partition, brief of, 231.
Pastures, in a grant *in liberam baroniam*, 43.

Paths, roads and paths in a grant of barony, 43.
Pauper, brief for supporting, 234.
Payment to Commissioners of Shires and Burghs, 151-3.
Peas, grant of a dish to the monks of Melrose, 38.
Peebles, rural deanery of, 176.
Peerages for life, 145-6.
Peerage and Consistorial Law, Riddell's, 18.
Pendicler, sub-tenant, 267.
Penicuik, reddendo for, 68.
Penny, silver, valued, 65.
Pennyland, where found, 275-6.
People (*populus*), how they were represented in the National Council, 106.
Pepper, pound of, valued, 66.
Perambulation, brief of, 231.
Perth, charter of the burgh, spurious, 87.
Petary, *cum petariis*, pertinent of land, 44; petary of Waltamshope, inquest concerning, 227-8.
Picts, settled on the eastern shore, 93.
Pigeons, grant of lands *cum columbis*, 45.
Pinkerton, neglected Church history, 13.
Pit, grant of a barony *cum fossa*, 58.
Pittance, King's, to the monks of Melrose, 38.
Plains, conveyed in a grant of barony, 43.
Planum, means arable land, 43.
Pleas at Dull, 206-7.
Ploughgate; extent of, 242; military service for, 247; rent of, in silver, 247; rent of, in the parish of Clatt, 250-1; rent, on the Forbes property, 255; rent, in a Lowland parish, 262; rent, in a Highland parish, 261; money extent of, 270; connected with taxation? 274.
"Points of the Crown," reserved in grants of barony, 60.

Pond (*stagnum*), used for fish or mill purposes, 44.
Poor, deprived of their rights in Commons, 155; brief for supporting a pauper, 234.
Popes; usurped the patronage of bishoprics, 178; disposed of the benefices of churchmen who died at Rome, *ib.*
Porter of the monastery, his duties, 170.
Portmuoch, St. Stephen and St. Moan's Church of, dedication of, 208.
Poultry lands, near Edinburgh, reddendo for, 67.
Poultry of Ross, estimated, 66.
Poundland, where found, 275-6.
"Practicks;" MS. volumes of decisions collected by lawyers, 5.
Pratum, a hay meadow, 43.
Prebend, the meaning of the word, 183.
Prebendary, 179, 183.
Precentor of the cathedral; his duty, 181.
Prelates in Parliament, 170.
Prerogative, Crown lawyers stretching, 4.
Prescription, founded on in the case of Monachkeneran, 215-6.
President of the Council; his office, 77.
Primogeniture, right of, in the earliest Scotch charter, 34-5.
Priors, specially summoned to Parliament, 123; prior and sub-prior, officers of the Cathedral, 170.
Privilege; persons admitted, but not allowed a vote in Parliament, 142.
Privy Seal, the, his office, 77.
Probi Homines; who they were, 36.
Process, forms of, 21, 22; earliest, 209.
Procuration, meaning of, 196.

Progresses, royal, 95.
Property, right of, precedes that of forest, 41.
Provostries, list of, 201-2.
Proxies in Parliament, 150.

Quæquidem clause in the charter, 39.
Quarry; grant of lands *cum lapicidiis*, 45.
Queen *Mary's Jewels, Inventories of*, 13, 293-4. *V.* Mary, Queen.

RABBITS, pair of, valued, 66.
Randolph, Thomas, receives earldom of Moray in regality, 40.
Rathel, witness in the case of Monachkeneran, 218.
Recognition, brief of, 231.
Records; rescued from decay by Thomas Thomson, 13; plea for the study, 286-8; books recommended, 288-296; publications, English and Scotch, 296.
Rector or parson of a church, 184.
Rectorial tithes, 186; distinguished from vicarial tithes, 193-196.
Reddendo clause, 61-8.
Red-handed, homicide taken, 210.
Reek hen, paid as custom, 257.
Reeves's, Rev. Dr., *Adomnan's Life of St. Columba*, 293; history of the Culdees, *ib.*
Reformation, Abbots and Priors in Parliament after, 141; excommunication before, 149.
Regality, extent of the grant, 40.
Regiam Majestatem, first proved by John Davidson to be copied from Glanvill, 16.
Registrum Magni Sigilli, edited by Thomas Thomson, 13.
Regular and secular clergy, distinguished, 161.
Relief, grant of a barony *cum releviis*, 50.
"Relig-Oran," origin of the name, 20.

INDEX.

Religious Houses; trial by ordeal given to, 61, 210; earliest information of rural matters from abbeys, 241.
"Removing of Tenants," by Walter Ross, 16.
Rent; rarely stipulated in old grants of land, 63; oldest information concerning, 241; small money rent paid in Badenoch, 258-9; money valuation in the West for rent or tax, 277.
Rental; of Abbey of Kelso, 243-8; of bishopric of Aberdeen, 250-4; of Forbes property, 254-6; of Gordon estates, 256-265; of Struan estates, 267-9; of the Isles, 278-9; of bishopric of the Isles, 279; of Orkney and Shetland, 279-280.
Representation; James I. attempts to introduce, 122, 123; Acts in favour of, 123, 136, 137; established in the reign of James VI., 123, 137; 20 commissioners for shires and 10 for burghs in the British Parliament, 139; burghs required to send each two commissioners, 141; afterwards one only, 142.
Residence, prebendary bound to, 183.
Restennet, charters of, in MS., 192.
Ressin, witness in the case of Monachkeneran, 218.
Restalrig, collegiate church of, 201.
Restoration, bishops in Parliament from, till the Revolution, 141.
Retours, edited by Thomas Thomson, 13.
Revocation, the King's prerogative of revoking all grants, 148.
Revolution; the clergy no longer an estate, 141.
Rice, Bruce's grant of a dish of rice and milk to the monks of Melrose, 38.
Riddell, John; his Peerage and Consistorial Law, 18; his MS. presented to the Advocates' Library, *ib*.

Riding of Parliament, 143.
Right, brief of, steps of procedure, 234-6.
Rinnes, deanery of, 176.
Roads, in a grant *in liberam baroniam*, 43; right of, encroached upon, 158; high roads in the time of William the Lyon and the Alexanders, 242.
Robertson, E. W., *Scotland under her Early Kings*, 291.
Robertson, Joseph; *Antiquities of the Shires of Aberdeen and Banff; Inventories of Queen Mary's Jewels; Statutes and Councils of the Scotch Church*, 13, 293-4.
Rome; disposal of the benefices of churchmen who died there, 178.
Rose of Kilravock's dispute with the Bishop of Moray, 237-8.
Rosemarknie, bishopric of Ross sometimes called, 175.
Rose-noble of gold, value of, 66.
Roslin, collegiate church of, 201.
Ross, Duke of, received his title of honour *ad vitam*, 145.
Ross, Walter, a learned Writer to the Signet, 16.
Ross, bishopric of, 175; sometimes called Rosemarknie, *ib*.
Rossinclerach, church of, dedicated, 208.
Rotheric Beg of Carric, witness in the case of Monachkeneran, 218.
Rouming, explained, 269.
Roxburgh, one of the burghs composing *curia quatuor burgorum*, 114.
Ruddiman, Thomas, wrote the preface to Anderson's *Diplomata*, 289.
"Runrig," 252.
Rural clergyman distinguished from cathedral vicar, 84.
Rural dean; his jurisdiction, 183.
Rural occupation, Lecture on, 241-285; earliest information from religious houses, 241.

X

Russell, John, a learned Conveyancer, 14-5.
Rutherglen, rural deanery of, 176.

SAC, jurisdiction in, 55.
St. Andrews; Bishop of, David, churches dedicated by him, 208; bishopric, 173-4; archdeaconries, rural deaneries, *ib.*; suffragans, 174-6; register of the bishopric, lost, 190; cathedral *invested* by Alexander I., 20; Priory, a house of the canons of St. Austin, 163—account of, 163-4; register of the Priory printed, 191; MacBeth and Pictish King Brude, noticed in the register, 29; archdeaconry of, 174; rural deaneries, *ib.*; University, register not printed, 191.
St. Clare, nuns of, branch of Franciscans, 172.
St. Columba, taking seisin of Iona, 20.
St. Cuthbert's, vicar of, 199.
St. Giles' College Kirk, chartulary printed, 191.
St. Mary's Isle, register of, lost, 193.
St. Serf's Isle in Lochleven, a house of the Culdees, 163.
Salic law, the Crown settled on the heirs-male of Robert II., 109-10.
Salmon, a fresh, valued, 66; barrel valued, 66; brief for putting down cruives, 236-7.
Salters, till recently "astricted," 50.
Salt-work, a pertinent of a barony, 49.
Sandilands of Calder, temporal lords of Torphichen at the Reformation, 169.
"Sang schuils," Act establishing, 129; origin of, 181.
Sarum, constitution of Cathedral of Glasgow formed after, 172.
Schools; Acts for establishing, 129-130; schools of Ayr, Master of,
judge in the case of Monachkeneran, 214.
Sciennes, Edinburgh, nuns of, 172.
Scone, Abbey of; inquest at, for assessing all property, 108; coronation of Robert III. at, 108-9; a monastery of the Culdees, 163—afterwards of the canons of St. Austin, 163; chartulary printed, 191; monks, had the jurisdiction of ordeal, 211; early contract of lease between the Abbot and the Hays of Leys, 248.
Sconin, St. Memma's Church of, dedication of, 208.
Scots language; version of the Statutes of Robert I. in Scots, 104; Records of Parliament in Scots, 110; language of the Acts of Parliament, 153-4; oldest specimen of Scots, 248.
Scotland; made up of several nations, 92; Proper, boundaries of, 92; constitution, different from that of England, 94; earliest court, 98; liberty of the subject, 149; divided into sheriffdoms, 222; *Scotland under her Early Kings*, 291; *Scotland in the Middle Ages*, 291; *Statutes and Councils of the Scotch Church*, 294.
Scots, settled in the West, 93.
Scott of Haychester, Sir Walter, created Earl of Tarras for life, 146.
Sealing of charters, 68-9.
Seals, preserved by the monks of Melrose, 168.
Seals, Ancient Scottish (Henry Laing), 294.
Seashore, encroached on, 155.
Secretary of State, 77.
Secular and regular clergy distinguished, 161; the secular clergy, 173-184; seculars members of collegiate churches, 201.
Sederunt of Parliament, an early 126-7.

Seisin, manner of giving, 19-20; brief of, 234. *V.* Investiture.
Senators of the College of Justice, in Parliament, 142.
Serfs; colliers and salters till recently "astricted," 50; attempt to "astrict" fishers, *ib.*; description of serfs, 50-1; serfdom died out first in Scotland, 159; brief of, 231-2; brief enfranchising a serf, 232. *V.* Native.
Serjeantry, tenure by, 62.
Services on the barony of Bolden, 244.
Session, Court of, origin and establishment, 119-122.
Sheep, a, valued, 66; white sheep exempted from taxation, 108; brief as to disease of sheep, 236; flocks of sheep belonging to the monks of Kelso, 243; small number of sheep in the Highlands, 263-4.
Sheer day's work, estimated, 66.
Sheriffdoms, Scotland divided into, 222.
Shetland, money measures of land in, 277.
Shillingland, tax or rent connected with, 275-6.
Shires; to send two or more wise men to Parliament, 122; grouped by Cromwell, 139; represented by 20 commissioners in the British Parliament, *ib.*; commissioners sat on "furmes," 142; commissioners paid, 151-3.
Signature, subscribed by the King, 68.
Sitting of Parliament, 143.
Skene, Sir John, as a legal antiquary, 3.
Skene, Mr. W. F.; his history of the Coronation Stone, 164; edition of Fordun's *Scotichronicon*, 292.
Skins; in the Gordon rental, 263.
Slavery, *V.* Serfs.

Smithy (*fabrina*), a pertinent of an estate, 48.
Soc, jurisdiction in, 55.
Sodor and Man, bishopric of, origin of the title, 177.
Soltra, collegiate church of, 201.
Sorryn, meaning of, 70-1.
Souming of sheep and cattle, 268.
Spain, constitution of the Cortes of Castille and Catalonia, 106.
Sparrow-hawk, valued, 66.
Speaker of Parliament, Act to elect, 122-3.
Spirituality of the Church, 187.
Sport, grant *in liberam forestam* refers to game, 41; forest of Glenrinnes reserved to my lord the bishop, 251.
Spurs, pair of gilt, valued, 65-6; pair of white, valued, 66.
Squires, lesser barons called, 135.
Stagnis, in, ponds conveyed in a grant of barony, 44.
Stair, Lord, author of our national Jurisprudence, 6.
States-general of France, their constitution, 106.
Statutes, Abridgement of, Lord Kames's, 10; Daines Barrington's *Observations on the Statutes,* 295.
Statutes and Councils of the Scotch Church, 294.
Steelbow, custom known as, 245.
Steel-bowman, sub-tenant, 266.
Sterling, coinage of the "Easterlings," 64.
Steward, chief officer of the Crown, 75; originally a Fitzalan, *ib.*; an early officer in Scotland, 96.
Steward, Walter, receives the earldom of Stratherne *for life,* 145.
Stewarts, pedigree of the, 167.
Stewart's "Answers," 4.
Stirling, one of the burghs making up *curia quatuor burgorum,* 114; register of the Chapel Royal, still in MS., 192.

Stone and lime, grant of lands *cum lapide et calce*, 45.
Strathbogy, rural deanery of, 175.
Stratherne; Earldom of, granted to the Earl of Athol for life, 145.
Stratherne or Dunblane, bishopric of, 175; founded by a subject, *ib.;* rural deanery of, 174.
Strathspey; rural deanery of, 175; a barony of the Bishop of Moray, 187.
Struan estates, rental of, 267-9.
Struther, Thomas (Englishman), grant of lands for his slaughter, 37.
Stuht, noticed in the Kelso rental, 245.
Styles; by Dallas of St. Martin, 14, 17; collection of, by the Juridical Society, 17.
Subletting in the parish of Fetternear, 251.
Subscription of charters, 68.
Subtenants on the Gordon estates, 265; different classes on the Drummond estates, 266-7.
Succession to the Crown, deeds regulating, 108-9.
Sucken, grant *cum molendinis multuris et sequelis*, 47.
Suffragans of Glasgow, 176; of St. Andrews, 174-6.
Summons to Parliament, persons specially summoned, 123; styles of summons, 150.
Swinton, Archibald, a learned Conveyancer, 16.
Symbols, instances of, 19-20, 85-91.

TAILLIE, the Crown settled on the heirs-male of Robert II., 109-110.
Tain, charter of the burgh, spurious, 87.
Tarras, Earl of, Sir Walter Scott of Haychester created, for life, 146.
Tarves, vicarage of, valuation of, 198.
Taxation; inquest at Scone for imposing a tax, 108; taxing the test of the power of Parliament, 111; taxation in the reign of Malcolm IV., 111; in the reign of William the Lyon, 113; in the reign of David II., 107-8; the rich monks paying taxes, but under protest, 169; *verus valor* and *antiqua taxatio*, 190; earliest marks of national taxation, 274; money valuation on the West for tax or rent, 277.
Taxing of accounts, early instance, 219.
Teaching, discouraged, 182.
Teinds, paid in the rental of Kingussie, 260.
Temporality of the Church, 187.
Tenancy; oldest description, 241; joint, in Merse and Teviotdale, 242; joint, on the bishopric of Aberdeen, 250; joint, on the Forbes estate, 254; joint, on the Gordon estates, 256.
Tenandries, grant of a barony *cum tenandriis*, 49.
Tenants; grant of a barony *cum tenentibus*, 49; extent of the right, *ib.;* different classes of tenants, holding of the Church, 245-6; improvements by tenants, 250, 252.
Tenure clause in a charter, 40; lands of Monachkeneran held for entertaining strangers, 215.
Terce, brief of, 234.
Terregles, charter of, 43, 69-73; savage state of society it shows, 73.
Teviotdale; archdeaconry, 176; rural deancries, *ib.;* measures of land, 241; rents and services, 244; extent of a plough of land in, 270.
Thanages, list of, 83.
Thane, Scotch, equivalent to Toschach, 79; different from the English Thane; his office, 80; the title changed into Toschach, 80-2.
Them, warranty or frank-pledge, 56.

Thol, right of exacting toll, 56.
Thomson, Thomas, as an historical lawyer, 11; editor of the Acts of Parliament; of Chamberlain Rolls; of the Register of the Great Seal; of the Retours; on Old Extent; rescues the Records from decay, ib.
Thorpe's *Ancient Laws of England,* 289-90.
Thrave of straw = 24 sheaves, 268.
Tithes; commissions for, noticed, 23-4; rectorial or great, 186; vicarial or small, ib.; rectorial and vicarial, distinguished, 193-196; settlement of tithes, 194-9; valuation of tithes, 197-9.
Titular, term explained, 204.
Topography of Scotland, 17, 290, 291.
Torphichen, Lord, 169; chief house of the Knights Templars, 169.
Torwood, letter from, 103.
Toschach; equivalent to Scotch Thane, 79; surname assumed from the title of thane, 80-2; Thane of Lochaber assumed the surname of *Mac-tosche,* 81-2; Toschach of Monivaird, originally Thane of Glentilt, 80-1—not connected with Clanchattan, 83.
Toscheochdorach, office of Toschach, 79.
Treason, dead put to trial, 150; "corruption of Blood," ib.
Treasurer, The; his office, 76; treasurer of the cathedral—his duties, 182.
Trinity College, Edinburgh, 201.
Trout-fishing, encroached upon, 158.
Tungland, register of, lost, 193.
Turbary, *cum turbariis,* pertinent of of land, 44.
Turf, cart-load of, valued, 66.
Tutory, brief of, 234.
Tyronensian monks, of the order of St. Benedict, 162.

Tytler, Patrick, noticed, 13.
Tytler, William, Writer to the Signet, 14.

Union; England and Scotland united during the Commonwealth, 139; law of treason imported by the Act, ib.; beneficial effects of. 149.
Unjust laws, notice of, 154-8.
Usher, the, his office, 77.
Uttingstone, rent of, 257.

Valliscaulium, of the order of St. Benedict of, 162.
Valuations of church benefices, 189; their usefulness, 190.
Vehicles used in Teviotdale, 242.
Verus valor, Bagimond's Roll, 190.
Vicar of cathedral, distinguished from vicar of parish, 184.
Vicarages, valuation of, 194-9.
Vicarial or small tithes, 186; distinguished from rectorial tithes, 193-196.
Vicinage, origin of the word, 223.
Vinarium, confounded with *viuarium,* 44.
Vivariis, in, fish-stanks in a grant *in liberam baroniam,* 44; sometimes used for parks, ib.; confounded with *vinarium,* ib.
Voting, old county qualification of, 270.

Wager of battle, 210; in use in the time of David L, ib.
Wair, grant of land with sea-weed, 45.
Waith, grant with right of waif, 45.
Wallace, Sir William, Guardian of the Kingdom, 102.
Ward, grant of barony *cum wardis,* 50; brief of, 231.
Warren, right of, 41-2.
Water, right *in aquis* in a grant *in*

liberam baroniam, 44; ordeal of water, 210.

Wattles, notice of a house of, 215.

Wax, pound of, valued, 65-6; stone of, valued, 66.

Way, right of, encroached on, 158.

Wedder, valued, 66.

Wemyss, David, W.S., as a Conveyancer, 16.

West Coast, money measures of land on, 271; valuation of land on the West for rent or taxes, 277.

Wheat; bread of, used by the monks of Melrose, 168; in the Gordon rental, 259.

White Friars, Carmelites known as, 172.

Whithorn, register of, lost, 193.

Wight, Alexander, *Law of Elections*, 11; *History of Parliament*, *ib.*

Wigton, Earl of, sells his earldom, 73.

Witnesses; facts not ascertained by, 209-10; examined in the case of Monachkeneran, 215-219; jurymen probably, 223.

Women, exempted from farm service, 245.

Woods, grant of lands *in boscis*, 42.

Wool; great produce of the estates of the Abbey of Kelso, 243; an item of rent on the Gordon estates, 263.

Wrak, grant of lands, with the right of wreck, 45.

Writers to the Signet, learned, 14-16.

Writing; no record in England before A.D. 597, 29; book of Deer, the oldest in Scotland, *ib.*; elaborate writing of monkish charters, 32.

Wyntoun's Chronicle, 292.

ZINZIBER, pound of, valued, 65.

www.ingramcontent.com/pod-product-compliance
Lightning Source LLC
Chambersburg PA
CBHW030003240426
43672CB00007B/802